WHO KILLED ETHEL AND MARTIN COHEN?

The police found Ethel Cohen in the loft near the landing. She was lying facedown, wearing a red, white, and blue flower print house dress but no pantyhose or shoes. Martin Cohen was in the second floor bedroom. A short man with a paunch, he lay in the middle of the room, partly on his right side, his feet pointed toward the door. He was wearing dark green slacks, but no shoes, shirt, or socks. The room was a mess. Every surface was cluttered and dirty.

The living room, kitchen, and bedroom had been thoroughly ransacked—papers, envelopes, pens, bills, everything was on the floor. Ethel Cohen's purse was on the floor but it didn't contain any cash, only dozens of discount cards for fast food chains, hundreds of grocery coupons, $200 in traveler's checks, and several Delaware Lotto tickets. The kitchen oven, still set at 350 degrees, contained a charred casserole. But the police found no signs of forced entry—no pry marks on the front or back doors and no broken windows. All the windows were locked.

It was getting very late—the couple's son still hadn't shown up. . . .

FALLEN SON

MIKE WALSH

FALLEN SON

AN ONYX BOOK

ONYX
Published by the Penguin Group
Penguin Books USA Inc., 375 Hudson Street,
New York, New York 10014, U.S.A.
Penguin Books Ltd, 27 Wrights Lane,
London W8 5TZ, England
Penguin Books Australia Ltd, Ringwood,
Victoria, Australia
Penguin Books Canada Ltd, 10 Alcorn Avenue,
Toronto, Ontario, Canada M4V 3B2
Penguin Books (N.Z.) Ltd, 182–190 Wairau Road,
Auckland 10, New Zealand

Penguin Books Ltd, Registered Offices:
Harmondsworth, Middlesex, England

First published by Onyx, an imprint of Dutton Signet,
a division of Penguin Books USA Inc.

First Printing, February, 1994
10 9 8 7 6 5 4 3 2 1

Acknowledgments

The author would like to thank everyone who was interviewed for this book. He would also like to thank the following individuals for their kindness, support, and assistance in this project: Gary and Donna Berkowitz, Kathy and Charlie Breuninger, Rick Henshaw, Michaela Hamilton, Sharon Lee, Lois Mathison, Lise Monty, Todd Moore, Judith Schaechter, John Downs and the New Castle County Police, Steve Walther and the Delaware Attorney General's Office, the *Wilmington News Journal,* and especially Mr. and Mrs. John M. Walsh, Jr.

Contents

Preface

Charles Cohen's thoughts are based on his letters, poetry, song lyrics, and other writings, as well as his court testimony, his statements to police, my interviews with those who knew or met him, and the court testimony of the three mental health experts who evaluated him.

The names of the following individuals have been changed to protect their anonymity: Albert McRea, Rick Muncey, Henry Posner, Ellen, Evan, Gary, Helen, Joanne, Karen, Li, Lisa, Marie, Mark, Nina, Paul, Rob, Stan, Ted, Tom, and Tim and Sandy. These changes in no way alter the substance of what happened.

part I

Nightmare Journey

chapter 1

- - - - - - - -

Raw Power

On Sunday afternoon, January 25, 1981, Henry Posner bashed in his father's head. He believed his father was the devil, so he had painted a cross on his bedroom door to keep his father out. His father had entered the room anyway, and Posner hit him on the head repeatedly with a jagged, two-foot metal bar.

Posner immediately called a priest and told him he had done a terrible thing. His father was rushed to a hospital, but there wasn't much the doctors could do. The elder Posner had multiple skull fractures and severe brain damage and had lapsed into a coma. Henry Posner was arrested and charged with attempted murder.

Posner was eventually taken to Delaware State Hospital near Wilmington, Delaware. He was diagnosed as paranoid schizophrenic, ruled incompetent to stand trial, and later found not guilty by reason of insanity. His father died a few weeks after the verdict.

Posner was held for one year in the hospital's secure ward for criminals. With medication and counseling, his condition improved. He took part in work programs and completed classes at the local technical college. He moved into a halfway house on the grounds of the hospital in 1987, and the hospital staff permitted him to work in the community.

Things didn't go as well for Henry Posner in 1988, however. He quit three jobs, lolled listlessly about the halfway house, and stopped cooperating with his treatment supervisors. He also took up drinking and became despondent when his girlfriend moved to California. On October 12, Posner was readmitted to a ward in the hospital.

On Monday afternoon, October 31, 1988, 41-year-old Henry Posner walked off the grounds of Delaware State Hospital. No one noticed that Posner was missing until five, when he didn't report to his treatment supervisor as scheduled. The police searched the surrounding area. They said Posner was potentially violent and asked the public to be on the lookout for him.

The police interviewed several staff members at Delaware State Hospital, including Dr. Martin Cohen, director of the institution. Dr. Cohen said that Posner had not "escaped" from the hospital. He labeled the situation as "unauthorized absence." He pointed out that Posner had not been violent during the past seven years, and he refused to sign a warrant for Posner's arrest. Cohen also told the police he thought that Posner had run off to California to be with his girlfriend.

"It is not an escape as you would think of it, where someone forcibly pushes past the staff or goes over a fence with barbed wire," Cohen told a local newspaper reporter. "He is no greater a danger to society, except that he still has symptoms of mental illness, than any one of us."

He opened a pack of Marlboro Lights and dropped the cellophane wrapper to the floor. He lit a cigarette and checked the parking area outside through the second-floor window. No signs of the police. Evidently the neighbors hadn't heard anything.

He crossed the hall, walked passed the corpse of the old woman and looked into the back bedroom. He flicked his cigarette butt at the body of the old man who lay there. He felt relieved. They had given him no choice. They had shattered his life, and they had paid the price. If anyone had deserved to die, those two wretches had.

He was trembling. He looked at his hands and arms. They were covered with blood. His shirt and pants were flecked with blood. The raw power of death was such a rush. He had created anarchy in a perverse world. Nothing mattered anymore, not even human life, his own or anyone else's. He took a shower.

He took the wallet from the old man's pants, pulled out a wad of cash, stuffed it in his pocket, and dropped the wallet to the floor. Now he needed to get high, very high, and he knew where he could score. He had a long drive ahead, and he had to maintain the rush. He felt giddy and excited, as if he had just begun to live.

Monday, November 14, 1988, was cool and cloudy. It had rained the day before, and everything was still damp. It was Naomi Wirt's first day back at work after a two-week vacation. Wirt had worked for over 28 years at Delaware State Hospital as an administrative assistant for half a dozen different hospital directors.

Wirt came in at seven-thirty and immediately noticed something odd. The lights weren't on in the director's suite of offices, and the door was locked. Since Dr. Martin Cohen had been named director of the hospital seven months ago, he'd always been in his offices by seven with the lights on and the door unlocked, reading his newspaper.

Wirt unlocked the door and turned on the lights. She

thought Cohen might be at an early meeting in another building on the hospital grounds and that he'd show up soon. Just to be sure she checked his secretary's appointment book, but his entire day was open.

By 8 o'clock the department heads had gathered for their daily staff meeting, but Dr. Cohen still hadn't shown up. They waited a few minutes for him before starting. Val Starcher, the deputy director, conducted the meeting. Afterward she asked Wirt about Dr. Cohen's whereabouts.

"He must've told Karen that he was taking a vacation day," said Naomi, referring to Dr. Cohen's secretary, who had taken the day off, "and Karen forgot to write it in his appointment book before she left for the weekend."

Starcher and Wirt assumed that Dr. Cohen would soon arrive or that someone would call with an explanation. Wirt went through the stack of papers that had piled up on her desk during her vacation, but she was worried. It wasn't like Dr. Cohen not to call or leave word if he wasn't going to be in.

When Dr. Cohen still hadn't arrived an hour later, Wirt called Personnel. They hadn't received notification that he was taking a vacation day. Wirt called Neil Meisler's secretary. Meisler, the head of the Division of Mental Health and Alcohol and Drug Abuse, was Cohen's supervisor. Wirt asked her if Meisler was having one of his breakfast meetings. He wasn't. Meisler was at a conference in Philadelphia, and his secretary hadn't received any word about Dr. Cohen taking the day off.

Starcher found out that Dr. Richard Winkelmayer, the medical director of the hospital, was attending a morning meeting at the Ramada Inn, just across Route 13. Maybe Dr. Cohen was at the meeting. The previous Friday had been a paid holiday for the hospital staff, so Starcher hadn't seen Cohen since Thursday afternoon. She found out from the switchboard operator that he had been in his office on Friday morning.

Wirt called the town house the Cohens rented in Hockessin, a small town in northern Delaware a few miles from the borders of both Maryland and Pennsylvania. The Cohens had moved to Delaware from Peoria, Illinois, last spring and hadn't yet bought a house. There was no answer. If Dr. Cohen were caught in traffic, his wife Ethel or their son Charlie would have answered one of Wirt's calls. Evidently, they weren't home either. Charlie was a student at the University of Delaware, so maybe Ethel was giving Charlie a ride to school.

As the morning dragged on Starcher and Wirt became more concerned. Wirt called the Cohen house every half hour or so but didn't get an answer. Wirt wondered if the heater in the new town house had malfunctioned. Maybe gas had leaked into the house. She tried not to think about such things and reassured herself that the confusion was just a minor foul-up.

Mae Lagana, Dr. Cohen's sister from Flushing, New York, called at eleven and asked to speak with her brother. When Naomi told her he wasn't in, Lagana became quite worried. She explained that she had phoned the Cohen household on Sunday morning, but no one had answered. She and her brother, Martin spoke on the phone nearly every Sunday morning. The Cohens were planning to spend Thanksgiving with Lagana in New York, so she wanted to make arrangements for their visit. She had called several more times on Sunday, but each time there was no answer.

"Don't worry. They probably just went out of town for a few days," Wirt said. "How about if we send a security officer to the house, see if the car is there. If it isn't, we'll know they've gone somewhere."

"Fine," said Lagana.

"We'll let you know the minute we hear anything," said Wirt.

Starcher asked Randy Reed, the hospital's director of security, to drive to the Cohen town house in Hockessin to investigate. She didn't want to panic. Dr. Cohen could walk in or call any minute. There would be an obvious explanation, and they'd all laugh about it later. But something bothered her. She hadn't known Dr. Cohen that long, but this was very unlike him. Dr. Winkelmayer returned to the hospital around eleven-thirty. Dr. Cohen hadn't been at the meeting at the Ramada.

At noon Starcher called Meisler in Philadelphia. "Marty didn't show up this morning," she told him. "We're worried. His sister called, and she's in a panic."

Starcher and Meisler were well aware of the problems Dr. Cohen and the hospital were having with the Sussex 1 ward. The ward had failed an important Medicare inspection in October, and millions of dollars in federal funding were at stake. As a result, Cohen had been under a lot of stress.

"Let's not get too worked up over this," said Meisler. "He probably said, 'Screw it,' and went away for a couple of days."

Reed called Starcher during lunch from the Gateway Townhomes. He said that everything looked fine from the outside of the town house. He'd looked through the front window, but he couldn't see much because the window shades were drawn. No one had answered the front door, which was locked, and neither car was in the parking area in front of the house. Reed had also talked to the woman who lived next door. She said there hadn't been much activity at the house the past few days.

"What else can I do?" Reed asked.

Starcher told Reed to come back to the hospital, but she was puzzled. If the Cohens had gone away for the weekend, why had they taken both cars?

* * *

Mrs. Lagana called back that afternoon, and with no word from her brother she was becoming hysterical. She had last spoken to Martin Cohen on the previous Sunday, November 6, and he hadn't mentioned any problems.

"I just know something's wrong," she said to Wirt.

"Look, we know which realtor they rent from, and we can probably get a key," said Wirt, "but we can't go in there unless we have a family member's permission."

"You have it," said Lagana. "Break the door down if you have to."

Starcher called the real estate office that managed the rental. The agent who handled the house had the key in her possession and wasn't scheduled to return to the office until later that afternoon. When Starcher finally contacted the agent, she agreed to leave the key in the office for them.

Starcher and Randy Reed left the hospital at 4 o'clock and headed for the real estate office. They both had a strange, ominous feeling and didn't speak much during the drive. They picked up the key and got to the Gateway Townhomes in Hockessin at four-forty.

Starcher sat in the car in the parking area in front of 532 Beech Tree Lane writing a note to Dr. Cohen. "Sorry to barge in. We were concerned, so we came to look for you. Call your sister. She's worried."

Reed rang the doorbell. No one answered. He inserted a key into the top lock. It was a deadbolt, and it wasn't locked. He slid a different key into the lower lock. The door opened into the living room as he turned the key.

The place was messy and dark. A pile of newspapers lay at the foot of a chair. Some papers had been knocked off the desk in the dining room, and a drawer or two had been left open.

Starcher called out, "Is anybody home?" No one answered.

"I'll look on the first floor, you look around upstairs," she said to Reed.

Reed went up the flight of stars while Starcher walked down the hall and looked in the first-floor bedroom. The covers on one side of the bed had been pulled down.

Reed called down to her. "Val, there's a woman up here, and she's not moving."

Starcher rushed to the stairs. "What do you mean?"

"She's on the floor," he said, "and she has a cane."

Starcher slowly walked up the stairs far enough to see Ethel Cohen's feet and the hem of her housedress. Starcher also saw a barbell on the floor near her.

"Oh, my God, it's Ethel," she said. "Is she dead?"

"I think so."

Reed turned, glanced down the hall through an open door into a bedroom, and saw the body of Dr. Martin Cohen. He was lying facedown on the floor.

"Oh, no," he said. "Marty's here, too."

"My God," Starcher shouted. "Is he dead?"

Reed had seen several dead bodies when he was in Vietnam, and he knew what they looked like. "Yeah, he's dead, Val. They're both dead."

Starcher intuitively knew what had happened. A terrifying thought suddenly occured to her. What if he were still in the house? She screamed, ran down the stairs, and out the front door. Reed was right behind her.

They ran next door. Starcher pounded on the door and told a neighbor to call 911. It was 4:47. Reed got on the phone and explained the situation to police. Starcher spoke with the neighbor, Carol Herington.

"Dear God, don't make it be what I think it is," said Herington.

"What do you think it is?" Starcher asked.

"I don't want to say what I'm thinking."

"Tell me, because I'm thinking something, too."

"The son," she said. "He's strange."

Starcher had been thinking the same thing.

chapter 2

- - - - - - - -

Extreme Trauma

It was 6 P.M., and everyone was standing around outside looking at the Cohen town house. The area was filled with police, who wouldn't let anyone near the house. Starcher and Reed were still there, along with Neil Meisler, who had rushed over after Starcher had called the hospital and cried, "They're dead! They're dead!"

Half a dozen New Castle County Police investigators were there, including John Downs, who had been assigned as chief investigating officer for the case. The Evidence Detection Unit (EDU) officers were ready to comb the inside of the house. Dozens of curious neighbors had gathered in the street. They were joined by several construction workers, who were at the site finishing up work on the subdivision. The emergency medical people had already left. The coroner's staff had arrived and were ready to remove the bodies, but they had to wait just like everybody else.

Assistant State Prosecutor Steve Walther was there, too. Walther lived in Hockessin, so he walked to the crime scene. The media were there in full force as well, including vans full of reporters and cameramen from the

Philadelphia television stations. The CBS crew had set up a tall retractable pole with floodlights. They wanted to get some shots when the coroner brought the bodies out. The police authorities wouldn't tell them anything, so the reporters could only wait.

Everyone quietly stared at the modern, gray, two-story town house as if they were waiting for someone to emerge. They knew, however, that Martin and Ethel Cohen wouldn't be walking out. A physician had examined the bodies an hour ago and had pronounced them dead.

The police had sent an officer to find the closest magistrate and obtain a warrant, and nothing could be done until then. There was no point in removing the bodies and risk disturbing a piece of crucial evidence until EDU had a chance to sweep the house for trace evidence.

In the meantime, police officers were stationed at the front and back doors. They put crime scene tape around the perimeter of the residence. Several officers searched the small yards in front and back of the house for evidence. They found a few cigarette butts and a ballpoint pen. They used the neighbors' phone to communicate with headquarters to prevent the media from listening in on their police radios.

The police also stationed a patrolman at the entrance of the development with instructions to hold Charles Cohen, the couple's son, if he attempted to enter the Gateway Townhomes. They expected him to return from school at any time, and they didn't want him to walk up and hear from a stranger that his parents had been murdered.

It was getting colder as it got dark, and John Downs was hungry. He'd been at home eating when the call came in, and within minutes he had been out the door and on his way. He knew it would be a long time before he'd get to eat again. Downs had been with the New Castle County Police for seven years, the first six as a patrolman. He had a reputation for being meticulous, dedicated, and intelligent. He'd never worked on a murder case that had gone unsolved.

While he was waiting, Downs spoke with Mrs. Herington, the neighbor. She told Downs what she knew about the family. The Cohens had moved into the development in May, just as the first few units were being finished, and they had been good neighbors. Ethel Cohen had needed a walker to get around and had been taking swimming classes for her arthritis. She had also been an occupational therapist and had worked two mornings a week at Delaware State Hospital. Their only son, Charles, was a college student, and he had a band that played loud rock music in the basement.

Mrs. Herington had last seen Ethel Cohen, whom she said was very outgoing and funny, at about 3 o'clock on Saturday afternoon. Ethel had gotten out of their big Ford and limped toward the Cohen town house. Mrs. Herington had met her outside, and they'd had a friendly chat.

Mrs. Herington told Downs that she and her husband hadn't heard any odd noises or disturbances over the weekend. The town houses were soundproof, and they had heard almost nothing from the Cohens except for the son's band. She and her husband had been awake early Sunday morning and had noticed that neither of the Cohens' cars were in the parking area.

The call came at six-fifty. They had a search warrant and could go in. The EDU officers began combing the place methodically for evidence. Downs went upstairs and found Ethel Cohen in the loft near the landing. She was a heavyset woman and looked to be about retirement age. She was lying facedown on top of two plastic trash bags. Her head rested partially against the half wall of the loft overlooking the living room. There was an indentation in the wall near her head.

A wooden cane was wedged at an odd angle under her body. Her right shoulder rested against a portable TV. Blood was splattered on the bottom of the wall near her head, and a puddle of blood twelve inches wide had soaked into the carpet under her head. Downs noted extreme trauma to the back of her head, and her hair was matted with coagulated blood. On the floor just three feet away was a ten-pound black wrought-iron Weider barbell with blood on it.

She was wearing a red, white, and blue flower print housedress but no panty hose, shoes, or socks. There were bloodstains on the top of the railing. The loft was cluttered with papers, magazines, clothing, dirty paper cups and plates, and a pair of Converse All-Star sneakers.

Martin Cohen was in the second-floor bedroom. He was a short man with a paunch and dark hair and looked to be about 60 years old. He lay in the middle of the room partly on his right side with both arms extending to the left, his feet pointed toward the door. He was wearing a pair of dark green slacks, but no shoes, shirt, or socks.

There were multiple wounds visible on the back of his head and deep, gaping cuts on his throat and neck. Both areas were covered with coagulated blood. Streaks of dried blood ran down his back from eight or nine stab wounds. There was a large quantity of blood on the floor near his head. A folding knife with a brown wooden handle lay near his hands. Its four-inch blade was covered with blood. The handle rested on his forearm, the blade between his arms in a puddle of blood.

Dr. Cohen's head rested partially on a blue notebook. His right rear pants pocket was turned out, and his black leather wallet was on the floor next to the pocket. Any cash he'd had in his wallet was gone. There was another barbell near his body, and it, too, had blood on it.

A pack of Marlboro Light cigarettes lay between his legs, and an empty cigarette carton was on the floor near his head. On the floor next to his body was an ashtray and a burnt cigarette. There were several cellophane cigarette pack wrappers on the floor of the bedroom as well. Cohen's glasses had fallen off and were lying next to his knee.

The room was a mess. Every surface including the floor was cluttered and dirty. There was a pile of men's clothing on the floor near Dr. Cohen's feet. The clothing appeared to have been folded before being thrown on the floor. Most of the dresser drawers were open and empty, and another pile of clothing lay in front of the closet, which was almost empty.

There were sprays of blood on three of the four walls in the room. There was no bed in the room, but blankets and bed covers had been laid out on the floor by the wall under the windows.

Downs found the handset of a portable phone on the bedroom floor between the doorway and a chest of drawers. It was flecked with blood. The base unit for the phone was in the loft. He also found a large sketch pad on the floor. It was opened to a page with a crudely drawn, bearded, muscle-bound man with a horrific face. His features were contorted in rage and hatred; his teeth were rows of pointed razors. Like almost everything else in the room, the drawing was flecked with blood.

The police found damp towels on the floor of the second-floor bathroom. They also found small amounts of blood on the bathroom door handle, on the light switch, and in the sink drain.

The living room, kitchen, and bedroom had been thoroughly ransacked. The fold-down lid of the desk in the dining room was open. Papers, envelopes, files, pens, bills, and other office items had been pulled out of the desk and onto the desktop and the floor.

A gray leather woman's pocketbook was open on the floor. Its contents were on the floor. A red wallet was on top of the pocketbook. It was Ethel Cohen's, and it didn't contain any cash. It did contain dozens of senior citizen discount cards for restaurants and fast-food chains, hundreds of grocery coupons, $200 in American Express traveler's checks, a 1958 Actors' Equity card for Sharon Wells, and several Delaware Lotto tickets.

The master bedroom had been torn up as well. Martin and Ethel Cohen's belongings were strewn about the floor, the tops of the two dressers, and the bed. Virtually every dresser drawer was open, and objects were left hanging out of the drawers. Jewelry boxes had been opened and dumped. The nightstand drawer was also open, the contents on the floor. Several small containers had been opened and their contents dumped on the bed. Downs discovered $700 in cash inside a brown American Express check holder on the bed.

The kitchen table and chairs were covered with piles of papers, letters, dishes, spices, and discount coupons. A Marlboro Light cigarette butt had been put on the kitchen tabletop and left there. The kitchen counter was similarly cluttered. Papers and mail had been knocked to the floor, and there were several cigarette butts in a pan in the kitchen sink. The oven contained a charred casserole covered with tin foil and was set at 350 degrees. An EDU officer turned it off.

Several hundred boxes took up most of the space in the basement with the exception of a small area that had been cleared for the band. Drums, amplifiers, a microphone, and a bass guitar stood among a tangle of wires. There were several more cigarette butts on the floor of the basement.

There were no signs of forced entry—no pry marks on the front or back doors and no broken windows. All the windows were locked. It was getting late, and the couple's son still hadn't shown up.

Downs soon had information on the Cohen family vehicles—a dark blue '83 Ford LTD Crown Victoria and a yellow '84 Nissan Sentra, both registered in Delaware. They weren't in the parking area in the Gateway Townhomes, and the garage was empty.

The police also obtained information about the son from the University of Delaware. Charles Cohen was currently enrolled in undergraduate art classes. Brown hair, blue eyes, five feet ten inches tall. Born on December 6, 1964, which made him 23 years old, just three weeks shy of his 24th birthday.

By ten-thirty the EDU detectives felt it was safe to remove the bodies, and the coroner's people came in. Downs helped. When they lifted Ethel Cohen, they found that her throat had been cut almost to her spine. They found a large gaping knife wound on the left side of Martin Cohen's neck, and his pants were urine-stained. Both had been beaten on the back of the head with a heavy, blunt object.

Dr. Ali Hameli, the chief medical examiner for the state of Delaware, gave a short statement to the press. He identified the preliminary cause of death as "multiple internal and external wounds caused by a sharp instrument." He placed the time of death from 24 to 36 hours before the bodies were discovered.

Walther also toured the crime scene. He had been a criminal prosecutor for the state of Delaware for thirteen years. He was second in command to state prosecutor Gene Hall, and he and Hall were responsible for assigning cases.

Walther realized that this wasn't your run-of-the-mill domestic dispute or drunken brawl variety of murder. Martin Cohen was an important and well-known civil servant, and the case would require one of their most experienced prosecutors and lots of investigation.

When Hall showed up at the crime scene Walther told him, "I'm keeping this one." Hall had no objections.

Several groups of patrolmen were sent to search for the Cohens' cars. They cruised through nearby quarries, dumps, construction sites, parking lots, service stations, farms, and side roads. One patrol team drove into Pennsylvania, and another searched the Delaware State Hospital grounds and the surrounding area.

The police also started interviewing the residents of the Gateway Townhomes. Starcher, Reed, and Meisler were taken to police headquarters and interviewed. A young woman named Darlene called the residence while the police were processing the scene and asked to speak with Charles Cohen. Two detectives were sent to interview her. A detective back at headquarters started calling the Cohens' relatives, trying to find out what he could about the family.

As the night wore on and Charles Cohen didn't show up, the focus of the investigation turned to his whereabouts. The police wondered if he had gone away for the weekend and still didn't know about the murders. They also considered the possibilities that he might have been kidnapped and killed or that he had committed the murders.

They soon found out that the Cohens had lived in the Illinois cities of Galesburg and Peoria before moving to Delaware, so they contacted police departments in both cities and told them that Charles Cohen, if still alive, might be traveling to Illinois in either of the two family cars.

Downs found names, addresses, and phone numbers of several of Charles Cohen's friends in his bedroom and went looking for them. He interviewed a University of

Delaware art student from Hockessin who car pooled with Cohen to classes in Newark, which was about six miles south. He also interviewed the ex-guitar player from Cohen's band, who said that Cohen had a cocaine problem a few years ago in Illinois and had gotten treatment. Downs woke up the bass player, Mark, at 3 A.M. He had a multicolored Mohawk, pierced ears and nipples, and several self-applied tattoos. All three claimed that they hadn't seen Charles Cohen in the past week. They also said that they knew nothing about the murders and that they had no idea where he was.

The police put out an all-points bulletin for Charles Cohen. They also asked all local police agencies to be on the lookout for the Nissan and the Ford. Stolen vehicle reports on both cars were entered into the National Crime Information Computer (NCIC), which is maintained by the FBI and is routinely accessed by police departments across the country.

At 4:30 A.M., Downs checked with local hospitals for Charles Cohen. Nothing. The EDU staff didn't leave 532 Beech Tree Lane until 9 o'clock the next morning.

chapter 3

- - - - - - - -

Eyes Without a Face

On Tuesday morning the police brought Darlene to head-quarters for an interview. She had a shaved head except for a four-inch lock of hair that hung down over her eyes. The 16-year-old was a chronic runaway and hung out on Main Street in Newark. She'd met Cohen two weeks ago through the guys in Cohen's band.

Cohen was strange, morbid, and moody, she said. "He talked about death all the time like he was gonna kill himself," said Darlene. About a week before the murders he told her, "I have an idea I'm going to get in trouble with the law."

Darlene had not seen him use any drugs, but he had asked her if she knew where he could get some cocaine. She also said that Cohen had a knife. He'd shown it to her. Her description of the knife matched the knife found near Martin Cohen's body.

Charles Cohen immediately became the prime suspect.

Neil Meisler went to the morgue on Tuesday morning to identify the bodies. It was worse than he had expected. Martin and Ethel had been beaten so badly he didn't see why the murderer had bothered to cut their throats. Whoever had done this hadn't wanted to simply end two lives. He or she had wanted to completely destroy two human beings.

Autopsies were performed on both Martin and Ethel Cohen later that morning. Martin Cohen had four gaping wounds on the back of his head. The coroner estimated that they had been made by at least six blows from a blunt instrument, and they were consistent in size and shape with the edges of the barbells. The blows had caused brain damage, brain hemorrhaging, and numerous skull fractures.

The coroner found a deep, hook-shaped cut on Cohen's neck, which had severed a major artery, and large indentations on the bridge of his nose and his right temple. He had small cuts on his forehead, nose, and one of his eyebrows. There were eight stab wounds on his back as well, two of which had entered his lungs.

He had several cuts on the fingers of both hands, which most likely had been inflicted while struggling to defend himself. The murderer hadn't simply knocked him out and quickly stabbed him. There had been a struggle, and Martin Cohen had died fighting for his life. The official cause of his death was listed as massive internal and external bleeding.

The two gashes on the back of Ethel Cohen's head were similar to those on her husband's head, with similar skull fractures, brain damage, and brain hemorrhaging. There was a six-inch-long, two-inch-deep gaping wound on the front of her neck just above her Adam's apple. It had severed her trachea and right jugular. The murderer had made at least three separate knife strokes inflicting the wound. The coroner concluded that the severing of the right carotid artery had caused the death of Ethel Cohen.

The coroner mentioned to the officers present that the

attacker knew exactly where to cut the main arteries on both victims. No alcohol was found in either victim's bloodstream or liver. Martin Cohen was 59 at the time of his death; Ethel Cohen was 64.

On Tuesday, New Castle County Police set up around-the-clock surveillance at the town house. Charles Cohen could show up at any time, and the police couldn't afford to miss him if he wandered back to Hockessin. One plain-clothes officer was stationed in an unmarked car directly across the parking lot from 532 Beech Tree Lane, and another was stationed inside the town house.

That afternoon Downs obtained another search warrant for 532 Beech Tree Lane. He and several detectives went through the house more thoroughly. He noticed that there wasn't much clothing in Charles Cohen's bedroom. The bureau had only two pairs of underwear and no socks. The clothing that remained seemed to be dirty or not needed.

Downs also found three drawings of the coffee table that was in Charles Cohen's bedroom. All three drawings showed a portable Sony cassette stereo on the table, but there was no stereo on the table. The spot was vacant.

He found several more pieces of artwork in the bedroom closet, including a watercolor and pencil drawing of several bottles, a small fish bowl, and a pair of eyes titled, "eyes without a face." He found a collage of several photocopied drawings. The edges of the collage were torn, and the phrase, "Never Tear Us Apart," was written on the back.

The detectives found checkbooks and credit cards from a dozen banks and financial institutions among Martin and Ethel Cohen's belongings. They also found a children's book entitled *Every Time I Think of You* with an inscription on the inside cover—"From Dad to Charlie, Sept. '72." They turned up a card from a florist in Ethel's belongings with the handwritten note, "You're still my best girl! Love, Charlie."

Tuesday was a hectic day at Delaware State Hospital. The phone rang constantly. Dozens of people called to confirm the Cohens' deaths. Karen, Martin Cohen's secretary, was hysterical and couldn't bring herself to go near the director's offices.

Two detectives went to Delaware State Hospital to search Cohen's offices and to interview people there. They learned that Dr. Martin Cohen had worked in mental health facilities for the state of Illinois for over thirty years, but he'd lost his job when the Galesburg Mental Health Center had closed in the mid-'80s.

"Was Martin Cohen depressed?" an investigator asked Starcher.

"What?"

"Did he ever talk about suicide?"

"Are you crazy?" she asked. She told them she thought Charles Cohen had murdered his parents.

The police discovered that Martin Cohen had been worried over recent events at the hospital. There was the failed Medicare survey, and Karen confirmed that Henry Posner's continued absence had been wearing on him as well. The hospital employees had hints of problems between Dr. Cohen and his son, but they didn't know anything specific. Whenever Dr. Cohen spoke about his son, it was usually in a very flattering manner. However, he had admitted to several people at the hospital that his son "hadn't found himself yet." There were rumors of the son's past drug use, but Martin Cohen never mentioned any problems at home. He showed no signs of violence, such as bruises or scrapes, and he hadn't missed a day of work in his eight months at the hospital.

The police also spoke with Dr. Richard Winkelmayer about Posner. Winkelmayer told them that Cohen had no contact with Posner other than seeing him in the ward occasionally. He didn't believe Posner was capable of murdering Dr. Cohen. Posner was lazy and didn't follow hospital rules, but he wasn't violent. "Posner would rather lie around and drink beer," said Winkelmayer.

The police also confiscated a painting and a small plaster sculpture by Charles Cohen from Martin Cohen's office. Starcher mentioned that she knew the director of the art therapy program at Hahnemann University in Philadelphia, Ronald Hays, and that it might be worthwhile to have him evaluate the artwork. Hays could look at the artwork and provide some insight into the mind of the person who had created it, said Starcher.

Charles Cohen had spent much of his youth and adolescence in Galesburg, Illinois, and after hearing about the murders, his friends and acquaintances in the quiet midwestern community were terrified that he would return. The newspapers were reporting that Cohen might be on his way back to central Illinois. Several of Cohen's acquaintances in Galesburg noticed that they were getting hang-up phone calls occasionally, and numerous residents thought they had seen Cohen in Galesburg. The police investigated each of the sightings, but they all turned out to be false.

After hearing about the murders on the radio while driving to work on Tuesday morning, Rick Muncey, a Galesburg resident, had to pull over to the side of the road. He simply couldn't drive anymore. He'd been one of Charlie's closest friends, and he couldn't believe that Charlie had killed his parents.

Rick thought that maybe Charlie had gotten involved with selling drugs again. Maybe he owed so much money that the dealers had come after him, and his parents had gotten in the way. Maybe Charlie had taken off in one of the cars, afraid that if he surfaced he'd be murdered, too.

That had to be it—a drug deal gone bad. Charlie couldn't have killed anyone.

Rick immediately contacted the Galesburg police and told them that if Cohen came to Galesburg, he would most likely come to the house he rented with some college buddies. Rick hadn't seen Charlie since before he had moved to Delaware seven months ago, but Charlie had written to him five or six times since then, and they'd spoken on the phone several times as well.

Rick also gave the police a tape recording he'd received from Charlie a few weeks before. It contained over ten minutes of Cohen chanting song lyrics and poems he'd evidently written. All the lyrics focused on hatred, destruction, pain, death, suicide, or insanity, and they were delivered in a frightening, maniacal rant. Rick mentioned that the weirdness of the tape was not particularly unusual for Charlie. He was always like that.

Rick didn't want to endanger his roommates, so he moved back home with his parents, who also lived in Galesburg. He didn't get much sleep, and he kept the doors locked. His father went out and bought a handgun. His three roommates in the rented house began sleeping in the same room with the lights on.

Greg, another Galesburg native who had briefly known Cohen, also came to the Galesburg police headquarters that day. He brought with him some of Cohen's sketches he had received through the mail at his parents' house. The drawings were gruesome and frightening, especially the one of a nude male holding a knife. Greg was worried. Obviously Cohen had his parents' address, and if he'd sent him this freaky artwork for no particular reason, he might do something crazy, like show up at his parents' house. They weren't even close friends, Greg explained. The Galesburg police forwarded the drawings and the tape to Downs.

When she heard that Martin and Ethel Cohen had been

found murdered and that Charlie was missing, Mrs. Nancy Harriman, another Galesburg native, called her son John at the University of Illinois in Champaign-Urbana. Charlie and John had been good friends, and she thought that Charlie might show up on campus looking for him.

Mrs. Harriman also prayed that Charlie was dead. If he were, it would mean he hadn't murdered his parents. If he had, she prayed that Ethel hadn't realized what was happening. She knew how Ethel had worshiped Charlie. It would've been worse than death itself for her to know that her only son had turned on her.

At 1 o'clock on Tuesday afternoon, two Philadelphia Electric Company employees found a yellow Nissan Sentra abandoned in a wooded area about a quarter mile from I–95 in Chester, Pennsylvania, a small city near Pittsburgh.

All four tires were missing from the Nissan, the hood was up, and the battery and air filter were gone. Both doors on the driver's side were open, and cigar boxes, a briefcase, floor mats, a window squeegie, papers, and maps were scattered on the ground near the doors. Materials from the glove box had been pulled out onto the seat.

The electric company employees contacted the police, who ran an NCIC search on the vehicle information number. The search revealed that the Nissan was one of the missing Cohen family cars. There were no signs that the car had been hot wired or that the ignition had been popped to start it. It had been driven by key, although the keys weren't in the car. The license plates were in the trunk.

While the Chester police examined the Nissan, they saw a man walking nearby along I-95. Upon questioning him, they discovered that his name was Albert McRea and that he was wanted on an outstanding warrant for vehicle theft. McRea, 34 and unemployed, had three previous arrests for offenses including assault, burglary, terrorist threats, harassment, discharging firearms in city limits, and endangering another person.

Two New Castle County Police officers went to Chester that afternoon. They questioned McRea, but he wouldn't cooperate. They had no idea if McRea had anything to do with the Nissan or the Cohens. They had the Nissan towed back to New Castle County Police headquarters.

That afternoon James Williams, an art instructor at the University of Delaware, gave the police a drawing Cohen had done for Williams's drawing class. Cohen hadn't attended class since Wednesday, November 2, when he'd handed in the drawing. Williams said it was disturbing, especially in light of recent events.

The assignment had been to sketch a group of objects that had been assembled by the drawing instructors and placed in the center of the classroom. Cohen had drawn everything in the assemblage, but he'd added two items— two disembodied human heads, one male, one female. According to Williams, the heads didn't resemble any of the students in the class.

Williams mentioned one more thing about Cohen. When he had first come to class in early September, he was dressed in normal clothing and his hair was cut in a conservative style. By the next class Cohen's appearance had changed drastically. He had a Mohawk haircut and was dressed like a punk rocker.

On Tuesday afternoon, Walther, Downs, and several other investigators met to review the case. Everything pointed to the missing son. Darlene had described the knife. Some of Cohen's belongings were evidently missing. Plus, the kid seemed weird, and his drug history was coming to light.

Even as a prime suspect, the main question remained: Where was he? As Downs told one of Cohen's friends, "At this point anything's a possibility. We are looking at friends, enemies, strangers. Our biggest problem is that Charles is not to be found. Now, that obviously creates a lot of questions as to why he is not around. If he did it, he's dangerous. If he didn't do it, we need to clear that out, so we can get back to the business of finding out who did do it."

Other than the empty wallets, there weren't any of the telltale signs of a robbery. There were no signs of forced entry, and valuables such as jewelry, TVs, and the VCR weren't taken. The investigators concluded that the murderer was someone close to the family, someone the Cohens had let into their house. From the Cohens' attire, police surmised that they had been up and awake at the time of the murders.

Another angle police were considering was someone with a grudge against Ethel or Martin. Maybe Martin had had an affair, and a jilted lover had gone off the deep end. It was just a theory because so far no evidence had turned up to support it.

The severity and number of injuries also indicated a family member or someone very close to the family. Typically, burglars don't murder, and when they do, they don't take the time to bash in someone's head, stab them repeatedly, and slit their throat. The murderer in this case, however, had been enraged and obviously had a great deal of animosity toward the Cohens.

It seemed likely that two people were involved in the murders since both cars were missing. One person couldn't have driven both cars away from the murder scene, certainly not at the same time. Since the Nissan had turned up, were the two murderers traveling together

in the '83 Ford? And how and why had the Nissan been
abandoned in Chester? Was one of the murderers from
Chester, or was Chester just a convenient place to dump
the car? Since Charles Cohen had a drug history and
Chester was an easy place to make a quick buy, it seemed
likely that drugs were somehow involved.

Posner was still a live possibility, and the police intensified their search for him, but there was no sign of him
anywhere. If Posner had shown up at the Cohen town
house, would Dr. Cohen have him let him in? Dr. Cohen
had told the police that Posner wasn't dangerous, so perhaps he would have.

And why were the bodies, especially Ethel Cohen's, on
the second floor? Most of the people who knew her said
she couldn't have climbed the stairs. In fact, the contrac-
tors had installed a handrail near the front door so she
could make it up the two front steps. She couldn't possibly have gotten up the thirteen steps to the second floor
without help, unless she had been motivated by pure
adrenaline and terror.

chapter 4

- - - - - - - -

All My Righteousness
Is As Filthy Rags

By 1980, John Downs had been the pastor of a Baptist church in Wilmington for several years. He felt he had done all he could at the church, so he started looking for another ministry.

Downs and his wife wanted to stay in Delaware, but Downs couldn't find a job opening for a Baptist minister in the area. In 1982 he heard that the New Castle County Police was accepting applications. He applied and was hired. He knew that someday he'd go back to the ministry, but he accepted his new profession as part of Jesus' plan for him.

When Downs started at the department, some of the officers and patrolmen were skeptical. They weren't convinced the ex-minister had what it took. They weren't sure he could be trusted when things got rough out on the street, so they tested him. They made him handle difficult situations without interceding on his behalf, and the ex-minister passed the test.

After five years as a patrolman, Downs was promoted to detective. He soon found that it wasn't a glamorous job. There was more drudgery than glamour, and the hours were ridiculous. But writing reports at home on weekends, being on call around the clock, and getting woken up at 2 A.M. didn't bother Downs. It was just like being a minister; you were always on the job. Human sinfulness didn't take evenings and weekends off.

The police searched for the '83 Ford everywhere. They even had a patrolman scour the area from a helicopter, but there was no sign of the Ford. Downs was certain that Cohen had fled the area in the Ford. He could be almost anywhere by now, even out of the country.

The week dragged on. Downs and his team of investigators kept getting sidetracked with false sightings and rumors. Each had to be tracked down, using up precious time.

Evidently a dark blue Ford LTD with Illinois plates was being driven around the Wilmington area. Several people had called the New Castle County Police Hotline, but the description of the driver didn't match Cohen. A truck driver from Delaware thought he had seen Cohen hitchhiking on an interstate in Pennsylvania. The suspect had approached him at a rest stop and asked for a ride in whatever direction the trucker was going.

Strange rumors about the Cohens and Posner swept through Delaware State Hospital. One alleged that Posner had played in Charles Cohen's band. Downs sent an investigator to Delaware State Hospital to check it out. He interviewed numerous employees but found no evidence that Henry Posner knew Charles Cohen.

Downs spent one afternoon going through pawn sheets, which contained records of all silver and gold transactions at pawn shops in the county. After four or five hours he discovered that Cohen had sold a 14K gold pendant at a jewelry shop in Newark on October 17 for $60. Downs suspected that the pendant had belonged to Ethel Cohen. Downs noticed that Cohen had written his old Peoria address and phone number on the receipt. Evidently, he didn't want anyone from the shop calling his parents' town house and inadvertently letting them know what he had done. A model child, Downs thought.

Downs decided to locate as many of Charlie Cohen's friends as he could until the kid came up for air. He found numerous Illinois phone numbers among the belongings in Cohen's room and on the family's recent phone bills. During the next few days, he called them all.

Cohen's Illinois acquaintances all claimed that they hadn't heard from him or seen him since the murders. Downs was naturally suspicious of everyone he interviewed, but he tended to believe Cohen's Illinois friends. Most of them were sincerely frightened that Charlie would turn up on their doorsteps. Real fear was hard to fake, and Downs knew it when he heard it. Downs urged them not to protect him if he showed up. "I understand he's your friend," Downs told one young man, "but he's in more trouble now than you can help him with."

Downs also interviewed several of Cohen's friends in Delaware. Most of them were teenage punkers who hung out on Main Street in Newark. Many of them were chronic runaways, and most of them hated authority figures like cops.

Downs learned that Cohen had been in and out of five different colleges during the past six years. He'd also enlisted in the Marines in December 1983, over his parents' objections. He had lasted only two weeks before being discharged for fraudulent enlistment.

At various times in his life, Cohen had told friends that he hated his parents. He felt that they were trying to run his life. He had moved out of the house on numerous occasions, but he had never made it on his own. He had always ended up back with his parents, financially dependent on them. Several people said Cohen had problems communicating, that he was a loner, kept to himself, and didn't have many friends.

He'd told one Illinois friend that he was adopted. However, the Cohens' relatives verified that he was Martin and Ethel Cohen's natural son. One of his aunts said that Charlie's major problem was that he didn't want to work. She said that his parents were always on him to get a job.

Downs also learned that in August 1988, several months after moving to Delaware, Martin and Ethel Cohen had given their son approximately $1,500 to buy band equipment, and he had invited his new friends from Newark to join the band. About this same time, Cohen seemed to change. He became angry and negative, according to one of his Delaware friends. He started dressing differently, more like the kids on Main Street.

Cohen had told several people in Delaware that he didn't use drugs anymore, but Downs learned that Cohen had acquired some cocaine and snorted it at a friend's house in Newark just a few days before the murder. He had told his friends that his grandfather had died and left him some money, which explained how he could afford the coke. Downs discovered that no one on either side of the Cohen family had died recently or left an inheritance for Charlie.

Approximately five days before the murders, Cohen had told a fellow University of Delaware student that a friend from his band in Illinois had just committed suicide. Cohen had said he felt compelled to do something radical in response. Downs found out that none of the band members in Illinois had committed suicide.

Downs also found out that Cohen had been arrested for shoplifting in Phoenix, Arizona, in 1986. According to Cohen's friends, he'd gotten in debt to some coke dealers and had fled Galesburg. He had ended up in Phoenix, where he was arrested for stealing some food from a fast-food restaurant.

Downs contacted the Phoenix Police Department. They had a set of Cohen's prints on file, and they immediately sent copies to Downs. The police compared Cohen's fingerprints to those found in the house. They discovered Cohen's prints on four of the ransacked items. They didn't find any prints on the knife or either of the dumbbells. They found only one partial print in the Nissan but couldn't match it. They also tested for traces of blood in the Nissan, but the results were negative.

Downs knew that the prints on the ransacked items wouldn't carry much weight in court. Even if Cohen's prints had been found on the murder weapons, they wouldn't necessarily help the case. Charles Cohen lived in the house, so naturally his fingerprints would be on many of the items in it.

Downs also found out that Cohen had known Anne Delaney, a 16-year-old who'd been reported missing by her mother in August. After running away, Delaney had crashed at Mark's place for most of July and August. The police hadn't been able to find her and had treated her disappearance as a standard runaway. She'd completely disappeared from the area in September, and the rumor was that she'd hooked up with some Deadheads and followed a Grateful Dead tour across the country to San Francisco.

Downs wondered if Delaney's disappearance had anything to do with Cohen. Since Mark, the bass player, and Charlie had become very good friends during the time Anne had stayed with Mark, certainly she'd met Cohen. Maybe she'd run off with him, or maybe she'd become another of his victims.

On Wednesday night word got back to Downs that a Catholic high school student from Newark was telling people he knew who committed the murders. The police traced the rumor to a young man named Paul. On Friday night Downs and another investigator found Paul on Main Street. Paul had a tall, pointed Mohawk and had to hold his head sideways to get into Downs's police cruiser.

It wasn't easy interviewing the kid. He was drunk or high on something. They were able to ascertain, however, that he'd been one of Cohen's closest friends in Delaware. He'd also been the singer in Cohen's band for the final couple of practices. He knew nothing about the murders firsthand. He'd simply repeated rumors he'd heard. Paul told them lots about Cohen, however.

"He was really strange in a lot of ways," Paul said. "He said weird things. He was very morbid."

"Why do you say that?"

"His lyrics were a lot about depression, and his paintings and drawings would usually wind up with death somehow. He said, 'Killing someone would be doing them a favor so they won't have to live on this earth anymore.' Most of his conversations revolved around death. He didn't like life. He didn't like much. He was really antisocial. He used to scream, 'Anarchy!' I know a lot of weird people, so I never really thought much of it."

"Is there anything else that you can tell me about Charles?"

"Just that he's a good guy except he's really weird, and I wouldn't be surprised if he was the one who did it."

A clerk at a Hockessin grocery store remembered the Cohens getting in shouting matches with their son. About a week before the murders, a neighbor two doors away from 532 Beech Tree Lane had heard a harsh male voice from the Cohen town house say, "Give me that fucking thing."

A video store owner had seen Cohen in her store approximately three days before the Cohens' bodies were found. He had rented *Angel Heart,* which has several bloody murder scenes, for the second or third time. The police had found the VHS tape of *Angel Heart* in the house. It was due back to the video store on Monday, November 14, the same day his parents' bodies were found.

On numerous occasions Cohen had spoken to the

woman who owned the video store, but she had never remembered his name. When he left the store the previous Wednesday, he said to her, "Someday you'll remember my name."

Downs also interviewed the maids whom the Cohens had hired to clean every two weeks. For some reason, Ethel Cohen had told them not to clean or to even go into her son's bedroom on the second floor. One of the maids said that the son seemed to live in his own little world.

Another maid was at 532 Beech Tree Lane during a band practice, which she described as "just banging." Mrs. Cohen had told the maid that she didn't pay attention to the noise. She was just happy to know where he was. Mrs. Cohen had also told the maid that she never went upstairs. If she needed her son, she just went to the stairway and hollered for him.

New Castle County Police detectives interviewed several of Cohen's University of Delaware classmates, who described him as quiet and strange. One young woman said he routinely made statements out of the blue that made no sense. Another coed said that Cohen had always smiled and said weird things to try to shock her.

Downs found out during his interviews that Cohen normally wore blue jeans, T-shirts, tan boots or sneakers, a black leather hat, and a black leather jacket. Downs had also been told that Cohen owned cassette tapes by Sinead O'Conner, the Sugarcubes, REM, the Misfits, D.O.A., and the Exploited. On Thursday, Downs and several officers searched the Cohen town house but couldn't find the clothing or the cassettes. One of the detectives found a large sketch pad in the basement. He opened it and found a drawing of an older man being shot in the head. The drawing also contained large letters that read, "Fuck you mom and dad."

* * *

By Thursday the police had collected numerous samples of Charles Cohen's artwork. As Val Starcher had suggested, the police contacted Ronald E. Hays of the Creative Arts in Therapy Department at Hahnemann University, a large medical school in Philadelphia, and asked him to evaluate the artwork. He agreed. The police took several drawings and a plaster sculpture to Hahnemann. They didn't tell Hays anything about the case or about Cohen.

Hays and Tracy Foedisch, an art therapist, examined the white plaster sculpture, which vaguely resembled a pelvis bone. The markings on the sculpture had obviously been made with a knife and had required a great deal of assertiveness, energy, and aggression to carve. It was as if the artist had attacked the sculpture, symbolically cutting into his or her pelvis or genital area.

They examined the drawing with the male and female heads. They immediately noticed that the attention to detail was much greater in the female head. The male head seemed incomplete, as if the artist had less feeling or even negative feelings for the male head.

They looked at a chronological series of charcoal drawings completed the previous June. The lines in the earlier drawings were precise, whereas the lines in the later drawings showed much less control. Many of them were applied with a slashing motion or with very heavy pressure. The deterioration indicated a loosening of boundaries and extreme mood changes. The artist had also cut large pieces out of the drawings, another assertive or aggressive act. A struggle was taking place in this artist's psyche to control his or her aggression, a struggle the person was losing.

Hays and Foedisch submitted a written report to the New Castle County Police. "It is our belief that the subject may be experiencing difficulty in responding appropriately to reality," they concluded. "The strong aggressive indicators in the artwork may reflect a potential to do harm to self or others."

By the end of the week there was still no word from Charles Cohen. He hadn't come home, he hadn't contacted any friends or relatives, and his body hadn't turned up anywhere. No one had any idea where he was. Posner was still on the loose as well, and that end of the investigation was just as cold. Downs pictured Cohen and Posner lying on a beach somewhere laughing at him. It was a big country, and he could only do so much from Delaware.

Downs was tired and frustrated, but he couldn't let it get the better of him. A good investigator had patience and persistence, but he was running out of both. Not one substantial lead had come in all week. Something had to break soon. He prayed silently at his desk for strength. Without the Lord guiding him, he knew he amounted to nothing. He remembered a passage in Isaiah: "All my righteousness is as filthy rags before the Lord."

Downs had a theory about the Cohen murders. He tried it out in a strategy meeting with Walther and the other detectives. It went like this: The night of the murders, Cohen drives the Nissan to Chester to score some coke. Sometime during the transaction, the car is stolen from him, and he has to hitchhike home. At home he gets into a violent argument with his father about the missing car, which ends in his father's death. His mother climbs the stairs during the argument and witnesses the murder, so Cohen kills her as well. He ransacks the house, steals whatever cash he can find, and splits in the '83 Ford.

Everyone agreed that Downs's scenario was plausible. However, some of the investigators still believed that two people were involved in the murders, possibly Cohen and a friend. Maybe he'd gotten in deep with a drug dealer.

Hadn't he run off from dealers before being picked up in Phoenix in '86? Maybe he had brought the dealer back to the town house to rip off and kill his parents, and they had taken off in separate cars. And you couldn't rule out the possibility that Cohen had been killed and was buried somewhere.

Downs wasn't buying it. He was sure the kid had acted alone. If drug dealers had killed Charlie and his parents, why would they take only Charlie's personal belongings? Why wouldn't they take the TVs and the VCR? No, this was a family job, Downs argued. The wounds were indicative of deep, personal hatred. You don't bash in two people's heads, slit one of their throats, and stab the other repeatedly in the back just to steal a boombox, a few cassettes, and some clothing.

While driving home on Friday night, Downs wondered why a young man would kill his parents. Cohen either had to hate them more than Downs could fathom or he had to be so high on dope that he didn't know what he was doing.

He didn't like the dope angle, and the more he thought about it the less he liked the stolen car/violent argument scenario as well. There was something sinister about the murders. How had one person killed two people without either of them calling the police? It was a logistical problem. He must've isolated his father in the bedroom and killed him without making much of a disturbance. But how had he lured his father into his bedroom? And how had he gotten his mother to climb the stairs without her using one of the phones on the first floor to call for help? Whatever had happened, it had been premeditated and well planned. Charles Cohen had thought long and hard about how to pull off the murders and have time to escape. It was chilling and ingenious.

Downs wondered where Cohen was and what he was feeling. Cohen had been running for several days. The enormity of what he'd done was probably just dawning on him, and he might try to contact a friend. But those first couple of days, Downs thought, must have been a complete haze.

chapter 5

- - - - - - - -

The Dead

He woke up with a start and didn't know where he was. The mattress and pillow were bare and smelled of dirt and mildew. He slowly looked around the room. The walls were cracked and dirty. The windows were covered with a gray film, and the old carpet was worn to the threads. It was like the empty, locked-up bedroom of a person who had died many years ago.

Images and sounds from the night before came back to him. The blood, the screams, and then the silence except for his breath as he inhaled deeply on a cigarette. Then the cold night, a wad of bills, cocaine, a gun pointed at his head, and driving around endlessly searching. He couldn't remember what he had been searching for, but he remembered being lost for hours on end. It seemed like a nightmare.

Then he remembered the girl. He could see the housing projects through the window. He was in Chester, Pennsylvania. It wasn't a dream. He suddenly felt sick to his stomach. He had a headache. The sun was going down. It was late afternoon, and he'd planned to be long gone by now. He must've slept twelve to fourteen hours. He was screwing up.

He checked his pants pocket. The cash was still there. She hadn't cleaned him out. A miracle. He'd seen her on the street the night before. She had smiled. Her deep brown skin had intrigued him. He'd never been with a black woman. He pulled over. She leaned on the car and said, "Wanna have some fun?"

When he saw her up close he noticed that she was just a teenager and rail thin. Her hair and the skin on her face were pulled back tightly. Her teeth were large and white, and her eyes were yellowish, deep-set, and unfocused.

"C'mon," he said. She got in.

"Ten bucks for a suck," she said. "Cash money up front. Once you shoot, you're done."

"I need a place to stay," he said and handed her a twenty. "I need to sleep."

"No problem, baby. I know a place."

She took him to a row house a block from the projects. It was her mother's place. They lay down on a dirty mattress in the second-floor bedroom. She worked one hand into his pants, but he was too tired, or maybe it was the coke. Besides, he knew she just wanted to get high. She was dead, worthless, human trash, just like him.

"Forget it," he said and pushed her hand away.

"Whatever you say, baby," she said. "Any time you in Chester, look me up. I'll take care of you."

The house was quiet when she was gone. He heard scattered sounds from outside, but he fell asleep almost immediately. Then he woke, and he didn't know where he was. On his way out of the house he saw a thin, middle-aged woman sitting on a couch in the living room smoking a cigarette and watching TV. He paused at the door, and they looked at one another.

She smiled and said, "You come back again, sweetheart."

He didn't answer. She laughed suddenly and said, "Don't be afraid, baby. No harm coming to you."

He was suddenly repulsed at the situation and at him-self. He rushed out, got in the Ford, started it, and fol-lowed the signs for a few blocks to the entrance for I–95 South. He had about $500 in his pocket. He'd been in-credibly stupid for going to Chester in the first place, and he considered himself lucky to get out alive.

Soon he was back in Delaware. He couldn't believe he hadn't made it out of Delaware yet. He wished he had never come there in the first place. He had to get out of the state as fast as he could. He was shaking so hard he could barely hold the wheel. He wanted to floor it, but he kept it below 65. He didn't want to attract any attention. Anonymity was important now, more important than any-thing else. That's how he would have to live from now on—a nobody, a ghost.

His life was so incredibly fucked up. Everything that could go wrong had. The horror of it was almost unimag-inable. He didn't know where to go or who to trust. He was alone, as he'd always been. It was over for him. He was more ghoul than human, more corpse than alive.

He took 95 South through Wilmington and picked up 13 South. He drove through Dover and through the flat farmlands and marshes of southern Delaware. He didn't stop until he refueled in Maryland. The Ford was a gas guzzler, but it was his most valuable asset. He had to keep moving. He continued south through the Delmarva Peninsula and crossed the twenty-mile Chesapeake Bay Bridge and Tunnel to the main portion of Virginia. He threaded his way through North Carolina and South Car-olina on small two-lane highways because he thought they were safer. There were too many cops on the inter-states, and they might be looking for him and the Ford by now.

Occasionally he got lost and couldn't figure out what road he was on, but as long as he was headed south he didn't care. The sun came up while he was in South Carolina. He tried not to think about Saturday night, but he couldn't help it. The more he thought about it, the uglier it got. On several occasions he had to fight the urge to floor it and turn into the oncoming lights of a tractor-trailer. Soon the whole world would know what he'd done—his friends, his high school teachers, his aunts and uncles, everyone. His stomach suddenly seized up. He hit the brakes, pulled over, and barely made it out of the car before losing his guts. He truly hated everything, including himself.

He made it deep into Georgia by late Monday afternoon, but he couldn't stay awake any longer. He'd been on the road almost 24 hours. He pulled into the next motel he saw. He gave the desk clerk a false name and paid with cash. The clerk didn't ask for ID.

He stole a Georgia plate from a car in the parking lot the next morning and put it on the Ford. If the cops had discovered the bodies by now, the Delaware plates could get him picked up. He looked at a map and noticed that the highway he was on, Route 319, meandered hundreds of miles south through Georgia directly to Tallahassee, Florida. Why not? he thought. No one would think to look for him there. He'd never been to Tallahassee before, and he didn't know anyone there. It seemed as good a place as any to hide out.

He was in Tallahassee by late afternoon. He got a motel room and drove around town. He liked the look of the place. It was clean and sunny. He could disappear into the throngs of Florida State University students. He'd make a whole new set of friends. Meet lots of girls. He was making decisions on his own, and it felt good. He had emphatically severed his ties with the past, and now he had a chance to start over. He would mold himself into someone different.

During the next couple of days he drove around the city looking at apartments, but he couldn't find anything he could afford. Apartments weren't cheap in Tallahassee. He would have to use every cent he had for the first month's rent, and he was already running low on money. He decided to head for Los Angeles. The West Coast would be much safer.

After paying his Tallahassee hotel bill he had less than $200 left. He drove west through the Florida panhandle and stopped along the highway near Pensacola for a haircut. The Mohawk had grown in and wasn't really noticeable anymore, but he didn't want to take any chances. He got a short, regular haircut. He was letting his beard grow in as well. Another couple of weeks, and the cops wouldn't be able to recognize him from recent photos.

He drove through southern Alabama and Mississippi without stopping. He spent a night in a motel near Shreveport and stole a set of Louisiana plates. He continued west, which made him think of James Joyce's story, "The Dead." He remembered a line from the story. "The time had come for him to set out on his journey westward."

His father, an armchair literary critic, would've appreciated the irony. Katie would have, too. Maybe all those college classes hadn't been a waste. He could interpret circles around those fuckers who attended every class, wrote perfect term papers, and got A's in every class. It was all such a joke. The system was fucked, and everyone knew it, yet no one did anything about it. Even his father, who had always wanted him to conform, had been screwed by the very system he advocated. Well, he had done something about it. He had risen up and struck back.

He had held back all of his anger for so long, but finally his power had been unleashed. All of his life he had been abused and humiliated. Now he had evened the score. He had meted out justice—short, swift, and merciless. He was stronger and smarter than anyone knew. Machiavelli said that violence was justified when absolutely necessary, and this time it had been justified. His life had been at stake.

He drove as far as he could, drinking coffee and popping Vivarins to stay awake. He bought food at grocery stores and ate as he drove. He was running low on money. The Ford cost him almost $25 for a fill-up. The boat was eating up every cent.

He drove through eastern Texas north of Dallas–Fort Worth and then north into Oklahoma. At night he invariably got lost on the long, dark, empty two-lane highways. There were few road signs, and many of the highways merged with other highways or suddenly took on new numbers. He didn't want to park by the side of the road and sleep because he was afraid a cop would pull up behind him and start asking questions. The two-lane highways didn't have rest stops where he could pull in and park, hidden among the big eighteen-wheelers.

He spent the night in a small motel in Oklahoma. The next morning he sold his guitar and amplifier for $50 to a shrewd Okie in a gas station. The equipment was worth more than $400, but the guy could sense his desperation and wouldn't go over $50. He couldn't blame the Okie. When you were in a position to take advantage of someone in difficult circumstances, that's exactly what you did. As Marx had said, the strong always exploited the weak.

North of Oklahoma City he picked up 270 and took it into the Oklahoma panhandle. Route 270 turned into 64, which he followed into New Mexico. Maybe it wasn't such a good idea sticking to the small roads. Maybe he should have zoomed out to the West Coast on the inter-states as quickly as possible or bought a plane ticket out of the country.

Highway 64 turned into 56 in New Mexico, and 56 ended at I–25, an interstate. The hell with it, he thought. He turned onto the ramp for I–25 and took it past Santa Fe to Albuquerque. He pulled over in a rest area somewhere along the way and slept, but most of New Mexico was a blur. In Albuquerque he picked up I–40 and followed it into Arizona.

He was mentally and physically drained by the time he reached Arizona, just as he had been when he'd gotten to Phoenix in '86. His clothes were dirty, he hadn't showered in several days, and he didn't know if he had enough gas money to reach L.A.

It snowed that night in Arizona. Everything was covered with a thin sheet of ice, and the roads were dangerously slick. It was like a dream, as if his approach had frozen over the entire state. Even in sunny Arizona he brought cold, ice, and death.

He slowed down because of the ice, but he was going too fast. The Ford fishtailed from side to side and suddenly skidded off the highway into a ditch. He was stuck. He got out of the car and walked around it. He was cold, and he didn't know what to do. He just wanted to get to the sun and the ocean where he could revive himself.

A road crew came by a few minutes later in a large truck and pushed him and the Ford out of the ditch. They dented the rear fender in the process, but he didn't care. He was just happy it had been a road crew and not a state trooper.

He continued on highway 40 for 200 miles across southeastern California to I–15. He picked up 10, the San Bernardino Freeway, just west of L.A. and took it directly into the City of Angels. He was flat broke, but the confused, nightmarish cross-country journey had come to an end. As a part of him understood, he hadn't escaped from anything. He was just lost.

Martin and Ethel Cohen were buried on Sunday, November 20, 1988. It was an overcast, cold, rainy day. A 20-minute funeral service was held at Sinai Chapel in Flushing, a neighborhood in the Queens borough of New York City. Approximately 50 people attended, including Val Starcher and Neil Meisler from Delaware State Hospital. Two Delaware police officers also attended the funeral in case Charles Cohen showed up. Everyone knew why the police officers were there, and everyone wondered if Charlie would actually make an appearance. Starcher kept fighting the urge to look over her shoulder.

The caskets were open and placed in the front of the chapel. The mourners slowly filed past. Dr. Cohen looked like a wax mannequin. There was no expression on his face. Starcher was stunned when she saw Ethel. A look of horror was frozen on her face.

The rabbi at the service gave a sketchy, vague eulogy. It was obvious that he didn't know the Cohens. A short procession of mourners followed the hearse to the Montefiore Cemetery. It was densely populated, with very little space between the graves. The rain was pouring down, and to everyone's exasperation the graves hadn't been dug. The mourners waited in their cars for the crew to dig the graves.

The funeral was depressing for Starcher and Meisler. Everything about it was without dignity. Martin and Ethel deserved better.

A memorial service for the Cohens was held in the chapel at Delaware State Hospital on Monday afternoon, November 21. A hundred of Martin Cohen's co-workers attended. The hospital employees also set up a memorial fund in Dr. Cohen's name. "The fund will be used for patients," Starcher told a newspaper reporter. "I'm sure that's what he'd want."

There was another homicide that weekend in Wilmington. Most of the investigators on the Cohen case were transferred to the new investigation. New Castle County Police also ended surveillance at the Cohen town house. The department couldn't spare the manpower any longer.

The Cohen case was all Downs's now. He somehow had known it would come to this. Cohen was out there somewhere, no doubt wreaking havoc, and it was his job alone to find him. But he was running out of leads, and he didn't have enough evidence to press charges.

Downs subpoenaed records from all financial institutions where the Cohens had held accounts. No credit card or bank accounts showed any activity since November 12. He also instituted a life insurance search to find out if anyone had recently taken out a policy on the Cohens, but no one had. Things started looking up on Tuesday, however, when Downs spoke with two people from Illinois who had known Charles Cohen as well as anyone.

Jonathan was the guitarist for Bourbon and Clorox, a fledgling punk band from Galesburg. He told Downs that Charlie had been the band's lead singer for one gig in April 1988. Jonathan explained that Charlie hadn't wanted to move to Delaware with his parents. He wanted to move in with his friends in Galesburg and play rock 'n' roll. Unfortunately, the band didn't have any other gigs lined up, and his Galesburg friends didn't want him to move in with them because his past behavior had been so erratic and disruptive. Charlie was insulted and reluctantly moved to Delaware with his parents.

Charlie had harbored a grudge against Jonathan over the snub, which became more irrational and melodramatic with time. He had written a letter to Rick Muncey, a mutual friend, that contained ominous comments about Jonathan. Jonathan also explained that Dr. Martin Cohen had been fired from his job as superintendent at the Galesburg Mental Health Center in 1984 and that Martin and Ethel had become very depressed as a result. Charlie had been deeply affected by his parents' problems and had become increasingly unstable.

"He would follow a pretty consistent pattern of getting more unrealistic and paranoid until he would get himself in such a condition, mentally, that he would start doing things that were relatively crazy and were obviously debilitating to his lifestyle," said Jonathan. "Then he would hit what he called 'rock bottom,' and he would come back and make peace with his parents, who would always take him back no matter what he'd done."

That same morning Downs spoke with Katie Adams, a young woman from Galesburg. She had dated Cohen in 1987 while he had been living in Peoria. Cohen had been very serious about their relationship, Katie told Downs. "It went on for three months, and he was ready to plan the rest of his life around me," she said. "He was a rather intense, possessive person."

She also told Downs that at one time he had a $2,500 per week coke habit. "He gets very violent when he takes that drug," she said. "A lot of people are scared of Charlie on drugs. When he's on coke, you don't know what he's going to do next."

She had broken off the relationship when she learned of his violent sexual fantasies about her. "I got some threats, rape threats," she said. "His sexual fantasies were violent, and that's what scared me, and that's why I backed out of the relationship." Downs felt that if Cohen were to look up any of his old friends, it would most likely be her. He told the Galesburg police of his concern, and they kept her under surveillance.

* * *

Downs and Walther were at a turning point. They had to make a decision about filing charges. They had exhausted virtually every avenue of investigation. They were certain Cohen had committed the murders and that he'd fled Delaware, but all the evidence against him was circumstantial. However, if he were picked up at 2 A.M. by a small-town Texas cop, and the cop couldn't find an NCIC warrant for him, he might let him go. They decided that they couldn't wait any longer. They needed the warrant.

On November 23, 1988, Charles Cohen was charged with two counts of first-degree murder and two counts of possession of a deadly weapon during the commission of a felony. Downs filed an eight-page affidavit outlining the evidence against Cohen.

"The victims were found upstairs, with Martin Cohen found in the bedroom occupied by Charles Cohen," Downs concluded in the affidavit. "The attire of the victims indicate that they were awake, but not entertaining. The master bedroom had not been slept in. Ethel Cohen did not normally go upstairs, but was found on the second floor. . . . A mobile phone was found at the doorway to Charles Cohen's room splattered with blood. Your affiant also noted that there were three phones downstairs all working on 11/14/88. This indicates that Ethel Cohen struggled upstairs, apparently tried to call for help but was killed before she could summon assistance. . . . There is no sign of any struggle indicating [Charles Cohen] was forced to leave, and his property is missing from the residence. Charles Cohen has not been in contact with any friends or relatives since 11/12/88. Charles Cohen has been expressing himself in morbid, threatening ways recently, and has been using cocaine. Charles Cohen has expressed written hatred of his parents. Your affiant believes that Charles Cohen became involved in a quarrel with his parents, and during that quarrel murdered them, and then fled."

The warrant was easy. Now came the hard part—catching him. Downs and Walther weren't confident that they could find him, but he had to turn up somewhere. He would make a mistake.

chapter 6

- - - - - - - -

Freak Show

Sunday, November 27, 1988, was a perfect day for the Christmas Parade in Hollywood. The weather was clear and warm. Mildred Dizacomo, a traffic officer, was at work keeping a section of the parade route and the temporary bus parking zones clear of parked cars.

At four o'clock she observed a white male drive a dark Ford LTD onto Sycamore Street. The driver looked at one of the temporary No Parking signs in the bus zone and drove off. Dizacomo returned fifteen minutes later and saw the same car parked there illegally. She wrote a ticket, noting the California plate number and the vehicle information number, which she could see on the dash through the windshield. Normally, she would have contacted the police station to have the plate number and the vehicle information number checked, but it was too hectic to do more than write the ticket and radio for a two truck.

Within a few minutes Mike Yamonti of Hollywood Tow arrived. He unlocked the LTD, made sure the emergency brake was off, and hooked it up. As he was waiting for the light at Hawthorne and LaBrea, he saw a white male with brown hair running down the street frantically waving at him. Yamonti knew that if a car owner discovered a tow truck hitching or towing his or her car, the driver must drop the tow, but he had no intention of doing that. He hadn't gone through all that effort for nothing. He made a quick right against the red light onto LaBrea without looking back.

About 45 minutes later, a young man in his mid to late twenties, about five foot ten inches tall with a medium build, light beard, and very short hair turned up at Hollywood Tow. He was wearing tan athletic pants and a baggy T-shirt.

Hollywood Tow did contract towing and storage for the City of Los Angeles. The Christmas Parade was always the busiest day of the year. Mark Werchowski was working the customer window in the office. He released cars when people paid their fines. It wasn't a pleasant job, especially when every other customer complained about the temporary towaway zones near the parade route.

The young man stood in the long line and waited his turn. When he got to the window, Werchowski asked him for the plate number. He didn't know it. Werchowski asked him for the car's make and model and the street it had been towed from. The young man gave him the information, and eventually Werchowski found the tow sheet.

"That'll be $62.50," said Werchowski, "and I'll need your driver's license."

"Look," said the young man, "I don't have any money. My wallet was stolen."

Werchowski shrugged. "There's not much I can do for you, sir."

"I'm starting a new job on Monday," said the young man. "Can I give you an IOU?"

"Sorry," he said. Werchowski had heard every excuse in the world, and he wasn't falling for that one.

The young man turned to the people in line and exclaimed, "Can somebody help me out here?"

Everyone in the crowded office ignored him.

"I promise I'll pay you back."

"We're going to need proof that it's your car," said Werchowski. "Do you have any ID at all?"

"I told you my wallet was stolen."

"Call a friend. Borrow the money."

"I just moved here. I don't know anyone in the area. Can't we can work this out somehow?"

"You'll have to come back and get your car when you have the money."

"Can I get a few things out of my car?"

"Step to the left, and someone will help you."

The young man walked out of the office and into the two-story parking garage. The first person he met was Pio Hernandez.

"Can you take me to my car?" he asked. "It's a blue Ford LTD."

Hernandez, who escorted people to their cars after they paid their fines, went to the office window and said, "What's with this guy?"

"Property only," said Werchowski. "He hasn't paid yet."

"Follow me," Hernandez said to the young man.

Hernandez escorted him up the ramp. The Ford was on the second level facing another car. Hernandez stood near the rear fender on the driver's side while the young man rooted through the car. Hernandez noticed that the car was very dirty. There were several grocery bags full of belongings on the seats and numerous papers and other items scattered on the dash.

The guy was taking his time. Hernandez tapped on the driver's window and said, "Let's go, sir. Just get your stuff."

"I have to find something," the young man replied. He

seemed a little strange. He didn't look Hernandez in the eye. Hernandez noticed the young man reach for the ignition with his keys. "Hey, you can't drive out of here," Hernandez said firmly.

Suddenly, the young man started the car and backed out of the space. Hernandez took several steps back. He stepped in front of the car and put his hands up as the car accelerated toward him. Hernandez jumped out of the way, but the left front fender sideswiped him and sent him rolling along the concrete surface.

The Ford turned toward the exit and roared out of the garage. Hernandez got up and saw the LTD go airborne for a second as it flew down the ramp. The south gate at the bottom of the ramp, which was normally locked, was open for the extra tow trucks on duty that day. Without slowing down, the LTD raced through the gate, peeled out into traffic and disappeared.

John Downs was at home relaxing with his family that Sunday night. He had worked on the Cohen case on Thanksgiving and through the holiday weekend. At ten-thirty he got a call from headquarters. A teletype had just come in from Los Angeles. The Cohens' '83 Ford LTD had shown up in a tow yard in Hollywood. A young white male matching the description of Charles Cohen had hit a lot attendant in the process of stealing the car from the tow yard.

Downs immediately called the Los Angeles phone number on the Teletype. He spoke with Detective Rick Wermuth of the Los Angeles Police Department, Hollywood Division. Wermuth explained that a suspect matching Cohen's description had duped the lot attendant, taken off with the car, and disappeared. The LAPD had no idea where he was. He'd hit the lot attendant, who hadn't been seriously injured.

Not until after the car was stolen from the lot had the

police run a check on the plate number and discovered that the California license plate had been stolen a few days before near Wilshire Boulevard in Los Angeles. After running an NCIC check on the vehicle information number, the Los Angeles police discovered that the car was wanted in connection with a double homicide in Delaware.

Downs called Walther and told him what had happened. "Well, John," Walther said. "I think it's time for you to take a trip to California." The next day Downs sent photos of Cohen to Wermuth. He wanted confirmation from the witnesses that the suspect was Cohen before traveling across the country.

That same afternoon Henry Posner called Delaware State Hospital from a phone booth at a bus station a few miles south of the hospital. Hospital security picked him up immediately. Posner explained that he'd left the hospital to purchase cough medicine, which he'd become addicted to. Publicity about his disappearance had scared him, and he had fled Wilmington on November 1. He had taken a train to Washington, DC, and then another to Miami. He had stayed in several cheap motels in Miami until his money and cough medicine had run out. Out on the streets, he'd become increasingly lonely and hungry. He had called his mother, who had wired him money for a bus ticket back to Delaware. The police looked into Posner's story, and it checked out.

Downs heard from Wermuth two days later. The two guys from Hollywood Tow had looked at the pictures and positively identified Cohen. Downs figured that Cohen had already left Los Angeles, so during the next few days he contacted numerous police agencies throughout California. Downs knew that Cohen had been to San Francisco in 1984 and had liked the Haight-Ashbury area, so he contacted various police officers there.

That Monday, Walther wrote a letter to the FBI office

in Wilmington requesting that they provide assistance in
the search for Charles Cohen. On Thursday, December 1,
1988, FBI agent Butch Hyden of the Wilmington bureau
issued a federal warrant charging Charles Cohen with a
violation of Title 18, U.S. Code, Section 1073, Unlawful
Flight to Avoid Prosecution.

Downs flew to Los Angeles on Friday, and Wermuth
picked him up at the airport. The next morning Downs interviewed Werchowski and Hernandez. He also interviewed Mildred Dizacomo, the traffic officer who had
ticketed the car. She was embarrassed that she hadn't run
an NCIC check when she'd had the chance. Downs also
spoke with the man whose license plates had been stolen.
He'd noticed that the plates were missing on Friday, November 25, when he picked up his car at an upholstery
shop, and had immediately reported the theft to the police.

Downs spent the next two days touring areas of Los
Angeles known for runaways and homeless people with
Wermuth. They interviewed numerous street people and
showed them pictures of Cohen. They talked to shop
owners and landlords of flop houses. They went to dozens
of shelters in the downtown area, east Los Angeles, and
Hollywood. They drove out to Venice Beach and talked to
many strange-looking people. No one had seen or heard
of Cohen.

They also cruised Hollywood Boulevard. Downs had
never seen anything like it. It was one big freak show. On
Main Street in Newark he normally saw five to ten kids
hanging out. Here he saw two to three hundred. A few of
the punkers in Hollywood thought they recognized Cohen
from the photos, but Downs didn't know if he could believe them.

After three days with the freaks, weirdos, runaways,
down and out, homeless, and mad street corner evange-

lists, Downs wanted to go home. He returned to Delaware on Monday. He'd slept through an earthquake the night before, and he was glad to get out of Los Angeles. Besides confirming Cohen's involvement in the tow yard incident, he hadn't accomplished much. Maybe Cohen was still in Los Angeles and maybe he wasn't. After all, Hollywood was known as "the runaway capital of the world." He could easily disappear into the thousands of disenfranchised on the West Coast and never come out.

chapter 7

- - - - - - - -

So Near and
Yet So Foreign

He gunned it out of the tow yard, pulled onto the street, and sped off. When he was several miles away, he laughed like hell. The look on that dude's face. Lucky he had jumped out of the way, and lucky there weren't any cops cruising the area when he made his high-speed getaway.

After the fit of laughter subsided, he realized that he both had to get out of Los Angeles and get rid of the car. The cops would be swarming the area as soon as they realized who he was. He saw a sign for Highway 5 south to San Diego and Tijuana, and he took the exit. It would be safer and easier to sell the car in Mexico.

Once he got out on the highway and had a chance to think about what had happened, he was infuriated with himself. That was a close call, too close. He had driven all the way across the country, and now the Delaware cops would know where he was. The last two weeks had been a complete waste. He felt so stupid. It was one fuck-up after another.

At least he'd gotten the car back, and he was proud of himself for the way he had done it. That would show the cops that they weren't dealing with a chump. He had balls, and he was willing to do whatever was necessary to stay out of jail. He also knew that his friends in Delaware and Illinois would be amused. Still, he couldn't pull these kinds of stunts, or he'd find himself in handcuffs.

The past week in L.A. had been weird, to say the least. He had been completely out of money when he arrived, so he sold his boombox and cassettes on a sidewalk downtown. He eventually wandered to Hollywood. The streets were full of runaways, old hippies, and punks.

After a few days he hooked up with some homeless kids, most of them punkers. They invited him to stay with them in an abandoned house they were living in. He didn't have anywhere else to go, so he moved in. It was dirty, and there wasn't any running water or electricity, just a few dirty mattresses and numerous piles of trash. When it was cold, they started small fires to keep warm. They used flashlights to get around at night. He didn't tell them anything about his past, and they didn't ask. The young squatters offered to share their dope with him, but he declined. He had to keep his wits about him. He didn't trust himself on dope anymore. Drugs had already cost him too much.

The punks were panhandling on Hollywood Boulevard to survive, so he tried it at a spot near McDonald's. After a few hours he had enough money for a meal. He couldn't believe how easy it was. If you stuck out your hand, people put money in it.

He tried to sell the car, but he couldn't get any takers. Everyone he approached about the Ford wanted to know if it was hot. At first he swore it wasn't. He didn't want to let anything slip about his background. After a few days he began admitting that the Ford was stolen. Everyone who looked at the car accepted his answer as if they suspected as much.

He saw a billboard for Tijuana as he drove through San

Diego. TIJUANA—SO NEAR AND YET SO FOREIGN. He'd heard
that Tijuana was one of the most corrupt cities in the
world. It couldn't be too difficult to sell a hot car there.
And once he got some cash, maybe he'd hitch south to
one of the resorts on the Baja and try to set himself up.

He made it to the border crossing by 10 P.M. He was jit-
tery. Were the L.A. cops following him? Would they
show up behind him with their lights flashing just before
he reached the border? And what about the crossing
guards? Would they check the California license plate on
the Ford? Would they want some ID? He pictured cops
rushing at him from all directions just as he was about to
cross. He had to stifle the urge to jump out of the car and
make a run for it. He was shaking so hard when he got
to the crossing he almost screamed, but a Mexican customs officer calmly waved him through. He almost wept
with relief.

He spent the first couple of days trying to sell the car.
He approached the owners of dozens of auto repair shops
in Tijuana but couldn't close a deal. Some young guys on
the street offered $200, but he wanted $400. Two hundred
dollars was the standard price for a stolen vehicle, they
said, and they wouldn't pay any more.

He parked near the banks of the Tijuana River each
night and slept in the car. He used the bathrooms in fast-
food places. He spent a couple of hours each day begging
for change in front of the hotels. He hated Tijuana. It was
a gauche resort packed with fat, ugly Americans. He
swore to leave as soon as he sold the car.

After several days he was befriended by a 19-year-old
named Joe. He was the shouter for a disco. His job was
to lure tourists into the club. Joe was interested in the
Ford, but he didn't have the money to buy it.

Joe could tell that he was in some kind of trouble, but
he didn't ask questions. Cohen told Joe that his name was
Tom and that he didn't have a place to stay. Joe offered

to help him sell the car for a cut and invited him to stay with his family in the meantime. Cohen was getting desperate, so he went home with Joe.

Joe's brothers and sisters, his wife, and his mother lived in the barrio outside the city and owned several shacks right next to one another. The smallest shack was empty, and Joe's family let him stay there. It had two rooms with dirt floors. The walls were made of cardboard and tin. The bathroom was a twelve-foot hole in the backyard.

He contracted a stomach flu almost immediately. He had diarrhea and nausea and was out at the hole several times a day. He became almost too sick to stand. The stench from the hole filled the shack and often made him feel even worse. Bugs bit him while he slept. His temperature was over 100 degrees.

Joe and his family did what they could. They brought him meals, but he wouldn't eat. He blamed the food for making him sick. They told him it was the water. Joe's mother prayed for him, but he wasn't getting any better.

He didn't know why Joe's family was being so nice. He wondered what they wanted from him. Maybe they expected a windfall from the sale of the Ford. Maybe they were afraid he would die, which might get them in trouble with the authorities.

With each passing day he felt worse. His parents' faces haunted him in his dreams. They became ghouls and crawled up out of the hole to get him. He dreamed of them dragging him to the hole and drowning him. He spent his 24th birthday in the Tijuana shack, sick as a dog.

One day Joe came with some bad news. He had let a cocaine dealer in the barrio test-drive the car, and the dealer had sped around town in it. The Tijuana police had arrested him for reckless driving and impounded the Ford.

Joe had helped him so much he could hardly be angry at him. Nevertheless, he took the news badly. He had no hopes of retrieving the car. He didn't have any money to pay the fine, and he wasn't up to another stunt like the one he'd pulled in L.A. The Ford was history.

"Hasta la vista LTD," he said to Joe, who laughed. He laughed, too, until his stomach hurt and tears came from his eyes.

Everything had gone from bad to worse. He had nowhere to go, no money, no food, no ID, no hope. He couldn't think of any reason not to end it all. Then Joe's mother presented him with a bus ticket to Bakersfield, California. She also gave him $10 and the name and address of some relatives there. She had called and explained everything to them, and they would help him.

Cohen didn't know why Joe's mother was helping him out. Maybe she felt guilty about the Ford or maybe she was sick of looking at him. He was just happy for a way out of the situation, and he got on the next bus headed north.

The bus trip took most of a day, and he was sick when he got to Bakersfield. A young couple with two daughters met him at the bus station and took him home. They were very kind, but he was so sick he hardly acknowledged them. The pain had moved to his groin. He thought he had a hernia. They took him to a free clinic. The doctors gave him some antibiotics, and he recovered within a few days.

When Downs got back from Los Angeles, he gave Butch Hyden of the FBI's Wilmington office a progress report on the Cohen case, which included a list of the people he'd interviewed and a summary of what they'd told him. Downs was sick and tired of Charles Cohen. He was the FBI's problem now. The FBI had resources that the New Castle County Police didn't. They could follow up every lead and chase the kid all over the country. The NCCP couldn't afford such an investigation.

The FBI might also have more luck with Cohen's associates, especially if one of them was in cahoots with Cohen. It was easy to lie to Downs over the phone, but it wasn't so easy to lie to an FBI agent in person.

Hyden sent a Teletype to every field office about Cohen. He also distributed copies of Cohen's fingerprints. Agents around the country were assigned to find and interview specific relatives and associates. They also continued the search for Cohen in Hollywood.

Downs spent much of December contacting police agencies throughout the country and sending them information about Cohen. Occasionally, he ran NCIC searches on the Ford, but he came up empty-handed each time. Cohen was placed at the top of Delaware's Most Wanted list.

On December 18, Anne Delaney, the teenager who had disappeared from Newark the previous summer, returned home from San Francisco. Downs interviewed her, but she hadn't seen Cohen since the previous summer.

The weeks rolled by, and Downs didn't hear much from the FBI, which wasn't good news. If they had been on to anything, he would've been the first to know. By the end of the year Downs was assigned to several new cases. He tried not to think about Cohen, but he knew it was only a matter of time before someone else got in his way.

In early December, Delaware State Hospital hired a new director to replace Martin Cohen.

chapter 8

- - - - - - - -

The Only Way

He hated Bakersfield and left Joe's cousins without so much as a goodbye or a thank you. He jumped a freight train and headed north. He got off at a railroad switching yard in Sacramento and wandered to the Salvation Army Men's Shelter. It was early January. The meals were free, it was warm, and they gave him a bunk to sleep on every night.

He adopted the name John Chadwick. He occasionally got work through the day-labor pools. He panhandled for extras like cigarettes, movies, and meals in fast-food places. He decided to stay until they told him to leave. The shakes, which he'd had since he'd gotten sick, subsided after a few days, as did the nightmares.

He checked the bulletin board in the shelter's job office and soon found a job at Pre–Pak, a produce packing warehouse. He was paid minimum wage, $4.25 per hour, to pack tomatoes, potatoes, onions, peppers, and other vegetables and fruits for shipping. Pre–Pak paid in cash and didn't ask for identification.

He found a room in a cheap hotel for $80 per week. There were no TVs in the rooms, the bathrooms were down the hall, and most of the residents were retirees, but it was better than the shelter.

He walked to Pre–Pak every morning. He worked ten to twelve hours a day, five or six days a week. The cold from the cement floors of the refrigerated warehouse seeped up into his feet and ankles through his beat-up tennis shoes. His entire body ached from lifting crates all day. He didn't get back to the cramped hotel room until after dark, and he was usually so tired he couldn't do anything except sleep.

He soon realized that the dismal packing job was about the best he would ever do. He didn't have identification, and he didn't have any salable skills. He couldn't even get a job in a fast-food place without a Social Security card. He was at the bottom of the economic ladder. He and the illegal aliens were fighting for the worst jobs.

He kept at it almost a month, but one day he decided not to show up at the warehouse. He couldn't handle it any longer. He didn't show up at Pre–Pak the next day either. When his money ran out, he went back to the shelter.

He became even more depressed. If he had a Social Security card, maybe he could make it, but he couldn't risk applying for a card with his real name. He'd have to use a false one, and he'd need other identification, which he didn't know how to get.

Without a job he had no money. Without money he was on the streets. On the streets he knew it was only a matter of time before he'd be caught. That was exactly what the cops were hoping for—that the pressure would wear him down and he would make a mistake. But he was stronger than that. He had to keep his composure and hold on.

One day he picked up some work moving furniture at one of the government buildings in Sacramento. He worked there the next day and the day after that. There was plenty of work moving furniture from one floor to another on the freight elevator.

His mood changed completely. He began to feel good about himself. Maybe he could make it. He was getting himself together. If he worked at it maybe he could turn the furniture moving into a full-time job or even a small business.

A few more days and he could afford another motel room, maybe even one with a TV. Later he could rent a small apartment with a private bathroom or share a house with some people. The counselors at the shelter would help him find roommates. He needed companionship and new friends. He had to get out of the shelters and off the streets. He was getting on his feet again. Life wasn't so bad after all. Maybe he'd stay in Sacramento. How had he ever doubted himself?

In late January representatives from the television program *America's Most Wanted* contacted John Downs and expressed an interest in producing a segment on Charles Cohen. Since Downs hadn't developed any new leads and the FBI didn't seem to be getting anywhere, Downs and the New Castle County Police decided to cooperate. They hoped the show might turn up something new.

A film crew and several actors from New York came to northern Delaware to videotape the segment in early February. Downs lent them some of the photos he had confiscated from the house and directed them to several of Cohen's associates. The owner of 532 Beech Tree Lane wouldn't let the film crew use the town house the Cohens had rented, but the crew found a similar town house for some footage and took exterior shots of 532 Beech Tree Lane for the show.

The segment's producers were very interested in the drug angle of the case, particularly Cohen's alleged LSD usage. They asked several of Cohen's Delaware associ-

ates to comment about his drug use on tape, but most of
them wouldn't cooperate. However, one young man,
whom Downs had never heard of during his investigation,
told *America's Most Wanted* that Cohen had said, "If I
don't get some more coke, I'm going to kill someone."

On Sunday night, February 19, 1989, Charles Cohen
was watching television in the recreation room at the Salvation Army Men's Shelter in Sacramento. *America's
Most Wanted* came on. He had suspected that they might
produce a profile on him, so he tried to watch the show
whenever he could.

At the end of the program, the announcer described the
cases they'd be profiling on the next week's show, including the case of a punk-rock drummer from Delaware accused of murdering his parents. He knew immediately
that it was him. His face was going to be broadcast on national television to millions of people. He couldn't stay in
Sacramento any longer. Too many people knew his face.
Someone would recognize him.

The show was scheduled to air the following Sunday
night, February 26. He had a week. He had to do something drastic. He decided to make a run for it. He had to
go someplace where he wasn't known and hide until
things cooled down. And he needed money desperately.

He had tried doing it the straight way, with jobs and
panhandling and the shelter, but it hadn't worked. Now he
had no other choice. Someone had to die. His survival depended on it. It was the only way. He would kill someone
and steal everything he could from the person. He would
soon be a famous criminal. One more corpse wouldn't
make any difference.

On Tuesday morning, February 21, Cohen headed for
San Francisco. He had a knife in his duffel bag, which
someone at the shelter had given to him. San Francisco

was only 80 miles away, and it was big enough that he could blend in for a few weeks. No one knew him there, so his chances of remaining anonymous seemed good. Besides, he'd been to San Francisco once before, and he'd always wanted to return.

chapter 9

- - - - - - - -

One More Fool

Fifty-one-year-old Conrad Lutz had worked at the Wells Fargo Bank in San Francisco for eighteen years, and eventually he'd worked his way up to Assistant Vice-President of Marketing. He lived alone in an apartment in the scenic Twin Peaks neighborhood. His apartment building, the Bayview, was situated on a ridge, and each apartment had a deck off the back of the building that provided a fantastic view of downtown and the bay area.

The Bayview was a short commute to the financial district where Lutz worked, but the two miles made it seem like a world away. Lutz could have afforded an expensive condo in one of the ritzier neighborhoods, but the Bayview was peaceful, quiet, and cheap. His one-bedroom apartment wasn't big or very modern, and the management wasn't good about maintenance. In fact, the Bayview was beneath a man of his means, but it suited him.

Conrad Lutz had a secret. He was gay. He had grown up in Texas and had always hidden his sexual orientation. Even in San Francisco, Lutz just couldn't come out. He couldn't let himself join the gay community, and he felt like an outsider in the conservative financial community. He knew he could never be a part of either world, and that realization often made him feel very alone.

Conrad Lutz also had an unusual hobby. He liked to pick up young male street hustlers. He knew it wasn't smart to bring such people into his home, and he knew they didn't care about him. Sometimes they ripped him off—one had even beaten him up—but he couldn't help himself. He craved their attention and would do almost anything for their affection.

By Thursday, February 23, Charles Cohen, aka John Chadwick, had been on the streets of San Francisco for two days. In three more he would be on *America's Most Wanted.* He was very tired and very hungry. He needed some money, and he needed it quickly. He had to get off the streets by Sunday night, when his status as just another anonymous face would end.

He'd thought about mugging someone, just running up to an old lady on a dark street and grabbing her purse, but he couldn't do it. The idea repulsed him. Instead, he decided to kill someone. A rich fag would be the easiest target. San Francisco was full of faggots. No one would miss one more fool, especially a gay fool.

He hung out on Market Street watching the business people scurry home. There were street people all about. A short, balding, middle-aged man in a suit and glasses approached and greeted him. Cohen smiled at the older man, who introduced himself as Conrad. They chatted amiably. Cohen knew an opportunity when he saw one.

Conrad offered to buy him a meal, and Cohen took him up on it. They ate in a fast-food restaurant. It was creepy, but the guy reminded him of his father. They were about the same height, weight, and age.

When they were finished, Conrad said, "So tell me, John, how do you like San Francisco?"

"I love it. I was here once before, and I've always wanted to come back."

"How long have you been in town?"

"Just a few days."

"You have the loveliest eyes," Conrad said, "and the nicest smile." He placed his hands on Cohen's under the table. "You look tired. Do you have a place to stay?"

"Not really," Cohen said.

"Why don't you come back to my place? Get a shower, do your laundry, get some sleep. You'll feel a lot better."

"Are you sure it's all right?"

"Don't be silly. It's no problem at all. Really. I love having guests."

Cohen smiled. It was so easy it was almost comical.

Lutz's apartment was nicely appointed with contemporary artwork, large plants, and modern furniture. Cohen liked what he saw—a stereo, CDs, records, tapes. Lutz was wearing an expensive watch and a gold ring. The old faggot was pretty well-off, and he had to have some cash somewhere in the apartment.

Cohen needed some rest and some food. The past few nights sleeping on park benches had worn him out. He needed to get his strength back. He decided to wait a night.

Lutz invited him to sleep with him. Cohen was almost asleep as he fell into the soft bed and sheets, but Lutz wouldn't leave him alone. Charlie shrugged him off a few times, but Lutz kept coming on to him.

"I need to sleep tonight," Charlie said.

"Okay," said Conrad, but he was persistent. He kept pawing Cohen and rubbing against him.

"Tomorrow night," Cohen whispered. "I promise. I'll take care of you."

But the promise made no difference. Lutz couldn't help

himself. Charlie finally rolled over and played with him until he fell asleep.

The next morning they got up early and took a bus downtown. Lutz gave Cohen some cash, and he spent the day at a cheap all-day movie theater. They met across the street from the Wells Fargo Bank at five and took a bus to Castro Street and ate dinner. They rented a movie and took another bus to Lutz's apartment. They spent the next several hours watching the movie and eating ice cream.

Lutz kept hinting about going to bed, but Cohen put him off each time. He would make him wait. He enjoyed watching him squirm. At ten Charlie decided he'd made Lutz wait long enough. He would give him what he wanted.

"How about a massage?" Cohen asked.

Lutz smiled. "I thought you'd never ask."

Lutz went into the bathroom. Cohen took off his shirt and tennis shoes and waited for him on the edge of the bed. He looked around the room. There was no telling what valuables he would find in the dresser and the closet.

Lutz came out of the bathroom wearing nothing but a towel around his waist. He lay down on the bed. Cohen looked at Lutz's body while he massaged his back. Lutz was pudgy and out of shape. He wouldn't be much trouble. Cohen almost felt sorry for him.

When Lutz seemed relaxed, Cohen whispered, "Why don't you roll over and close your eyes? I've got a surprise for you."

"I can hardly wait," said Lutz. He rolled onto his back.

Cohen hurried into the living room and got the knife from his bag.

"Keep 'em closed," he said as he tiptoed into the room with the knife behind his back. He took the knife from the sheath, dropped the sheath to the floor beside the bed, and climbed on top of Lutz.

"Are you always this playful?" Lutz asked.

"Oh, yes," said Cohen as he plunged the knife with both hands into Conrad Lutz's heart.

Lutz's upstairs neighbors, Ted and Rob, came home from a dinner party at about 10 that night. They lived on the top floor of the Bayview, directly above Lutz's apartment, and their apartment had the same floor plan as Lutz's.

Around ten-thirty they went to bed in their futon, which was on the bedroom floor. Almost immediately they heard strange sounds coming from the apartment below. People were yelling and banging around. It sounded like two drunks fighting or having some very rough, kinky sex. Ted and Rob had never heard any noise from their downstairs neighbor before. In fact, they didn't even know his name.

They'd seen him around the apartment building occasionally, and he made them feel uncomfortable. He was always leering at them on the elevator, and he never said a word when they passed him on the stairway. It was obvious to them that he was gay, closeted, and uptight about his sexuality.

Rob had seen their weird neighbor commute to work frequently on the bus. He'd also seen him riding the bus home from downtown with transient and homeless types. They looked like pickups to him.

"I had no idea the old codger was so sleazy," said Ted. "And we're living in the same building with him."

The muffled noises continued. They heard someone shout, "Get out! Get out!"

"God only knows what he dragged home tonight," said Rob. "Sounds like a rough one."

"I'm complaining to the manager first thing tomorrow," said Ted. "He's the type who gives gays a bad name."

They heard a very loud thud that sounded like someone collapsing to the floor or falling against a wall. It was followed by a loud moan. Then it was quiet.

That was enough for Ted. He got up and dialed 911. He told the police he'd heard sounds of a struggle and cries for help coming from the apartment below. He exaggerated the situation to make sure the police looked into it.

After the first thrust of the knife, which was deep and in the left portion of his chest, Conrad Lutz screamed and fought wildly. He managed to push Cohen off the bed, and they both rolled to the floor. Lutz got to his feet and fought to keep his attacker away from him. He screamed at him to get away. Cohen continued lunging at him with the knife, sometimes missing and sometimes making contact.

They fought out of the bedroom and toward the front door where an alarm was located. The landlord had installed the alarm just a few months ago. Cohen knew about the alarm, and he positioned himself between Lutz and the front door. He pushed Lutz back and stabbed at him to keep him from getting to it.

Lutz held his arms up to protect himself, but the knife kept coming down. Several times it cut into his hands and arms. He bounced off the wall in the hallway and fell to his knees in the foyer. The alarm was only a few feet away, but he couldn't get to it. Lutz continued to fight but with less energy. He slowed down more and more each time the knife pierced him. He soon stopped moving altogether.

Charlie stood over him, trembling, just like the last time. They were both covered with blood. He nudged Lutz's back with his hand. Lutz was perfectly still.

With the first thrust of the knife the blood had literally squirted out of Lutz's chest into his face, momentarily blinding him. Lutz had been able to push him off the bed and get up because he couldn't see him. What if Lutz had AIDS? he wondered. Was it possible to get AIDS through your eyes?

There had been lots of screaming and banging. Lutz had been tougher to take out than he'd anticipated. Cohen wondered if the neighbors had heard anything. He knew it would be best if he got the hell out, quickly.

He took a shower to wash off the blood and began to ransack the place, looking for anything of value. He pulled the rings and the watch off Lutz's bloody hands. Then he heard a knock at the door and froze.

Ted stood on the sixth-floor front balcony of the Bayview and waited for the police. Two police cars arrived at eleven with their emergency lights flashing. They sped up from opposite sides of the building, one car blocking the driveway. Two cops rushed to the door of Lutz's apartment. They knocked. No one answered.

One of the officers barked, "Open up, police. We had a report from your neighbor. Open up."

They tried to open the door, but it was locked. There weren't any windows on the front of the building, so they couldn't see into the apartment. One of the cops looked at Ted and said, "Where's the manager?" Ted gave him directions to the manager's apartment on the fourth floor.

Ted ran back to his bedroom and listened again with his ear to the floor. Oddly, the apartment below was completely silent. If two drunks were down there fighting, he expected to hear something—conversation, a toilet flushing, anything.

He came back out to the balcony in time to see one of the policemen leave in a hurry with the lights on his cruiser flashing, as if he had gotten another call. The other policeman left more slowly, as if he'd given up. Neither cop said anything to Ted before leaving. He assumed that they'd made contact with his neighbor below and with the manager and that everything was okay. But he hadn't heard the front door of his neighbor's apartment open.

Cohen sat on the sofa trembling and didn't make a sound when he heard the police at the door. After they left, he stuffed compact discs, records, cassettes, cuff links, a watch, and a gold ring into his duffel bag. He got about $20 in cash from Lutz's wallet and took his bank card and some checks. He rummaged through the apartment for more cash, going through every drawer and closet, but he didn't find any.

When it was quiet in the apartment complex, he called a taxi and took it downtown. He got a meal at an all-night burger and coffee joint. He stayed up the rest of the night walking the streets, trying to wear down his frayed nerves.

Ted stayed up until 4 A.M. with his ear to the floor listening for sounds from the apartment below. Even though the police had come and gone, he still had an eerie feeling. He'd heard some banging noises below, but they didn't seem to involve two persons, and they didn't sound violent.

The next morning he called the apartment manager and complained about his downstairs neighbor. "I'm fed up with this creep below us," said Ted. "What kind of people is he bringing into the building? What if one of them has a gun and fires a shot and the bullet comes up into our apartment?"

"I'll look into it," said Roberto Narvios, the elderly landlord.

"The least he can do is keep his kinky sex quiet."

"I'll talk to him and make sure he behaves in the future. Maybe we'll even get him out of the building."

"And what did the police tell you last night?" asked Ted. "I feel I have a right to know."

"What police?" Narvios asked. Ted explained that the police had been to the building the night before. Narvios said he had gone to sleep early the night before and hadn't been awakened.

"Oh, my God," said Narvios. "I saw Conrad bring home a mean-looking one last night."

Narvios hung up. A short time later there was a knock on Ted and Rob's apartment door. It was Narvios.

"Conrad's newspaper is still in front of his apartment," he said. "I knocked on the door and rang the bell, but there was no answer, and his alarm is off." A small red light on the outside of Lutz's apartment door blinked when the alarm was set. It wasn't blinking.

"I don't think he'd mind if you opened the door and checked his apartment," said Ted.

"Okay," said Narvios, "but you come and be my witness that I don't steal anything."

Ted and Rob went downstairs to Lutz's apartment with Narvios. The manager opened the door with his key, and there was Conrad Lutz. He was lying in the apartment entryway on his stomach in a pool of blood, naked and blue.

"Conrad, Conrad," said Narvios, but Conrad didn't answer. A cat with its fur saturated in blood wandered to the doorway whining for food. A small white poodle, its coat also splotched with blood, stood by Conrad Lutz's body barking at them silently. The dog's vocal chords had been removed so its barking wouldn't bother the neighbors.

"He's dead," Narvios mumbled. "He's dead."

The police soon arrived, as did the coroner and the press. They found Lutz's body in the short hallway that ran from his bedroom to the front door. He'd been repeatedly stabbed in the chest. A trail of blood led from the bed to the hallway. He had deep cuts, scrapes, and bruises all over his body. A large pool of blood lay underneath him and a bloody handprint was on his back.

There were sprays, drops, and smears of blood on the walls in the hallway, bathroom, and bedroom. Numerous bloody footprints were found on the bathroom floor, and several bloodstains were found in the bathroom sink. There was blood in the bedroom on the doorway, curtains, lamp, bookcase, and floor. The bed was disheveled, and the stylish black-and-white-striped sheets were heavily soaked with blood. A knife, with the brand name Texas Tickler, was found under the covers of the bed. It had a 3½ inch blade and a black handle. A black knife sheath was found on the floor near the bed. The contents of almost every drawer in the apartment had been dumped on the floor. Clothing and other belongings were strewn about in every room.

One of the cops fed the cat and the dog. The SPCA was notified, and they came and took the animals. The police spent all day in Lutz's apartment and soon realized that his rings, watch, and wallet were missing.

Narvios told police that at about 9:30 the night before, he had seen Lutz and another man enter the apartment. Narvios described the man as a white male between 25 and 30 years old, five foot eight inches to five foot eleven inches tall, medium build, wearing a brown long-sleeve shirt and brown pants. Narvios said he looked unkempt, like a street person. Narvios also told police that Lutz had been robbed several times by the people he brought home, so Narvios had installed a burglar alarm on the front door just a few months ago.

Ted wanted to know why the police hadn't done more the night before. The police told him that they didn't have the right to bust someone's door down unless they had reasonable suspicion.

"What if it had been you in there?" Ted asked. He didn't get an answer.

The next day Cohen took a bus to the University of California campus at Berkeley. He sold most of Lutz's CDs, records, and cassettes to students on Sproul Plaza. He made about $200. He tried to withdraw money with Lutz's bank card at ATMs all over San Francisco and Oakland, but he couldn't figure out the PIN number. He also filled out a check to John Chadwick from Conrad Lutz and tried to cash it at a check-cashing business, but he was refused.

He got a cheap room in San Francisco and decided to hole up until the *America's Most Wanted* storm had passed. He registered under the name Bob Lydon. He liked the sound of his new name. Lydon was the last name of one of his favorite rock musicians, Johnny Lydon, and Bob was innocuous enough.

He couldn't use the name John Chadwick anymore because that had been his name in Sacramento. He felt relatively safe because he knew the cops couldn't trace John Chadwick from Sacramento to San Francisco. Only one person in San Francisco had known him as John Chadwick, and that person was dead.

Cohen was full of nervous energy the next day. He knew it would be best if he stayed in while *America's Most Wanted* was on, but he didn't have a television in his room, and curiosity about the show was killing him. He was far too restless to just sit. After all, how many chances did a person get to be on national TV? He set out to find a dark bar where he might be able to watch the program.

He walked for a long time. None of the bars had their televisions tuned to the right channel, and he didn't think it would be wise to draw attention to himself by asking to watch the show. He found a quiet diner that happened to be showing *America's Most Wanted* on a small black-and-white, so he ordered a cup of coffee and watched part of the show. It was him, definitely, on national TV. He was a celebrity. What a rush.

The *America's Most Wanted* segment on Charles Cohen aired nationally on February 26, 1989, on 135 television stations in the U.S. It included photos of Cohen at different ages, the most recent showing him with a Mohawk haircut.

The show depicted Cohen as a punk rocker with a drug problem, advancing the theory that he may have been under the influence of drugs during the murders of his parents. It alleged that Cohen had distanced himself from his parents and refused to speak with them, even though they lived together.

The profile also included a dramatization of a band practice and of Downs's theory that the '84 Nissan was stolen from Cohen in Chester while he was attempting to make a drug buy. The missing car sparked a violent argument between Cohen and his parents in the dramatization, which ended in their murders.

Steven Dolgin, Charlie's cousin, appeared on the program and said, "If there was anything we might have been concerned about, we usually put it on the back burner because Uncle Martin was a bright psychologist. We always had a sense that nothing could be terribly wrong because, if it were, Uncle Martin would be able to identify it." The commentator also quoted an FBI agent as saying that Cohen had gone "from the All-American boy to Charles Manson."

Downs appeared on the show and was at the Fox Network studios in Washington, DC, to help field calls. A total of 200 came in from across the country. *America's Most Wanted* viewers had sighted Cohen in almost every state of the union. People with Mohawk haircuts and drummers in rock bands were the main suspects, as were numerous people with the last name of Cohen. Many of the calls were anonymous, and none of them demanded immediate attention.

An anonymous caller from San Francisco said he had seen Cohen during the previous week in an area frequented by gay male hustlers. The person he suspected to be Cohen looked like a male model. He was dressed in blue jeans and had a short, trimmed beard. He was in his early twenties and about five feet, ten inches tall. The caller said he seemed out of place. He wasn't all "punked out" like the other hustlers. On March 5 a call came in to *America's Most Wanted* placing Cohen in a skinhead hangout on Haight Street in San Francisco.

The FBI and Downs started interviewing callers and tracking downs leads. Many of the anonymous calls were ignored because the police had no one to contact for further information. Downs investigated the 60 or so calls originating from Delaware, and the FBI handled the rest.

The San Francisco city coroner performed an autopsy on Conrad Lutz the morning of Monday, February 27. The coroner found five stab wounds 1 to 2½ inches deep, two of which had penetrated Lutz's lung. Another stab wound went all the way through Lutz's heart. It was 5½ inches wide and 2½ to 3 inches deep. He would have lived only a few minutes after suffering such a serious heart wound.

He also had a cut on his elbow and one on the back of his hand, wounds he most likely had sustained while trying to protect himself. The coroner found six other superficial wounds caused by a sharp instrument. Lutz also had numerous abrasions and bruises on his head, knee, bicep, forearm, forehead, neck, lip, and the bridge of his nose. No evidence of semen, alcohol, or drugs was found in his body. The coroner concluded that Conrad Lutz had died from multiple stab wounds.

* * *

On Tuesday, February 28, John Downs sent a set of
Charles Cohen's fingerprints to the California Department
of Justice, Fingerprint Division, in Sacramento to have
Cohen's prints checked through the state fingerprint computer system. If Cohen had been arrested under a false
name in California, the prints would still be in the state's
system.

The state of California maintains several large computer databases of criminal fingerprint information. The
fingerprint division also maintains a separate database of
unidentified fingerprints, most of which had been lifted
from the scenes of unsolved crimes.

Cohen's prints were compared with those in the California databases. The results were negative, and the prints
were returned to Downs.

Inspector O. E. 'Whitey' Guinther of SFPD Homicide
was assigned to investigate the Lutz murder. He had been
on the force for 23 years, with 10 years in homicide.
Guinther went to the video store where Lutz had rented
the film. A clerk remembered seeing Lutz in the store the
night he was murdered along with another man. The clerk
gave Guinther a description of the man, which was similar to the apartment manager's description.

After comparing Conrad Lutz's fingerprints to those
lifted from the apartment, the crime scene experts discovered that two prints didn't match Lutz's, one on a water
glass and another on the phone. Quite possibly they belonged to the murderer. They ran the prints through the
city's computer database of fingerprints and later through
the state's fingerprint system in Sacramento. Neither
search found a match.

Guinther interviewed several of Lutz's acquaintances.
They told him about a street hustler named Ralph who
was known to associate with Lutz. He was their best
prospect, so Guinther and several other officers searched

likely hangouts for Ralph, but they couldn't find him. They picked up half a dozen other hustlers and brought them in for questioning and fingerprints, but none of them were viable suspects.

On March 2, Guinther got a break. Wells Fargo Bank notified him that someone had tried to use Lutz's bank card at the Berkeley ATM branch. The person had unsuccessfully attempted to withdraw money from Lutz's account several times on Saturday morning, February 25. A camera at the ATM had taken shots of a white male in his mid-twenties with medium length brown hair and a beard attempting to withdraw cash. The card was rejected because of an invalid PIN number. The bank gave Guinther several photos of the young man.

Now Guinther had a fingerprint, a description, and a photo. He distributed photos of the suspect to all police stations throughout the city. He canvassed the Bayview apartments and showed the photo to several tenants and to Lutz's acquaintances. No one had ever seen the person before. He went to a few gay bars that Lutz was known to frequent and showed the suspect's photo around, but no one recognized the guy.

He distributed the photo of the suspect to the media. It was broadcast on television news programs and printed in various newspapers. Guinther got over 100 leads from callers on a police hotline. He and several other investigators began tracking them down. They spent several weeks on the leads, but none of them panned out.

In mid-March they found Ralph. Guinther thought that they had broken the case. They interrogated him, gave him a polygraph test, and fingerprinted him. He passed the polygraph, and his prints didn't match those found in Lutz's apartment.

Downs had contacted the SFPD homicide division in November and December. He had also sent them a wanted poster for Cohen. One of the homicide detectives distributed the poster to all of the police stations in the city, but in January they closed the case when they didn't get any leads.

Conrad Lutz's sister and mother came to San Francisco. They arranged a quiet viewing. Several of Lutz's friends attended. His sister and mother then took his body back to Texas for burial.

chapter 10

- - - - - - - - -

The Chill That's in the Air

Charles Cohen spent another nine days in the cramped, dank San Francisco flophouse. The room was dismal, but it was cheap, and it was a lot better than a park bench. He didn't go out on the streets much because he was afraid he would be recognized.

He had started writing a diary at the shelter in Sacramento, and he continued working on it in the room. He decided to send it to Rick Muncey, a friend from Galesburg. Rick had remained a friend through all the pain, betrayal, and failures of his past and hadn't judged him.

Charlie's relationship with his other friends had always broken down, every last one of them. He had given so much of himself to his friends, practically idolizing them—Jonathan, Dan, Katie, Pete, Kevin—but he never got anything in return.

But Rick was different. He'd always given something back. He felt Rick's presence despite the thousands of miles separating them. It was as if they were communicating right at that moment. He wrote to Rick explaining everything, and he knew Rick would appreciate the explanation. He would somehow understand.

He had some paper from Pre-Pak with the company's address and phone number, so he wrote part of the letter on that paper. A clue for the cops. So what if they traced it? He'd be long gone by the time they got it, and this little clue would drive them mad.

As he had learned from *America's Most Wanted,* the FBI was on the case. Avoiding the Delaware cops had been easy, but evading the FBI was the ultimate test for a criminal. They were everywhere, but he was smarter and faster than them. It felt good to elude capture. It was an exciting game, a challenge. They were such fools with all their stupid rules. Rules weren't for him. He had destroyed all rules and freed himself in the process. He knew the truth, and it made him strong.

On March 7 he stuck the envelope with the letter and the unfinished diary in a mailbox. Wait until they get ahold of this, he thought. Maybe he'd even get more press out of the letter, become even more famous. He wanted more recognition. Manipulating the media—that's what fame was really all about, playing the idiots like puppets.

He still had Lutz's ring and cuff links. What a dumb, vile bastard, he thought. He got what he deserved, that's for sure. He had done humanity a favor. Who was going to miss him? Nobody.

He was wearing Lutz's watch. There was a little blood encrusted on the watch face, but it was nice to take a memento of his gracious host along with him. He sold the gold ring and the cuff links to a gas station attendant for $15.

He hummed the *I Dream of Jeannie* theme song as he walked out to the highway. He had no idea where he was going or what would happen to him, and he didn't care. His destiny was now ruled by pure randomness, which would drive the FBI crazy. He felt confident and strong, better than at almost any point in his life. He stuck out his thumb and smiled.

On March 10, 1989, Rick Muncey picked up his mail and found a large manila envelope addressed to him. It was postmarked March 7 in San Francisco. There was no return address, but he immediately recognized the handwriting. It was Charlie Cohen's.

Rick stared at the envelope. He felt all the fear of November and December rush back. He'd been hoping that it had gone away, but it hadn't, and it wouldn't until they found Charlie or he turned himself in.

It was all so crazy it made him dizzy. For months he'd fought against thinking about it. He went through his daily routines, but he felt shell-shocked. Whenever he went home, walked up the stairway of the apartment house, put his key in the door, turned the key, and opened the door to the dark apartment, all the fear came rushing back. As he turned on the light, he always expected to see Charlie sitting there smiling at him, covered in blood, a knife in his hand. He didn't want to think about insanity and hatred and knives and blood and people dying. Sometimes he wanted to run away and hide.

It was almost too much to comprehend. His best friend had most likely killed his parents and was running from the law. The only way he'd found to escape the craziness was to look through his closets every night and constantly work on what he'd say if Charlie showed up. The closets were always empty, but no matter how hard he tried he could never think of anything appropriate to say. The best he could come up with was something lame like, "Hi, Charlie. How's it going?"

He put the envelope on the kitchen table and looked at it. He didn't want it in his house. He didn't want to be involved. Why did Charlie have to put him through this up-heaval, fear, and confusion all over again? Couldn't he comprehend the trauma he had caused? No, of course not. If he could have, none of this would've happened.

He'd have to call the FBI. He had felt guilty when they interviewed him in January, like he, too, was somehow responsible. Even his parents had been pissed off at him for being pals with a parent killer.

He thought about just ripping up the letter, burning it, and pretending it never existed, but he couldn't. He had to know what Charlie had written. He opened the envelope. It contained numerous loose pages of handwriting, many of them different sizes. Some of the pages were torn and ragged. One page had the name and address of a fruit and vegetable packaging company in Sacramento. So that's where the crazy bastard was. At least he was thousands of miles away.

> *Dearest Rick,*
>
> *I'm sure you have been hurt and disturbed by my actions of late. I can't blame you for feeling alienated by me, but it was my own alienation which led to these "tragic" events. Bear with me and listen to my own recollection of the events which have brought shame on myself and all who loved me. I don't think you realize how hard it was for me to leave Illinois. I tried to be subdued in my emotions, but it was a painful move. After reestablishing my ties with Galesburg and my past (before the cocaine incident), I felt better than ever. You were the first person who helped me cross that bridge.*
>
> *The move to Delaware was a sort of rebirth for my father who was deteriorating rapidly without work. Although I didn't want to leave Illinois I knew my father and especially my mother would need support in Delaware. And so I sacrificed my own happiness for them.*

*I felt I owed them my youthful humor and physical
zeal, for they had given me a great deal of love and respect in earlier years. Since my bout with drugs, however, much of their devotion had been replaced by
distrust and bitterness. They felt obligated to shelter
and clothe me, but the feeling that I had betrayed them
was always in the forefront of their minds. Even after
going to a health club every day for a year, getting almost straight A's in Jr. College, and working at St.
Francis Hospital. Even after helping them through two
moves and with doing almost all the physical chores of
the household. Plus being drug and alcohol free! They
still treated me as though a failure. For about the first
year I accepted this treatment as fair. I was sorry for
what I had done and knew that only time and my actions would prove myself worthy of their love and trust
once more. I stood proudly by my father's side at his
trial to recoup what the state had denied him. Upon
his victory at the trial I should have seen the change
that had overcome him. My father had become obsessed with money.*

*I am keeping a log of my journey through this night-
mare which national celebrity has brought upon me.
So far my journey has taken me across the heartland
of this country to the land of the beautiful people (California), and twice to the land of ugliness and poverty
(Mexico). I have driven boldly into south central L.A.
where the bloods and crips treated me with some respect (possibly owing to the fact that I had a large
bomb between my legs). I strutted briskly down Hollywood's walk of fame and then daringly stole my car
from the tow-truck thieves.*

*I have accepted the fact that I will probably die of
a fatal drug injection or electric shock. This does not
bother me. What only concerns me is that my side of
the whole sordid tale be told. You are the only one who*

I feel will do justice to my final wish. I realize that what I ask of you is very difficult, but you are also the only one I know who might muster the courage to do it. My suggestion to you would be to lock these papers away somewhere safe. Don't let anyone else see them. When I am eventually captured sell it to the highest bidder. Something good has got to come of all this. I release all rights of these and future stories and letters to you Rick. Who knows, someday these may make you a wealthy man.

Rick continued reading. The handwriting was hard to understand and much of it didn't make sense. Some parts of the letter seemed to consist of random thoughts and ideas.

No one really looks at you in the city. You are lost in a sea of faces. A bisexual with fatal kidney and heart problems told me that when he looked at me he saw only a mask; no face, just a mask. . . .

There comes a time when you realize that trying to win is futile—can't win—life is a game—can't win—see Bill shine—the hot white sparks shoot out his nostrils through his mouth and. . . .

There are very few people who value honesty and friendship. Just look around you—who can you really trust and turn to for help. You're lucky if even a single person comes to mind. Remember, sometimes peoples' good intentions and apparent niceness is really a fraud for some wicked scheme to use you. . . .

People do remember you. If you treat them with distrust, vulgarity, general coarseness of nature—they respect and admire you—oh yes, people remember. Conversely if you are sympathetic, attentive, compassionate, and understanding, your name is dirt—your face is forgotten. . . .

You cannot touch me. You would not dare. I am the chill that's in the air....

The coffee shop is a refuge, an oasis in the desert of cold concrete and hard glances. There are still good people out there—for 69¢ you get a cup and refill of blood warming java and a warm plastic seat for several hours, a chance to shake the heat, the cold, the bogeyman out of your system. At twelve a sparkling four course hot lunch is served (worth the wait), it's weight in gold—the church people really do care....

The pages also seemed to contain a story about a homeless shelter. The homeless were represented by monkeys, and the food they were given was laced with mind-controlling drugs. The minister at the shelter wore a black patch over one eye. Charlie also wrote, *This diary is done in a fictional manner. All the characters are based on real peoples lives.*

The scribblings ended with, *What blessing have you to bestow upon me brother, cigarettes, coffee, friendship, conversation, weather, what?—money—God bless you brother—Amen.*

Muncey called the FBI, who called Downs, who immediately got in touch with Muncey. Rick read the letter over the phone to Downs. The desperation and craziness of the letter got Downs's adrenaline flowing.

After the phone conversation, Downs reevaluated the situation. That "nightmare which national celebrity has brought upon me" business evidently referred to *America's Most Wanted.* The part about dying by electric shock or lethal injection worried Downs. He still was very dangerous, and he seemed to enjoy his wild-goose chase with the cops and the FBI.

The letter clearly established that he was running from the law, and he all but admitted the murders. He seemed to know what he was doing, so an insanity defense was unlikely. The case was iron-clad. No way a good lawyer could wiggle him out of this. But maybe he really was crazy. Any kid who could kill his parents and at the same time trade a comfortable life for one of poverty, homelessness, and drifting—it didn't make any sense.

Cohen had given them lots of clues. He had been to Mexico, Los Angles, San Francisco, and Sacramento. Maybe he was still in San Francisco. If he stayed there, the local police or the FBI were sure to find him. If he had moved on, they were just a few days behind him.

Downs contacted the Sacramento Police Department and the San Francisco police division in Haight–Ashbury and told them that Cohen might be in the area. He didn't contact the homicide division of the San Francisco police. They already had photos and information on Cohen.

Muncey turned the letter over to one of the FBI's Midwest agents on March 11. Downs waited patiently for a copy of the letter. He assumed that the FBI was doing the obvious follow-up work—tracing the postmark, contacting Pre–Pak, scouring the homeless hangouts in Sacramento and San Francisco, and searching for a shelter director with a black eye patch. He didn't need to go to northern California to look for Cohen. The FBI had agents on the West Coast who could do the job much better than he could.

chapter 11

- - - - - - - - -

The Edge of Nowhere

He was picked up hitchhiking by some Romanian gypsies heading for Fresno. They liked him and offered to put him up, and he accepted. He used the name Dan Springfield.

The gypsies made money by ripping off insurance companies with fraudulent auto and medical claims, and they wanted to include him in their scams. They told him that he could make a quick two grand by taking a fall in a McDonald's after someone had just mopped the floor. He thought of all the crazy stunts he had pulled in fast-food joints in Galesburg and was tempted to do it just to show them how good he was, but he thought better of it. He didn't want to get involved in anything that could bring the law sniffing around. He wanted to keep moving. He was too close to San Francisco.

One of the gypsies, John, was visiting his relatives in Fresno. He lived in El Monte, a suburb of Los Angeles, and claimed to have an electronics business. He offered Cohen a job. Charlie accepted, and they took off for El Monte.

John's electronics business amounted to cruising various neighborhoods on trash night and picking up discarded TVs and pieces of electronic equipment, which he attempted to fix and sell on the sidewalk in front of his home. Cohen spent a few days helping John, but he soon discovered that John wanted a boyfriend. Cohen wasn't interested. It was just another messed-up scene, so he left and started hitchhiking east.

He didn't have a cent in his pocket when he reached Las Vegas. He panhandled for a few bucks and then won a $100 jackpot on a slot machine in a 7–11. To celebrate he got himself a room in a Motel 6.

The motel was only two blocks from the strip. He went out looking for work each day, but he hated Las Vegas. The lavish casinos, the lights, the drunks, the greed, the con artists, the extravagance, the whores, and the general all-around sleaze disgusted him. He hit the highway again. He figured he was lucky to get out of Vegas with more money in his pocket than when he'd arrived.

He got a ride about 20 miles to the outskirts of a small resort near the Hoover Dam, but it was getting dark. He knew he wouldn't get another ride until morning, so he built a small fire and spent the night sleeping on the ground.

The next morning he spent three or four hours in the blazing sun waiting for a ride. Finally, a young man in a pickup truck gave him a lift. His name was David Flanders. He was from Los Angeles and was going to the Superstition Mountains near Phoenix to pan for gold. Charlie wanted to chill his head someplace where he wouldn't have to look over his shoulder every minute. A mountain range in the desert seemed like an ideal spot. He decided to settle in and do some prospecting with Mr. Flanders.

* * *

By April, Downs and the FBI had tracked most of the leads generated by the *America's Most Wanted* profile, but they led nowhere. They had also interviewed all of Cohen's relatives and dozens of his acquaintances in Illinois and Delaware. They had gathered lots of information about Cohen's past but still didn't have any strong leads concerning his whereabouts.

The FBI checked vehicle registration records throughout the United States and Mexico. They performed numerous NCIC searches. They ran a search of the U.S. Customs computer that recorded the license plate numbers of vehicles entering the United States from Mexico. They continued to search for him in Los Angeles.

The FBI also sent copies of Cohen's fingerprints to the states that had computer fingerprint systems. They requested that the fingerprints be compared against the state databases, but the results were all negative. Cohen hadn't been arrested or fingerprinted in any of those states.

Downs waited patiently for a copy of the Rick Muncey letter from the FBI. Weeks went by without any word. Downs didn't get the letter from the FBI until April 3. It had been stalled in FBI channels for over three weeks. He also discovered that the FBI hadn't contacted the Sacramento police, gone to Pre–Pack, or checked the homeless shelters in Sacramento. No one had traced the postmark, searched for a shelter director with a black eye patch, or analyzed the cryptic short story. The trail was cold and getting colder.

Downs was more frustrated than ever. He couldn't rely on the FBI; he had to do it himself. He immediately contacted the Sacramento Police Department. He also contacted Jeff Brosch, a homicide investigator with the San Francisco Police Department, and told him about the letter, but by then it was too late. Charles Cohen had given them a tantalizing clue, daring the FBI and police to find him, but by the time they followed up on it, he was long gone.

* * *

Charles Cohen and David Flanders camped in the Superstitions for three weeks in late March and early April. Cohen was still using the name Dan Springfield. The area was mostly desert with scattered peaks that rose to 6,000 feet. They hiked many miles looking for suitable panning sites. Flanders had camping equipment and some food. He also had a shotgun, and he showed Charlie how to use it.

They read in a local newspaper about a recent murder in the desert, and it made them a little jumpy, especially at night when the desert was dark, cold, and full of sounds. They took turns sleeping with the loaded shotgun, just in case some nut snuck up on them.

Cohen was deeply touched by the stark beauty and peacefulness of the desert. His existence was trivial in relation to the awesomeness of the desert, and his problems seemed to disappear. It was the edge of nowhere, and it put his mind at ease. The cops would never find him. If God existed, he decided, it was in the desert.

They did a lot of panning, but they didn't find any gold. Soon they were out of food and money, so they went to the Salvation Army shelter in Apache Junction, a small town on the edge of the Superstitions. They did some panhandling around supermarkets for cigarette money and looked for work. They put up signs on bulletin boards for furniture moving and landscaping. It was beautiful near Apache Junction, and Cohen thought he might stay for a while, but he and Flanders couldn't find any work.

Charlie realized it was time to move on, but he felt bad about abandoning Flanders. He told Flanders that he had lots of valuable stereo equipment in a friend's apartment near Los Angeles. He promised to sell the stereo equipment and come back and set them up in an apartment or a trailer near the desert. Flanders fell for it. In fact, it sounded so good that Cohen thought about giving it a try.

Flanders gave him some of his camping equipment to prepare him for the journey. Cohen walked out to the highway, but instead of heading west toward Los Angeles, he turned south toward Tucson. He never saw David Flanders again.

He got a ride with a guy to a motel just outside of Tucson, and the guy got him a room. The next day he hitched rides to Las Cruces, New Mexico, and spent the night at a truck stop. In the morning someone in a station wagon picked him up. They drove straight through New Mexico and Texas, and the guy took him all the way to Little Rock, Arkansas. He slept on a picnic table in a rest area that night.

The following day he made it as far as East Memphis, Tennessee. It was raining, so he called a shelter. They told him to call the police, who would pick him up and deliver him to the shelter. It was standard procedure in East Memphis, he was told. He called the cops, knowing that they wouldn't take the time to figure out who he really was. They gave him a ride to the shelter without any hassle.

After a few days he hitched south to New Orleans. He ended up on a park bench in the square near the French Quarter and fell asleep. When he woke up it was getting dark. Some young guys on a park bench nearby were smoking a joint. "Want a hit?" one of them asked.

He got high with them and told them about his travels. When they learned that he didn't have a place to stay, they offered to help. They took him to an old plantation-style house. The house was owned by a young guy, Kreiger, who rented rooms. Kreiger agreed to let him stay as long as he helped with the maintenance of the place. For a week Charlie scraped old paint off window frames and painted to pay his way, but he hated the work, so he hit the road again. He headed for Miami Beach. He was familiar with the area from his family's vacations there, and he was beginning to feel a little homesick.

Within a few days he was in a shelter in St. Petersburg, where he complained to one of the counselors about his circumstances. "I'm completely broke. I can't get a job unless I have ID, and I don't have any way of getting my birth certificate so I can get ID. I need a job real quick, and I'm sure I can work my way through this."

The counselor felt sorry for him and gave him a fake voter's registration card bearing the name Michael David Jarman. He was proud of himself. He had conned the counselor as well as Flanders, Lutz, Kreiger, Joe and his family, and all of the people who had put him up on the road. He had made up complete lies on the spot, and they had believed every word. He had easily convinced them that he was a good, honest person who had fallen on some hard luck.

He worked up his courage, went to the St. Petersburg Social Security office, and applied for a replacement card under his new name. They told him to come back in a few days. The more he thought about it, however, the more he worried. He was sure FBI agents would be waiting at the Social Security office to nab him, so he never returned.

By early May he had drifted to Miami Beach. He had always liked the beaches, the warm weather, the lush vegetation, the boardwalk, and the Art Deco district, but now he saw the city in a different light. Like Las Vegas, it was another playground for the well-heeled. The extravagant beachfront hotels weren't friendly environments for a homeless person.

He had come to realize that the only option left to him was to hustle gay men. He was desperate. He needed food, clothing, a shower, and a comfortable place to sleep, the kind of things that money could get you. If he didn't come up with some money soon, he wouldn't survive. They would catch him or he would die.

He started working the boardwalk at 21st Street. He met many gay men, some wealthy, some not. Some of them felt sorry for him, and some were frightened by him. Most wanted to screw him, but he wouldn't let them. He let them suck him off, but that didn't pay as well, so he didn't make much money. He tried to give a guy a blow job once, but he couldn't go through with it. He always tried to barter for a place to sleep from his customers, but he ended up spending most nights on the beach.

On May 17, 1989, a cop from Sacramento called Downs. Cohen had been identified in a Sacramento homeless shelter two weeks ago. Also, a Sacramento TV show styled after *America's Most Wanted* had run a profile on Cohen in May, and they were still running down the resulting leads.

Downs also heard from the FBI in late May. They had put up wanted posters for Cohen throughout the Fisherman's Wharf area in San Francisco and had received several tips. It was possible that Cohen was still in the area.

In May a Philadelphia television station featured Cohen on *Philadelphia's Most Wanted*. Fifteen calls came in from various locations in the city and the surrounding area. One of the callers said Cohen was the drummer for a local rock band. On a Friday night Downs and two Philadelphia police officers went to a nightclub where the band was playing, but the drummer wasn't Charles Cohen. He didn't even look like Cohen.

During the daytime Cohen frequented the Miami Beach branch of the Dade County Library at 21st and Collins, just a block from the boardwalk. It was air-conditioned, and it had bathrooms where he could wash up. He read newspapers and magazines. He also read several novels by authors he had grown fond of earlier in his life, like William Burroughs and Albert Camus. They somehow made him feel justified for what he had done.

He frequently slept behind the library. It was a shady, quiet spot, and he thought he could sleep there without anyone hassling him. One afternoon, however, he was woken by a pain in his ribs. He opened his eyes. A Miami Beach policeman was poking him with a nightstick. The cop frisked him and barked questions at him. "What's your name? Where do you live? Why are you sleeping out here?"

He politely answered the questions. The cop seemed a little crazy, and he didn't want to make him mad.

"Don't you know this is a tourist area?" the cop yelled. "We don't want your kind around here. Go to Miami. Go anywhere. Just get the hell out of here."

Cohen immediately gathered up his few belongings and headed for the nearest highway. He didn't like encounters with the law, and if he stayed in Miami Beach he was sure to run into that cop again.

He spent the next few days in Palm Beach, but he had a run-in with the cops there as well. Two patrolmen put him in the backseat of their cruiser while they ran a computer check on him. He was shocked to find out that Michael David Jarman was wanted for a parole violation in Wisconsin. He vociferously claimed that he wasn't *that* Michael David Jarman. He didn't match the description in the computer record, so they released him.

During the next few weeks he hitched through Florida, Georgia, South Carolina, North Carolina, Virginia, West Virginia, Ohio, and Pennsylvania. He eventually decided to go to New York City. The largest city in the U.S. seemed like a good place to lay low. Since he had committed a murder on the West Coast, the East Coast would be the last place they'd look for him.

On June 24, 1989, he showed up in a shelter in Easton, Pennsylvania, which was only 65 miles from New York City. An employee at the shelter took an interest in his tale of woe and put him up in his house for a night. The next day the guy gave him $50 and bought him a bus ticket to New York City.

chapter 12

- - - - - - - - - -

I Never Sang for
My Father

He arrived in New York City two days later and wandered to Washington Square in Greenwich Village. It was full of skateboarders, joggers, tourists, students, ranters, dope dealers, police, and homeless people, who pushed their belongings in shopping carts or slept on benches or in the fountain.

He asked a few street people about a cheap place to stay, and someone suggested the Fulton Hotel, a flophouse above a grocery store on the Bowery. A room was only $8 per night. The lobby was cramped and dismal, the front desk was screened in by thick wire-mesh glass, and the clerk was surly.

The Bowery was a dangerous neighborhood. Hundreds of bums hung out drinking wine and getting high, and people were frequently robbed in the area. None of this fazed him. He was just glad to have a room and a bed.

He quickly figured out where he could get picked up. A few nights later he was sitting on a bench in front of Boots and Saddles, a gay bar on Christopher Street in the Village. He approached a balding, middle-aged, white guy, who was obviously drunk, and introduced himself as Frank Watts. The man's name was Don.

"Some people told me that I look like a hustler," said Charlie. "What do you think?" He had hair over his ears and collar, a beard, and he was somewhat disheveled.

"Yeah," said Don, slurring slightly, "you look like a hustler. Either a hippie or a hustler, and I don't know which is worse. I can see that you're not from the city."

Cohen told him that he was from the Midwest and that he had just arrived in New York.

"Really. I'm from the Midwest, too. This may be the start of a beautiful relationship," said Don. "Now don't tell me. Let me guess. You hitchhiked."

"Yup."

"And you don't have a nickel to your name."

"How'd you know?"

"You remind me of any number of people I met during my hippie days in the Sixties," said Don. "Might I presume that you're looking for a place to stay?"

"You could say that."

"Well, you could stay at my house for the night, if you like. I've got a sofa-bed in the living room. Not luxurious accommodations, but it beats a park bench."

"I wouldn't want to impose."

"Impose? Oh, for goodness sakes, are you kidding? What's the big deal? It's like old hippie days. Take it or leave because I'm going home. Dear Lord, I'm hungover already."

They took a cab to Don's apartment on the Upper West Side. Cohen slept on the sofa.

The next day Don gave him a tour of Central Park. Cohen told him that he had a job in Queens, loading trucks, but he wouldn't be paid for several more weeks. Don, a 42-year-old English professor, felt sorry for him and agreed to let him stay in his apartment until he got on his feet.

During the next several weeks, Charlie got up every morning and left Don's apartment, ostensibly to go to work. Instead, he panhandled and spent hours in the main branch of the city library at 42nd Street and 5th Avenue.

Cohen never had more than a few bucks on him, so Don helped him out with a little money here and there. He bought the groceries and picked up a pack of cigarettes everyday for his new roommate. When they went out to dinner, Don paid his portion of the bill. Don really didn't mind. Cohen wasn't costing him enough to worry about, and he enjoyed having him around the house. His new roommate was pleasant, considerate, intelligent, and funny.

Charlie was surprised that Don wasn't pushy about sex. In fact, Don hadn't laid a hand on him since he'd moved in. Cohen was used to his pick-ups demanding sex and then getting rid of him as quickly as possible, but here was someone who put him up and asked for nothing in return.

"Why don't you want to sleep with me?" he asked Don one day. "Is there something wrong with me?" They began sleeping together that night.

They both loved watching movies, so they spent many evenings in front of Don's television and VCR. Cohen particularly liked *I Never Sang for My Father,* a 1970 movie staring Gene Hackman and Melvyn Douglas. Hackman plays an estranged son who tries to reconcile with his elderly father. He does everything he can to please his father, but he is never satisfied. In the end the son leaves his father.

Charlie continued to get up and go out every morning. However, he never got paid when he was supposed to. Once he told Don that his boss hadn't shown up on payday. Another time he claimed that his boss didn't have the money to pay him.

After a month Don finally said, "This nonsense has to

stop. I thought you were trying to get yourself together, but it's very obvious that you aren't getting anything together. You don't even have a job, do you?"

Cohen didn't answer.

"I'm sorry, but you're going to have to leave," said Don.

Don left early the next morning, and when he came home Cohen was gone. So were his CDs, records, and many of his books. Cohen had also stolen some clothing and a pair of shoes. He left behind his dirty, worn-out clothing and a note with just one word—"Learn?" Oh, yes, he had learned something, thought Don. No good deed ever goes unpunished.

A few days later Charlie went to the library and saw a girl with blond hair smiling at him. He started talking to her. Her name was Anne. She had just gotten off a bus from Chicago, and she was in New York sightseeing. He volunteered to show her the city.

They went to a museum and ate lunch in a restaurant. He started kissing her. She had some money, so he suggested they get a hotel room. They got a cab and asked the driver to take them to the cheapest hotel in the city. He took them to a place that rented rooms by the hour. They had sex twice before their time ran out.

They had dinner, and since she was running low on money, they decided to spend the night on the subway. By the middle of the night the subway was populated almost exclusively with homeless people and drunks. They harassed Anne and leered at her. Cohen was intimidated and afraid to defend her. Neither of them got much sleep, and they both were embarrassed by the ugly episode.

The next day they continued to tour the city, but their moods had soured. They were tired, and she was almost broke. He suggested they stroll through Central Park on their way to the Metropolitan Museum of Art. When they reached a secluded area, he leaned her back against a boulder and began kissing and fondling her. He unzipped her jeans and pushed them down.

"No," she said, "not out in the open."

"Don't worry," he said. "People get it on out here all the time, especially the fags."

"I don't want to," she said. "Stop it." But he had his weight on top of her, and she couldn't push him off.

"What's the matter?" he said. "Nobody cares."

"All right. Just hurry up."

He turned her around facing the boulder.

"No, not like that," she said.

"Oh, for Christ's sake," he said. He turned her around to face him, and he leaned her back against the rock. She cried quietly when it was over.

"What the fuck's your problem?" he asked. "Maybe you should just go home."

He zipped up his pants and left her.

The next day Cohen met a woman named Donna, an actress in her 30s who was writing a screenplay. She invited him to her apartment, which wasn't far from Don's. She said she would help him get a job. When it got late he suggested that they go to bed. She was willing. Afterward, he left and never saw her again.

He decided against spending any time in the New York City shelters. He had heard too many stories about people being robbed in those places. Besides, the people who ran shelters were wary of homeless with no ID. They asked too many questions. They might even alert the cops about him if they were suspicious enough.

He started sleeping at an old church on the northwest corner of 5th Avenue and 55th Street, just a few blocks from Central Park. There was a four-foot-wide landing at the top of the steps, and he curled up behind one of the marble pillars each night. The church was in the midst of dozens of ritzy 5th Avenue shops and hotels, almost directly across the street from the Trump Tower.

He soon changed his name to Jesse Connors. As with the name John Chadwick, he liked the initials. They seemed appropriate for someone who slept on the steps of a church. Frank Watts had been a useful enough name, but Don had probably reported him to the cops.

A few other people slept in the church entranceway, too, including a part Indian, part black woman named Gypsy. Soon she and Cohen were sleeping together on the steps of the church and having sex. Ever since high school, having sex at a church had been one of his fantasies.

From the moment he met her, he knew that Gypsy was crazy. He could see it in her eyes. She was volatile, unpredictable, and couldn't be trusted. When she got mad, she was liable to start screaming and cursing, no matter how many people were around. Dealing with the mentally ill, he discovered, could be a real pain in the ass. He started avoiding her.

One morning he woke up in the church entranceway and discovered that someone had stolen his shoes. Actually, he had stolen them from Don, but they were the only shoes he had. He slowly limped along the busy morning sidewalk, completely humiliated. He had always tried to hide his homelessness by keeping his clothing clean and neat, but now he couldn't hide it. Anyone who looked at him immediately knew he was a drifter. The Midtown business people gave him a wide berth. He was one of the untouchables, a leper. He didn't mind it from the men, but looks of revulsion from attractive young women crushed him.

Within a few blocks he had splinters and several small cuts on the soles of his feet. He openly wept. A few people gave him coins. He thought of going back to Don and begging for help, but Don would probably just call the cops.

He wandered over to Columbus Circle at the southwest corner of Central Park. The area was crowded with homeless people. He was befriended by several old black men, who found him some shoes and gave him pointers about surviving on the streets. Columbus Circle quickly became his home.

He slept on a bench in the corner of the park or on the subway grates along Central Park West. He could always find a large piece of cardboard behind one of the newsstands to sleep on. The cardboard kept the early morning dampness from seeping into his bones. Various charities delivered hot meals to the homeless at Columbus Circle as well, so he was assured a meal every night, as long as he lined up early enough.

He soon fell in with a bunch of crack addicts at Columbus Circle. They took him to various locations throughout the city to get high, including crack dens, Harlem apartments, and the dark service tunnels under Grand Central Terminal. He didn't care where he went as long as he got stoned. He frequently woke up in a gutter in a strange section of town, unable to remember how he had gotten there. On several occasions he got so high that he didn't know who he was, which was just fine with him. Once some cops saw him getting high in Central Park and chased him. He thought it was funny and took a hit from his crack pipe while he was running. They didn't catch him.

He eventually settled into an abandoned building in Riverside Park that had become a thriving crack den. It was a dangerous place, with lots of fighting and prostitution. The crack was only a few bucks a hit, and he managed to scrape up the change to get high every day. The city had become a horrible, dirty, nightmarish circus, and his life a crack haze. People were pathetic and disgusting, he concluded. He may have committed heinous crimes, but he decided that he wasn't much worse than anyone else.

He managed to get a few days' work painting an apartment, and he collected cans and turned them in for five cents a piece at recycling centers, but he spent the money getting high. He stayed fed by frequenting soup kitchens.

He soon discovered that selling used books on the sidewalk was the only legal street hustle in the city. He wouldn't need a license or a Social Security number. As long as he stayed within a certain amount of space, no one would hassle him.

He went to a warehouse on the Lower East Side and bought two grocery bags full of books for $20. He laid the books out on some cardboard on the sidewalk. He sold paperbacks for 50 cents to $1 and hardbacks for $2 to $3. His first day he took in over $60.

He found a permanent spot on the sidewalk at 51st and Broadway and sold books at the site almost every day for a month. He even sold books to a few celebrities, including Bill Murray. He could've gotten off the streets selling books, but he spent every cent on crack and eventually didn't have any money left to buy more books.

He occasionally slept on the subway platform at 86th Street on the Upper East Side. He would get two cardboard boxes and put his head in one and his feet in another. The trains ran all night long and lulled him to sleep.

He learned that the subway police would let him ride a train all night if he told them he was homeless, so sometimes he spent the night on the subway. He helped a few other homeless people construct some clapboard huts under a bridge in Riverside Park, and sometimes he slept there.

For a while he slept in the Staten Island Ferry Terminal

at the south end of Manhattan. Sometimes he slept in Battery Park, which was clean and had working bathrooms. He drifted to the World Trade Center Concourse occasionally, which was heated in the winter and air-conditioned in the summer. For several weeks he was a fixture at Grand Central Terminal, where hundreds of the homeless lived.

In the fall he wandered to Tompkins Square Park, which was surrounded by tall row homes and expensive apartments in the East Village. Homeless people were living under the band shell and in tents throughout the park. It was much more peaceful than the other homeless areas of the city, and it gave him a chance to lay off crack for a while.

One day on the subway he noticed a young cop with a German shepherd looking at him like he knew who he was. The cop approached him. This is it, he thought. I'm going down. By then he had changed his name to James McDowell, the last name in honor of the star of *A Clockwork Orange*.

"Have you been on Staten Island recently?" the cop asked. The dog growled at him. Cohen had heard about a recent murder on Staten Island and wondered if he looked like the suspect.

"No," he answered.

The cop escorted him off the subway at the next stop. He tried to convince the cop he hadn't been to Staten Island, but the cop wasn't buying it. When the policeman turned his back, Cohen jumped a railing, hopped two flights of stairs to a different platform, and jumped into a Brooklyn-bound train. He hung out in Brooklyn for the rest of the day before returning to Manhattan.

On October 15, 1989, *America's Most Wanted* reran the episode featuring Charles Cohen. Once again sightings came in from all over the country. The FBI followed up each of the leads, but it was another bust, and hundreds of man-hours were wasted.

Everyone involved in the investigation was surprised that Cohen had been able to elude capture for so long. He had no criminal record and no prior dealings of any note with the police, so he certainly wasn't street-smart.

From what Downs knew of Cohen—five different colleges, in and out of the Marines, drug abuse, very little work history, financial dependence on his parents—he hadn't been able to cope with any type of adversity, so how could he cope with it now? Maybe he had been killed or had starved to death.

Downs knew that Cohen was reasonably intelligent. If a few people helped him out, he might be able to elude capture for a long time. He could use a false name and work under the table. It was a big country, and if he was careful, he could run loose for a long time. Even if he got picked up for a misdemeanor, the police in the local jurisdiction wouldn't know who they had unless they sent his fingerprints to the FBI, which was unlikely.

For the first time Downs faced the fact that they might not ever catch Cohen. He'd never worked on a murder case that hadn't resulted in a conviction, but he knew it was bound to happen sooner or later. Finances prohibited what Downs could do. He was tied up on other cases. If Cohen had fled to Canada or Mexico, they might never find him.

chapter 13

- - - - - - - -

Know Body Can Make Me
Feel the Way I Do When
I'm with You

Nina was a 22-year-old security guard at the mid-Manhattan branch of the New York City Public Library. She was also a regular viewer of *America's Most Wanted*. She had noticed a young man in the library on numerous occasions. He had brown hair, blue eyes, a beard, and a warm smile. She could tell by his appearance that he was homeless, but he seemed too young and too clean to be living on the streets. She felt sorry for him. She also noticed that he carried a psychology textbook around with him. He had noticed her, too, and he often greeted her or smiled at her on his way in and out of the library.

One afternoon about two weeks before Thanksgiving, Nina fell asleep at her desk. She was woken by a noise and jumped. It was the young man with the blue eyes and beard. He was standing in front of her smiling.

"You look beautiful when you're sleeping," he said.

Soon he was coming by everyday and chatting with her. He told her his name was James McDowell. She enjoyed his attention.

"Your face is familiar to me," she said to him once.

"I don't see how."

"I've seen you somewhere before. I'm sure of it."

A few days later she invited him to her place for Thanksgiving dinner. Her apartment was in the projects in the Bronx near 134th Street. Her husband had moved out a few months before, and she lived alone with her young son. The apartment complex was made up of half a dozen 20-story buildings. The streets were littered with trash, and people hung out on every corner in the vicinity.

Nina and Cohen had a long conversation that night after dinner. He was funny, and she enjoyed talking with him. She just wanted to hold the young man with the beautiful blue eyes and take care of him. He looked like he needed love and affection. He spent the night.

She saw him in the library the next day at closing time.

"It's really kind of cold outside," she said. "You could come back."

He looked at her with a quizzical expression.

"You know, to stay with me, in my apartment."

"Really?"

"I mean, like, until you find a job and get a place of your own."

He moved into her apartment that night. He had very few belongings. Nina was determined to help him find work, and she tried to clean him up a bit. "The way you look, I mean, oh my God, it's impossible for you to get a job," she said.

She bought him a pair of pants, some shoes, and a shirt. She disliked his beard as well and talked him into letting her shave it off. She said he looked much more handsome without the beard. "And them blue eyes look so damn innocent," she said.

They had very little money between them, so they didn't go out much. He liked to lay around the apartment watching TV. They rented lots of videos. Sometimes he drew or wrote in an old appointment book. He celebrated his 25th birthday in the Bronx with Nina.

He and Jason, Nina's six-year-old son, took to one another immediately. Charlie took Jason out to play in the nearby playground almost every day. He bought candy for him, and they watched TV together. He walked Jason to and from school.

Cohen told Nina that he was from Illinois. His parents were dead, he said, and he was an only child. He had been alone for a long time. He also claimed that all of his possessions had been stolen from him when he had first gotten to New York. He didn't have a place to stay, a job, or any money, clothes, or friends, so he was forced to live on the streets.

It was a sad story, and Nina believed every word. He was getting good at these off-the-cuff fantasy autobiographies. He enjoyed embellishing them. It was a challenge to create a different but believable background each time he met someone.

One morning he asked her for some money. She said she didn't have any, but he had just seen her give $5 to Jason. He demanded that she give him the money. She refused.

"I'm trying to get a job, but I can't if I can't afford a subway token," he said, beginning to shout.

"I don't make enough for all three of us," she said, "and Jason comes first."

"You waste money on stuff like junk food and beer."

"It's my money," she shouted back at him. "I can spend it any way I want!"

Jason started to cry.

"You don't want to see me get nasty," he said.

"You don't want to see the bad side of me neither, dude."

He pushed her. She punched him in the eye. That was the end of the argument. He stormed out, but he came back that night, and they made up.

A few days later, Cohen heard about an opening at a

health food store. He applied for the job, using the alias James McDowell, and was hired full-time restocking shelves. The manager gave him some paperwork to take home and fill out. He filled out everything except the W-4, which required a Social Security number. He told the manager that he had left the form at home and promised to bring it in. He knew he wouldn't last at a legitimate job because he couldn't give them a valid Social Security number, but he hoped to get at least one paycheck from them before it became a problem.

One night Nina's husband called and wanted to meet with her. Cohen didn't want her to go. She told him she was going anyway. He insisted that she tell her husband that she was living with him.

"No, not yet," she said. "I can't."

"Bullshit," he said.

"What do you want from me? You been here, like, what? Two weeks. You don't have no money. You gotta give something before you go demanding shit."

"It always comes down to money with you, doesn't it?" he asked.

"Look," she screamed, "I don't let nobody tell me what to do." She slammed the door and left. When she came back, he wouldn't speak to her. When he woke the next morning, he found a note on the kitchen table.

> *Dear Jim,*
> *I know this may be strange or childish but I'm better with writing than say what I have to say face to face. So I'm telling that you was right but I also felt you was a little jealous because when I came back upstairs you started acting very funny towards me. And I don't think it is fair because I proved my feeling to you because I don't think there is any woman who will tell there husband that there sleeping with another man. I think that maybe I had a little doubt about your feeling*

and you have some for me but I feel a lot for you but at any time you feel like leaving I'm not going to stop you because I did what I wanted and that was to help you get out of were you didn't belong and I want nothing in return. Anyway we both have been acting like assholes so lets just kiss and make-up because I want you and not just for love-making because I can get that anywhere and so can you. Know body can make me feel the way I do when I'm with you and if that's wrong then take me to court. That's all I have to say for now.

Love, Nina

He couldn't take it any longer. She was so headstrong, and the apartment was so small. He wasn't ready to assume the father role either. She and Jason were obviously better off with her husband, so he left without saying goodbye or leaving a note. It was Friday, December 15, 1989.

He had a paycheck coming from the health food store, so he went to pick it up. He told the manager that he was quitting and that he wanted his money. The manager told him that he hadn't handed in a W-4, so they couldn't process his paycheck. He filled out a W-4 with a false Social Security number and birthdate. It was a serious risk, but he needed the money. The manager told him to come back for his check in two weeks.

He called Nina at work and told her that he had quit his job and had moved out of the apartment. Then he hung up.

Street News: America's Motivational Not-For-Profit Newspaper. Helping America's Hungry By Rejuvenating America's Work Ethic. Any homeless person can go to the Street News Sales Center on 9th Avenue between 45th and 46th in Midtown and get a free starter kit of five newspapers. Each paper is sold for $1. Sell-

ers can purchase more copies at the sales center for
25¢ per copy.

After a few days of drifting around Manhattan, he
heard about *Street News*. Homeless people were selling it
and making money. He tried it, and after a few days he
had enough money to move back into the Fulton.

As soon as he got the paycheck from the health food
store, he planned to get out of the city. He couldn't cope
with it anymore. Eleven months had passed since the
Lutz incident, and he felt he could safely move on.

In December 1989, John Downs was promoted from
detective to patrol supervisor. He worked a regular shift
in a patrol car supervising other patrolmen. He was getting better pay, but he wasn't doing what he enjoyed—
investigating crimes.

No one in the department was actively pursuing Cohen.
The FBI was still on the case, but he didn't know if they
were doing anything. He was still the department contact
on the case, and occasionally he got calls from other departments, but they never amounted to anything.

Someone thought they had seen Cohen walking along a
highway in Hockessin. Dozens of patrolmen searched the
area, but they came up empty-handed. One of Cohen's
classmates from high school thought he'd seen him in
Galesburg, but that, too, was a false alarm. Every now
and then a hitchhiker was picked up in Delaware by the
state police, who thought it might be Cohen, but it never
was.

The investigation was at a dead end. It was depressing
to think about, and Downs was quickly losing his interest
in his new job. He was a cop, not an administrator. For
the first time since joining the force he seriously thought
about going back to the ministry. Life had seemed less
complicated then. He had put in over eight years with the

New Castle County Police. Maybe there was a congrega-
tion who needed him.

In early January, Charlie got his paycheck, and he took
a bus to Hyannis, Massachusetts. He stayed in the shelter
there for a week getting some rest. He soon made his way
out to Provincetown, a small seaport and arts community
at the tip of Cape Cod. Provincetown had a large gay
population, as well as lots of bars, restaurants, shops, gal-
leries, and small inns.

He was hungry, broke, and depressed. Everyone else in
the small town seemed to have lots of money. He had a
knife he had picked up before leaving New York, and he
desperately needed money. He decided to use the knife.

He cruised the bars. He didn't want to kill another
man. He wanted to kill a woman, preferably one of the
rich lesbians. They were so content and confident. They
thought they were superior to men. He could tell from
their expressions that they hated him. He was absolutely
disgusted at the thought of two rich bitches getting it on.

He toured the bars looking for a deserving victim, but
the right opportunity never presented itself. After a few
days he wearied of the hunt and hitched back to Hyannis
and the shelter.

He thought about getting a job and staying in Hyannis.
He liked the town, but he began to feel claustrophobic.
There was only one highway off of the Cape. The FBI
could trap him with his back to the ocean. He would have
nowhere to run.

He left Hyannis on a warm day in February 1990. He
was headed for Boston, but once he got out on the road,
he started thinking about New Orleans. There was a large
artist community there, and it was a cheap place to live.
Perhaps he could make a fresh start in New Orleans. It
would soon be Mardi Gras, and he enjoyed a party as
much as anyone.

chapter 14

- - - - - - - - -

Hey, Babe,
I'm Psychedelic

Charles Cohen arrived in New Orleans on Friday, February 23, 1990, four days before Fat Tuesday. He sat on a bench in Washington Square near the French Quarter. On his second day on the road after leaving Cape Cod he had gotten a ride right through Delaware. He couldn't help but smile: if the Delaware cops had only known.

He stayed at a couple of shelters along the way when he needed food and rest. The homeless shelters throughout America were very convenient, he thought. How kind of them to make his life on the road so hospitable.

A heavyset born-again Christian picked him up under a viaduct near Charleston, South Carolina, during a rainstorm. The guy took him to his mother's house for dinner and put him up for the night. A minister gave him a ride the next day all the way to a shelter in Atlanta and gave him a few bucks to boot. What was it about people that made them want to help him? he wondered. Did it make them feel good about themselves? Maybe there was something about the way he looked. No harm done, he decided. They had done their good deeds, and they would never know who they had helped.

* * *

Greg Fitch took off from work early on Friday afternoon. It was the first day of Mardi Gras, and he didn't want to stick around the office all afternoon. It was carnival time. Fitch had grown up in Canton, Illinois, a small town near Peoria. He was 20 years old and had gone to college in Illinois for a year and a half before moving to New Orleans. Fitch, who was six foot one and 145 pounds, worked for ACORN, a nonprofit organization.

He walked through Washington Square and saw a guy sitting on a park bench with a large duffel bag beside him. Fitch asked him for a light. The guy lit his cigarette, and they sat on the bench smoking and talking.

His name was James, and he said he was from the Bronx. He looked tired and disheveled, and Fitch could see that he had been hitchhiking. It was also obvious that he was carrying all of his worldly possessions in the duffel bag.

They went to Molly's on Toulouse Street for a drink. Cohen was carded, but he had a New York ID card in the name of James McDowell.

"Do you have a place to stay?" Fitch asked.

"Not really."

"I could put you up for the night, and I might be able to find you a place to stay. Are you hungry?"

"Yeah, sure," said Cohen.

"Let's go get a hamburger."

They walked to a fast-food joint on Canal Street and had a hamburger. Afterward they ran into a friend of Greg's on Canal Street.

"James is new in town. He's from New York," said Greg. "He's looking for a place to stay. Can you put him up at your place? He's cool."

"Sorry. Normally I would," said Greg's friend, "but I don't know him well enough."

As they walked off, Greg said, "What the hell. You can

move in with me. My apartment is small, but I'm not home that much. Now we need another drink, and we need to find some women."

Fitch took Cohen to some bars on Bourbon Street, which were packed with Mardi Gras revelers, and they joined in. Cohen was exhausted, but he was delighted to have found a place to stay so quickly and easily.

"Mardi Gras is the perfect time for picking up women," Fitch said. "They come to New Orleans because they know they can get away with anything down here."

Before long they were pretty loaded, and they were hitting on every woman they saw. They met two young women from Chicago, who were friendly, drunk, and wanted to party. They paired off, Fitch with the hospital administrator and Cohen with Amy, a nineteen-year-old travel agent.

The Chicago girls invited Greg and Charlie to their hotel room at the Radisson. Cohen had a funny feeling walking through the hotel lobby. He and his parents had stayed at the Radisson during a mental health convention almost two years ago.

There was more drinking and partying in the hotel room. The two couples spent the night in separate double beds. Fitch and Cohen left the next morning and headed directly for Molly's, where they drank several toasts to the young ladies from Chicago.

That afternoon they ran into one of Greg's friends, Lisa, from Illinois. Fitch hadn't seen her for well over a year. She and her friend Ellen were staying at a campground on the other side of Lake Pontchartrain. They also had a car, so the four of them decided to head out to the campground. Greg made it with Lisa in the car at the campground that night, and Cohen made it with Ellen in the tent.

The next day all four decided to go back to the city for the Bacchus parade. By the time they left the campground, Cohen was thinking about Amy, the travel agent from Chicago, not Ellen. He was convinced he was in love with her.

As they were driving back into the city, he remembered that Amy and her friend were staying at the Airport Hilton that night and were flying home the next morning.

"I want to get out," he said suddenly. "I want to see Amy at the airport before she leaves."

"What's the matter with you? Are you obsessed with this woman?"

"Yes."

"How are you going to get back? The buses don't run out here."

"I'm getting out. Stop the car."

"But we aren't anywhere near the airport."

"I'll hitchhike."

"You don't know where you're going," said Fitch as they came to a stop sign. Charlie suddenly jumped out of the car and took off on foot. He spent the next several hours hitching rides and finally made his way to the Airport Hilton. He asked for Amy's room number at the desk, but the desk clerk wouldn't tell him without her permission.

He called her on the hotel phone. Amy was sleeping and terribly hung over.

"I really want to see you before you leave," he said.

"But I'm too tired," she said.

"I think I'm in love with you."

"You've got to be kidding."

"I really enjoyed the time we spent together."

"This is crazy. It'll never work."

"So do you want to just forget the whole thing? Just like that."

She paused before answering. "Well—yeah."

It was late, and he couldn't get a ride back to the city. The hotel security wouldn't let him sleep in the lobby, so he spent the night in the baggage claim area of the airport. He didn't make it back to Fitch's apartment for two days.

Fitch had an efficiency at 2127 Carondelet Street on the first floor of a two-story building. Fitch's apartment wasn't fancy, but it was livable and cheap. Cohen slept on the couch.

Carondelet Street was just outside the French Quarter, about fifteen blocks from downtown. Realtors referred to the area as "transitional." The atmosphere at 2127 Carondelet was friendly and casual, and most of the tenants knew one another. Many of them worked in the French Quarter at night as waiters, waitresses, and bartenders.

Word had gotten around to the other tenants that Fitch had dragged a guy named McDowell in off the street, so they were slightly wary of him. Despite living on the streets for over a year, Cohen presented a well-groomed, clean-cut image. Once the other tenants got to know him, they liked him. He was quiet, well-spoken, conservatively dressed, and very polite—the perfect gentleman.

Besides setting him up in the apartment, Fitch brought Cohen to the ACORN office every day and gave him work. Charlie was technically a volunteer, but he was paid under the table. He didn't earn much, but he was quite happy to have any work at all.

Cohen couldn't believe his good luck. The whole setup was too good to be true. It was just what he wanted—a job, an apartment, and a friend he could trust. After fifteen months of hell, he finally had it going good.

He didn't tell Fitch much about his past, but he did tell him about his eight months on the streets of New York City. He talked about Nina and about selling books on the streets. He bragged about having sex on the steps of a church at 2 A.M. and about his escapades with crack. Cohen also told him that a housewife had picked him up in the middle of nowhere while he was hitchhiking and had taken him to a motel for a romp in the sheets.

When Fitch asked about his parents, Charlie answered simply, "They're dead." He added that he was an only child. He also told Fitch pleasant, sentimental stories of his childhood with his parents, as if he missed them, but he never told Fitch that he had grown up just 45 miles from Canton, Illinois.

Fitch believed the stories, and Cohen was proud of himself. He had gotten damn good. How else could he have survived so many close calls during the past fifteen months? He couldn't be touched. He was too smart. Not that he was conning Fitch. He couldn't tell him the truth. The guy was helping him with very little encouragement. He thanked Fitch several times for the help and promised to do a good job at ACORN and to help with the rent, but Fitch wouldn't hear of it.

"If I were in your situation," he said, "I'd want somebody to help me."

Cohen was convinced he wasn't the same person he had been a year ago. Violent thoughts no longer appealed to him. He had mellowed out. He wanted to go clean. This was a chance to make a fresh start and to lead a normal life.

From an ACORN leaflet:

ACORN is the Association of Community Organizations for Reform Now, a nonprofit neighborhood-based membership organization that organizes citizens to win more power in decision-making on issues that affect their lives, whether it be rape and sexual assault, utility rates, banking or housing. The key to ACORN's success lies in our ability to mobilize large numbers of citizens and directly confront our politicians and public officials.

ACORN has offices in over 24 U.S. cities and is one of the largest nonprofit organizations in the country. In 1990 it had over 4,000 members in New Orleans and about two dozen employees.

On Cohen's first day at ACORN, Fitch, a campaign organizer, sent him out to do a can shake. He stood at a busy intersection, shook a coin can, and solicited money for ACORN from passersby and motorists. He raised over $50 in three hours. Fitch was delighted. The dude could hustle. He let him keep the money.

On Saturdays, the two ran a tag operation. They rounded up a dozen or so inner city kids to solicit money. The kids got to keep a percentage of the take. Fitch and Cohen also kept a percentage. Within a few weeks Charlie was running his own tag team.

Occasionally Fitch and Cohen would canvas one of the nicer neighborhoods in New Orleans. They'd go door-to-door, explain the issue they were working on, and ask for a donation. Cohen got a healthy cut of the money he collected, which was crucial. If he didn't get donations, he didn't get paid.

Fitch paid for most of their food and drinks when they went out, but Cohen was such good company he didn't mind. His roommate could be witty and unpredictable. He wasn't afraid to approach total strangers and start conversations with them. One night at the St. Charles Tavern, he walked up to a young woman, pulled off his sunglasses, and said, "Hey, babe, I'm psychedelic. Wanna party?" Fitch just about died laughing.

One of their favorite hangouts was Igor's, a bar and laundry down the street from their apartment building. One of the bartenders, a young woman named Goldie, didn't like Cohen. She didn't trust him. He asked her out once, but she turned him down. On another occasion he asked her to front him a hamburger. She wouldn't do it.

"That guy is a creep," she told Fitch. "He's one of those people who tries to connive you with his good looks."

"You just don't know him," Fitch answered.

At the end of March, James McDowell became an official ACORN employee. Fitch gave him a W-4 to fill out. Cohen used the same Social Security number he had used at the health food store in New York. About that same time Fitch told Charlie that he would soon be moving out of the apartment and in with his girlfriend. Cohen could take over the apartment after Fitch moved out, but he was going to have to carry himself. Fitch couldn't pay his rent and food bill much longer.

Cohen began talking to Fitch about moving, too, which didn't make any sense, but Fitch didn't question him about it. Fitch was busy with a new campaign at work and didn't have time to worry about it.

Cohen was no longer happy working at ACORN. He had worked hard for over a month, putting in lots of hours every week, yet he still wasn't making enough money to survive. He also knew that ACORN would eventually find out about the bogus Social Security number. Someone would come around asking questions. He couldn't risk staying there much longer.

He became depressed and began spending more time alone in the apartment. Fitch tried to get him to go out. "C'mon," he said. "Maybe you'll meet a good-lookin' chick and get lucky." But Cohen preferred to stay in. He didn't have the energy to face people. He was too depressed.

Fitch helped him look for a job. He bought the newspaper and went through the Help Wanted ads with him. He asked around about work. Charlie was looking for a construction job or perhaps some house painting, something that paid cash under the table.

Fitch could see that Cohen was becoming more alienated and unhappy. He tried to buck him up. "Look, man, you've got to hang with it," he said. "You'll find some other work sooner or later."

One afternoon they were at a sandwich shop near the office. A guy pulled up and said he needed someone to do some painting, so Cohen worked for the guy for the next few days. The guy had more painting work, and he paid in cash, but Charlie didn't want to continue.

"That guy's gay," he told Fitch.

Fitch was confused. Cohen wasn't making sense. He had a job with ACORN, but he didn't want it. He had a cheap apartment, but he wanted to move. He had gotten other work, but he had quit because the guy was gay. What was his problem? Cohen knew. He had a secret that was eating at his insides, and he was about to rupture.

He received his first paycheck from ACORN made out to James McDowell on Friday, March 30, 1990. He and Fitch went to a grocery store across the street from the office to cash their checks. The store clerk refused to cash McDowell's check because he didn't have sufficient ID, but Fitch, who was known in the store, intervened, and Cohen got the money.

chapter 15

- - - - - - - - - -

Like Abbott and Costello

Charles Cohen spent Sunday night sleeping on the street in the French Quarter. The noise of the traffic woke him up early Monday morning. He sat up in a doorway and looked around suspiciously. It was there again, just as it had been the past few days, weeks, and months: that feeling that he was being watched. Only now it was worse. The Feds were trailing him, getting closer and closer, and soon they would make their move. They would jump him, several men in suits and topcoats, and they would rape and kill him.

The FBI didn't like being led on a wild-goose chase. He could sense their humiliation at being outsmarted by a 25-year-old and their hatred. They were psychotic. Somehow they had sniffed out his trail. They had known it would happen sooner or later, but he wanted to stretch out this sick game for as long as possible.

He had split up with Fitch on Friday night. He had spent the first night in a cheap motel out by the airport and slept on the streets the past two nights rather than risk leading the Feds directly to Fitch's apartment.

A couple of office workers walked by. He held out his

hand and said, "Spare change?" A woman dropped a nickel to the sidewalk near his hand, and he scrambled on all fours for it as it rolled away. He looked up and saw a familiar mixture of fear and disgust on her face. He threw the nickel back at her. It bounced near her feet and rolled into the gutter as she hurried away.

He had gotten moderately buzzed with some friends the night before, and his head wasn't feeling too good. A cup of coffee might help. He felt his pockets. No money. God only knew what had happened to the money, not that it was very much to start with. Got paid $96 plus change on Friday, and now he was cleaned out. Typical. That's how things had gone during the past sixteen months. It was a never-ending nightmare. Just when he thought he finally had his feet on the ground, something went wrong, like getting the LTD towed in L.A., getting sick in Tijuana, or turning up on *America's Most Wanted*.

He found a small piece of folded paper in his back pocket. He opened it and sighed. Just enough for two quick lines. He couldn't remember buying the coke, but at least it explained where the money had gone. He carefully brought the paper to his nose, snorted the contents, and licked the sheet. He leaned back against the doorway, closed his eyes, and breathed deeply. Yes, indeed. That helped. Nothing like a little self-medication.

He thought about returning to his apartment, but he wasn't sure he could trust Fitch any longer. Fitch was acting like he knew more than he was letting on. Fitch had psychic power. He was a vampire, draining his energy, fighting to control him.

Cohen knew the FBI would catch on about the phony Social Security number; he just didn't know they would catch on so fast. The problem cashing his check on Friday was just the first sign of trouble. The lack of a valid Social Security number had been his albatross.

He couldn't work for ACORN or live in Fitch's apartment any longer, but he couldn't bear the thought of living on the streets again. He needed a new job, a new place to live, and a new identity. Everything was falling apart, just like it always had.

He had to get out of New Orleans and get back to the West Coast, but how would he get there? There had to be an easier way than hitchhiking, especially without a cent in his pocket. If he just had a car. A long, quiet drive would give him a chance to forget and to relax. He thought back to his drive from Delaware to California in his parents' big, comfortable Ford. It seemed like a lifetime ago.

He'd have to steal a car. It couldn't be that hard. He thought of Metairie, a rich suburb out by Lake Pontchartrain. He had seen plenty of nice cars in Metairie when he and Fitch had canvassed the neighborhood for ACORN. Those rich bastards stood for everything he hated, for conformity and authority and the system and selling out. They didn't care about anyone but themselves and how much they could own. They wouldn't miss one car. Everybody in Metairie probably had two or three, plus enough insurance not to worry about losing one.

He spotted a man in a phone booth looking his way. Another goddamned Fed. Charlie tried not to look at him. He didn't want to let on. It was a game they were playing, a vicious psychological game. He had to make a move, but he couldn't run for it. That would show weakness.

Cohen leisurely ambled down the sidewalk right past the guy in the phone booth. He walked across Elysian Fields, but he saw the guy again, this time with another agent. They were standing near a dark sedan, your basic unmarked car.

He suddenly realized that he was only two blocks from Kreiger's house. He had spent a week at Kreiger's a year ago, just before he had split for Florida. He walked

around the block just to be sure the Feds weren't following him, and he slipped down an alley to the house. He
peeked through a window in the back but didn't see anyone. He climbed through the window and sat on the floor
breathing heavily, trying to regain his composure. He
needed to be strong.

He stayed in the same spot for an hour. It dawned on
him suddenly that Kreiger might have seen him on *America's Most Wanted.* He heard a voice from the second
floor. He had to check out, pronto. He climbed out the
window and headed for the French Quarter.

On April 2, 1990, at approximately 9:30 A.M., Abed El
Hackam Khalil pulled his Rollins Cab over to the curb at
the corner of Burgundy and Esplanade, and a young man
with a thin beard and a wrinkled blue shirt got in. It was
a bad part of the French Quarter, known for drugs, and
the kid looked a little scruffy, but Khalil had seen worse.
He wanted a ride to Metairie, a 20- to 30-minute drive
north of downtown New Orleans.

Khalil and Cohen began chatting during the drive.
Charlie mentioned that he had lived in the Bronx. Khalil,
originally from Egypt, had spent five years in New York
before moving to New Orleans. Cohen told Khalil about
his life there. He said that he had been hooked on crack
while living on the streets of New York. He talked about
several close calls with the cops in New York and about
getting his shoes stolen. His voice got louder and faster,
and Khalil could tell he was stoned. He bragged about
getting laid on the steps of a church. He ranted about going down into the tunnels under Grand Central Terminal.
He was making Khalil a little nervous.

As they entered Metairie, Cohen accused Khalil of
working for the FBI, of following him, and of plotting to
kill him. He cursed at Khalil, insulted his manhood, and
called his mother rude names. This last insult was more

than Khalil could withstand. He pulled the cab over. Charlie jumped out without paying the $26 fare and took off. Khalil grabbed the tire-iron he kept under the driver's seat and chased after him.

Cohen ran through a few lawns of the well-trimmed neighborhood. When he looked back, he could see the cabbie chasing him with a tire-iron. The Arab was going to club the shit out of him. Maybe he really was a Fed.

Within a few blocks the kid had disappeared. Khalil ran back to his car and decided to search the neighborhood in his cab. He couldn't have gotten very far.

At 10 o'clock that morning 79-year-old Hilda Sonderberg was hosing a flower bed of hibiscus and rose bushes in the front lawn of 4908 Reaser Street in Metairie, where she lived with her daughter, Gayle, and Gayle's husband, Ronald Rowbatham. It was a two-story house, about a hundred yards from Lake Pontchartrain. The neighborhood was quiet, clean, and safe.

On most mornings Ronald and Gayle Rowbatham were at work by 10. Gayle worked at Macy's. Ronald had a gift shop down by the Superdome, and he represented several large gift shop distributors throughout Louisiana. But this particular morning both Ronald and Gayle were home meeting with a saleswoman who was pushing a new line of stuffed animals.

Hilda saw a young man coming across the neighbor's lawn. She thought he was the gas man coming to read the meter, so she continued with her watering. Cohen saw the old woman and the two cars in the driveway. He didn't see the cabbie behind him, so he made his move. He grabbed Hilda's arms from behind. Hilda immediately felt pain shoot from her elbows to her shoulders.

"Let's go inside," he said. He tried to drag her toward the house, but she screamed and fell, cutting her elbow on the edge of the cement driveway. He tried to pull her up, but she was too heavy, and she kept screaming. He stared at her, not knowing what to do.

Just then Gayle Rowbatham stepped outside to check on her mother and saw her on the ground. A bearded young man in a blue shirt was standing beside her.

"Mother, what's the matter?" asked Gayle as she rushed to her. Gayle thought that her mother had fallen down and that the young man was helping her up, but then he grabbed Gayle and said, "Give me your car keys."

"Ahhh, help!" Gayle screamed. "Ronald, help!"

Rowbatham heard his wife scream and ran to the door. He saw his mother-in-law on the ground and his wife wrestling with a scruffy young man.

"Hey, you," he shouted. "Let go of my wife!"

When Cohen saw the six-foot two-inch, 215-pound Rowbatham rush toward him, his confidence deserted him. He tried to pull away from the woman, but she had her nails dug into his arms and wouldn't let go. Cohen took a swing at her. Gayle let go and ducked, and the punch just missed her.

Rowbatham and Charlie grabbed each other. Rowbatham hadn't been in a fistfight for so many years he could barely remember how it was done. Instinctively, he planned to grab the guy in a bear hug and fall on him, but Rowbatham couldn't get any leverage on the kid. They moved together in an odd circular dance, locked arm in arm.

"What are you doing?" Rowbatham yelled.

Gayle hit at Cohen and screamed, "Get out of here! Leave us alone!"

Cohen tried to kick Rowbatham in the groin. He missed but stomped down on one of his bare feet in the process. Rowbatham groaned and let go. Charlie swung his fist again and connected cleanly with the side of

Rowbatham's face, breaking his glasses. Then he took off running.

Rowbatham was furious. "Call the cops," he shouted to his wife and took off after the intruder. He had worked all of his life to buy a nice house for his family in a nice neighborhood, and some cretin was trying to ruin it all. He chased him down the middle of the street. At the end of the block, Cohen took a right. Rowbatham followed in hot pursuit.

Cohen was about a half block ahead of Rowbatham, who was running in his bare feet and couldn't keep up. Charlie took another right and continued down the middle of the street.

Rowbatham noticed that a cab was slowly following them. He waved at the cab driver and yelled, "Help! Help! Help!" The driver ignored him and continued following at a safe distance behind. Rowbatham realized that the cab driver and the kid were probably in cahoots.

Just then Rowbatham heard the cab accelerate behind him. He jumped to his right. The kid ran up on some lawns to the left and hurdled a few hedges. The cab roared past him and drove up on a lawn, knocking down a mailbox, and cutting off Cohen's escape.

Khalil jumped out of the cab with the tire-iron. Charlie knew he was trapped. Things had gone from bad to worse, from *America's Most Wanted* to Abbott and Costello. He didn't think the end would be so pathetic. He had hoped for something slightly more glorious.

He saw the tire-iron and pleaded, "No, don't hit me. I'll give you $50 if you just get me out of here."

"Now you ask me for a favor," said Khalil.

"My roommate's got the money. I promise I'll get it for you."

Khalil told him to hide in the backseat. They both jumped in the cab. As Rowbatham approached the cab, it took off, grit shooting from its rear tires. It roared down the street to the next intersection and hung a left.

Rowbatham hobbled home, breathing heavily. He told his whimpering mother-in-law not to move until an ambulance arrived. He also called the police and told them that the perpetrator wasn't on foot any longer. He was in a cab.

Deputy Robert Rotherham, Jr., of the Jefferson Parish Sheriff's Office, was in his cruiser and had been dispatched to the scene of an armed robbery at 4908 Reaser Street. The perpetrator was described as a white male about 25 years old, on foot, wearing a blue shirt. Rotherham was 25 years old and had been on the force just 2½ years.

Rotherham was about two blocks from Reaser when he saw a cab heading toward him. Suddenly the cab stopped, and the driver jumped out and ran over to Rotherham's cruiser, waving frantically.

"He's in the backseat," the driver said. "The backseat!"

Rotherham drew his revolver and cautiously approached the cab. He looked in the backseat and saw a white male fitting the general description of the perpetrator lying facedown on the floorboard as if he were trying to wiggle under the front seat.

He opened the back door, pointed the gun at the back of the young man's head, and shouted, "Show me your hands." Cohen put up his hands. Rotherham ordered him out of the car. Charlie did as he was told. Rotherham frisked him for weapons.

Several other police cars arrived momentarily, and numerous spectators gathered. The police sent a unit to the house on Reaser to bring a witness to the scene for identification. Within a few minutes the cruiser returned, and Ronald Rowbatham stepped out.

"Do you see him?" a policeman asked Rowbatham. The young man with a thin beard and wearing a light blue shirt was leaning against the side of a police car. He didn't look at all worried. In fact, he looked cool as a cucumber. Rowbatham promptly identified him.

At 10:21 A.M. at 4412 Folse Drive, Deputy Rotherham arrested a young man who said his name was James McDowell and read him his Miranda rights. He charged him with attempted theft and simple assault.

Rotherham took Cohen to the East Bank lock-up, where he was booked. He had no identification or money and nothing in his pockets except two shoelaces.

Rotherham noticed that the young man seemed oddly relieved, as if he had been through the arrest procedure before. Rotherham asked if he used drugs, if he was mentally ill, and if he had ever been arrested before. To all three questions Cohen answered, "No." Rotherham didn't believe him.

That evening Charles Cohen was taken to the Jefferson Parish Correctional Center in Gretna. His bail was set at $5,275.

chapter 16

- - - - - - - - -

Good God Almighty,
Let the Truth Come Out!

Greg Fitch was concerned when McDowell didn't come home on Friday or Saturday night. He knew McDowell was a little crazy, but he had never disappeared before. McDowell had gotten paid on Friday, so maybe he had gone on a binge. Maybe the cops had locked him up in the drunk tank for the weekend. He was impulsive and he had been acting kind of strange lately, so maybe he had just taken off to be by himself. Maybe he'd met some chicks and gotten lucky. Fitch tried not to worry too much. After all, he wasn't responsible for the guy.

His roommate didn't show up for work at the ACORN office on Monday. Fitch didn't have a phone in his apartment, so he kept expecting a call from him at the office. The week went by with no word. By Friday Fitch was seriously concerned. Where could he be? People just don't get up and disappear without a word. If he had split, why hadn't he taken his stuff with him? All of his belongings were still in the apartment.

Fitch considered the possibility that he had gotten drunk or really high and couldn't find his way home. Maybe he'd passed out in a gutter, hit his head, and gotten amnesia. Maybe he'd been mugged. He had seemed normal on Friday and hadn't said anything about leaving.

Fitch called the local hospitals and the Orleans Parish police lock-up. No one had a James McDowell. Fitch went to Igor's, Molly's, and their other hangouts and asked the bartenders and the regulars about him. He talked to some of the tenants at 2127 Carondelet. No one had seen him.

By the beginning of the second week Fitch and everyone else at the office assumed that McDowell was dead, and they expected his body to turn up any day. Fitch called the coroner's office and asked if they had any unidentified white male stiffs. They didn't. Fitch even filed a missing person report with the Orleans Parish police.

A few days later Fitch answered a phone at the office. "A collect call from an inmate at the Jefferson Parish Correctional Center. Will you accept the charges?"

Fitch accepted the charges. It was McDowell. "My God, what's going on?" Fitch asked.

Cohen told him the story of his arrest, but it didn't make any sense to Fitch. "Why did you run on a cab fare?" he asked.

"I don't know. It was stupid. I didn't have any money."

"Why did you go to Metairie?"

"I was in the Quarter, and I saw these people, and they were following me."

"What people?"

"I don't know, just people. They kept looking at me. I just freaked out."

Fitch asked him if he had gotten drunk or if he'd gotten ahold of some bad dope, but Cohen said he hadn't. Fitch couldn't help thinking that he wasn't telling him the whole truth. Something was wrong with the story.

"I just had to get out of there," Charlie repeated several times.

Fitch called Rollins Cab and offered to pay the fare, but they refused to drop the charges. He called the bail bondsman. He assumed the bail wouldn't be very high, especially for running on a cab fare. The bail bondsman informed him of the assault charge. Fitch was shocked. James hadn't told him anything about assaulting an old woman. This was more serious than he thought. The more he thought about it, the more angry he became. What was his problem?

The bail was over $5,000, but he needed only ten percent to spring McDowell, which was about $500. Fitch had enough money, but he couldn't decide whether to do it.

"Don't bail him out," said Goldie, the bartender at Igor's. "The guy'll walk for sure. Let him stew for a while. It's probably the best place for that weirdo."

After this episode, maybe it was better that he had some time to think about it, Fitch decided. He'd already helped him enough. What was to keep him from skipping bail or pulling another crazy stunt? He was too unpredictable and unreliable.

Fitch called Scott Brannon and told him of McDowell's predicament. Brannon, also a community organizer, had become one of Cohen's only other friends in New Orleans. Brannon asked some people he knew for money to help bail him out.

"Look, he's from New York," said Brannon. "He's in on a minor charge. Why don't we try and get him out? He's a nice guy. We're friends. I can vouch for him."

But everyone refused to help because they didn't know him well enough. Brannon tried to get him registered for a drug rehab program so he would qualify for lower bail or an early release, but the program had a year-long waiting list.

One afternoon Fitch and Brannon wrote a letter of recommendation for their friend. They pointed out that he had a job at a nonprofit charitable organization, they vouched for his character and his honesty, and they requested that his bail be reduced. Greg's supervisor signed the letter. Fitch and Brannon sent the letter to the bail bondsman, the police, and the prosecutor's office, but it didn't make any difference. Cohen's bail wasn't reduced, and he stayed in jail.

Fitch and Brannon couldn't afford to hire a lawyer for him. Cohen would have to be represented by the Indigent Defender's Bureau, or IDB as it was commonly known. Fitch called them about the case, but they were too busy to look into it before the arraignment. He was going to stay cooped up until his arraignment on May 24 and probably longer.

Once he had a day or so to think about the fiasco in Metairie, Cohen was infuriated at himself. It had been the irrational act of a scared, confused idiot. He was humiliated. His pride was shaken. He wasn't one of America's most wanted criminals. He was one of America's dumbest criminals.

After a few days his attitude changed. So what if he were held in a crummy little prison? No one knew who he was, and they probably wouldn't figure it out. The Feds could comb the country, but they wouldn't find him. He hadn't seriously injured anyone and hadn't stolen or damaged anything, so they wouldn't hold him for very long. If he played it cool he could probably get through this without anyone realizing who he was or what he had done. He'd just relax with a bed and three square meals a day, compliments of the fine upstanding taxpayers of Jefferson Parish.

As the weeks went by, Cohen didn't have much to do but think. There weren't many activities available to the 700 inmates of the Jefferson Parish Correctional Center.

The jail was a temporary holding facility for prisoners who were awaiting trial or transfer to other prisons.

Charlie went to the law library and looked up the sentences for attempted theft and simple assault. They weren't too bad. He wouldn't do a long stretch. He was also interviewed by a clerk from the IDB who said it was very possible he'd be released early because of prison overcrowding.

But prison life—the bars, the cement floors, the awful food—was taking his arrogance away. He tried to decide what he was going to do with the rest of his life. He wasn't sure he had the strength and stamina to go on running forever. The constant strain had taken its toll. He'd been worn down by the streets, the shelters, and the hustling. He'd often gone without food and sleep. It was a hard way to live, and he knew he would eventually be caught.

His life until the night of November 12, 1988, had been comfortable. Everything he'd needed had been provided for him. Now his life was a constant nightmare. He had tried to forget that night, but he hadn't been able to, and he never would.

Cohen thought about all the people who had helped him while he was on the run, even though they barely knew him. Everywhere he had gone people had helped him, and what had he done? He had been rude and manipulative. He had stolen from them. He had even murdered.

He didn't want to live like that anymore. He was sick of the fear, loneliness, hatred, and depression. He was fed up with lying, stealing, hustling, and panhandling. To continue with that life was no life at all.

Brannon knew Jefferson Parish Judge James L. Cannella, so he went to see him.

"Judge, James McDowell is a good person," said

Brannon. "He's working for ACORN. You know me, Judge. Could you release him on his own recognizance if I pay the fine for the cab?"

Brannon showed him the letter of recommendation from ACORN. Judge Cannella read the letter. He seemed to be mulling the request over in his mind. Finally, he said, "Where is Mr. McDowell from?"

"He's from New York," said Brannon.

"I can't release him if he's from New York. I can't take the risk. If he was from New Orleans, I might be able to help you."

There were several ardent born-again Christians on Cohen's pod in the prison, and they gave him some Christian literature to read. The prison chaplain also gave him a Bible. Cohen didn't have much else to do, so he started reading the materials. It helped pass the time.

He admired the Christians. They were the kindest and most content inmates. They passionately believed in their religion. It was like they were high, and he envied them. They spoke with him at length about becoming a Christian, and they urged him to let Jesus into his life.

Charlie started going to the religious services at the prison, and he began attending the Bible studies in the pod. He spent much of his time alone in his cell reading the Bible. He sketched pictures of crucifixes and scenes from the Bible, and he gave the drawings away as gifts. Most of the other inmates avoided him. They didn't want to talk about the Bible or Jesus Christ, and that was all he would talk about.

One of the chaplain's favorite topics during his sermon was salvation. "Let the Lord get ahold of you," he said. "He can change your life. If you have things on your conscience, you can be free of them. Christ turns you away from the bondage of sin and gives you eternal life, but first you must repent of your sins."

Scott Brannon visited him in prison a few times. They sat in a small booth facing one another through a thick piece of glass and spoke over telephones. Cohen told Brannon of his new interest in the Bible and Christianity. Brannon, a very religious person, knew that his friend was being born again. He would need help and guidance during this time of growth. Brannon tried to teach him what he could about Jesus.

During one of their conversations Cohen said, "I don't know how I made it through the last seventeen months without being killed or hurt. Nothing violent or even threatening happened to me while I was on the streets. I was shielded. Somebody was looking out for me."

"Jesus chose you, James, for something special," Brannon said. "He was watching you and protecting you. Jesus knew this day would come."

Charlie decided that he had become an evil and repulsive sinner, and he came to believe that the only way he could live with himself would be to turn his life over to Jesus Christ.

On Wednesday, May 16, at 11 P.M., Charles Cohen confessed every sin that he could remember, and he cried out for Jesus to save him. He felt cool air fill his cell. It seeped through his skin and filled his body. He felt an incredible release. The burden of his sins was being lifted from him. Jesus was forgiving him. No matter what else happened to him, his soul would rise to heaven when Jesus returned. Cohen knew he didn't deserve to be saved, but Jesus saved even the most wretched of sinners. He had committed terrible sins, but now he was forgiven. He had finally found peace. It was the greatest moment in his life.

Cohen asked the chaplain to baptize him. It would symbolize the death of his old self and his rebirth. Baptisms were performed in the prison on Saturdays, so

Charlie was scheduled to be baptized on Saturday, May 26, just two days after his arraignment.

Now that the Lord had forgiven him, Cohen had some earthly matters to straighten out. Unless he made a clean break with the horror of his past, he couldn't start his new life. He had to make sure that the people who were hurt by what he had done and afraid of him—his aunts, uncles, cousins, and friends—were notified as quickly as possible. He wanted to explain to them why it had happened and how a person who had done something horrible could be saved. It would take all the courage he could muster, but his salvation was at stake. It would create a great deal of chaos, but that didn't matter. This life was nothing compared to the eternal life that awaited him.

Brannon visited Cohen just a few days before his arraignment. A woman in the next visiting booth was praying very loudly. "Dear Lord, please let the truth come out," she said, half chanting, half singing the words.

Cohen told Brannon that he'd been saved by Jesus. Brannon praised the Lord.

"Let the truth come out, let the truth come out," the woman chanted louder and louder. She was sweating and trembling. Brannon knew she was speaking in tongues, and he could sense spiritual turbulence in the room. God had placed the woman there for a reason.

"What about your parents?" Brannon said. "Maybe you should contact them. Maybe they could help you out of this mess."

"They're dead," said Charlie.

"I'm sorry, James. I didn't know. What happened to them?"

"I'm not ready to talk about that yet," said Cohen, "but everything will soon be clear."

"No matter what you've done, dude," said Brannon, "God will forgive you."

"Let the truth come out!" the woman shouted. "Good God almighty, let the truth come out!"

"Amen," said Brannon.

"Whoa, almighty Jesus!"

"Amen," said Charles Cohen.

part II

Only Child

chapter 1

- - - - - - - -

The Little God

Martin Cohen and Ethel Weissler met in the early 1960s
at the Jacksonville State Hospital, an institution with over
3,000 patients. Jacksonville is a small town in southern
Illinois, about 35 miles west of Springfield, the state capital.

Ethel Weissler was born in Chicago and served in
World War II as an instrument mechanic for the Army Air
Corps. She was discharged in 1946 as a Private, First
Class, and received several good service medals. She had
a round face, thick eyebrows, stood five-foot five-inches
tall, and weighed 175 pounds.

After the war Ethel went to college in Chicago on the
GI Bill. She held a number of different jobs in the '50s,
including stints as recreation director at military bases in
Europe and the United States. Her first love, however,
was acting. She was funny and she could sing, so she set
her sights on Broadway. She went to New York and began auditioning.

In July 1956 she got her break. Harold Prince invited
her to join *Pajama Game* as an understudy. She signed a
contract for $140 a week. She used her stage name,

Sharon Wells, and joined the company on tour. Two weeks later one of the actresses dropped out, and Ethel was in the show. She finished the tour with the company and appeared on Broadway for a short time. When the tour ended, she waited for the next offer, but it never came.

Not one to wait long, Ethel looked for another career. She had always liked arts and crafts, so in 1958 she enrolled in the master's degree program for occupational therapy at New York University. The state of Illinois subsidized her studies provided she work in the state for an equal number of years upon graduating. She graduated in 1960 and was assigned to Jacksonville.

Martin Cohen grew up in New York City. At age 26, he was hired at Jacksonville as chief psychologist immediately after earning a Ph.D. in psychology at the University of Denver. Cohen was respected at Jacksonville for his intelligence and his diligence. By the early 1960s he had published half a dozen articles in professional journals and had presented papers at a number of conventions for mental health professionals. He was clearly destined for bigger things.

Cohen was known as a sensitive, kind man. He was very principled about the care of patients. If he felt that a particular activity or regulation was not in the best interests of the patients, he said so bluntly, even if it meant criticizing someone. In a dispute between a staff member and a patient, Cohen almost always took the side of the patient. He also had uncompromisingly high expectations for the performance of his staff. Consequently, Martin Cohen developed a reputation as being difficult to work for.

Cohen was extremely sentimental, particularly when it came to his mother, Bessie. He was the "baby" of his family, and he missed his mother very much. She had died by the early '60s, and he kept a picture of her on his desk, which he was known to kiss and talk to.

Cohen was short and a little overweight. With his thick glasses and large cigars, he looked like a short Ernie Kovacs. He was a fastidious dresser. His shirts were pressed, and his tie and socks always matched. Even in casual situations he dressed carefully, making sure that everything was coordinated.

He got along well with women, particularly older women. He constantly flattered them at work and bought them gifts on their birthdays. The female employees at the hospital enjoyed his attention, and he became their favorite.

Dr. Cohen liked older women so much that he married one. In 1957 he married Mary Elizabeth Zachary, a hospital employee. She was twelve years his senior and had two children from a previous marriage. Mary was from a socially prominent Jacksonville family, and her family set them up in a large house in a nice section of town.

The marriage did not go well. They didn't have enough in common. Martin wanted children, but Mary was past her child-bearing years. They were divorced in 1961.

Ethel Weissler was different from most of the women in Jacksonville. She didn't like playing bridge or drinking tea in women's clubs. She liked the theater, arts and crafts, and collecting antiques and junk. She didn't wear makeup, stockings, or girdles, and she didn't have her hair permed. She like to joke and laugh, loudly at times, and she wasn't afraid to poke fun at herself, particularly about her weight. She had some unusual ideas, too. She spoke openly with patients about subjects such as reincarnation and Buddhism. She was the very antithesis of the conservative, small-town, midwestern ideal of femininity, and she didn't care what other people thought of her.

Consequently, Ethel was not very well liked by the folks in Jacksonville. Dr. Martin Cohen, however, felt differently. He admired her intelligence and wit. Ethel was just five years older than him, and she was Jewish, too.

Many of the women who doted on Dr. Cohen were not at all happy when he began bestowing most of his attention on Ethel. They didn't think she was good enough for the promising young psychologist. Nevertheless, in 1963 the two were married.

They desperately wanted a child. Ethel, who was 40, had two miscarriages. Her third pregnancy was difficult, but on December 6, 1964, Charles Mark Cohen was born in Chicago. Martin Cohen was in the delivery room, and just minutes after the birth he held Charlie in his arms and smiled proudly. He finally had a son.

Charlie quickly became the center of Martin's and Ethel's lives. He was their pride and joy. They treasured him, and they were willing to give him anything. He was all they lived for and all they talked about.

One of their friends remembers: "Ethel was a typical Jewish mother. There's nothing that the son could do wrong. There's nothing that you don't do for the son or give to the son or forgive a son. The sun rises and sets on the son. That's how they were. The boy is always right, and nobody was going to do anything about disciplining the boy. She'd had a bad time having him and was not capable of having any more children. He was a little God on a pedestal. He never had a baby-sitter. Too precious to leave with a baby-sitter. Everywhere they went, everything they did, there was no question that Charles was part of it."

In the early 1960s, *community mental health* was the newest approach to the treatment of the mentally ill. Its proponents argued that psychiatric hospitalization was not necessary for most patients. They advocated the removal of the mentally ill from the big state institutions in favor of treatment in smaller centers closer to their homes. The idea was that they would be better off integrated into their communities at jobs and in their homes rather than locked up in large institutions. This approach could also provide more services to more people for the same amount of money.

The Illinois Department of Mental Health was enthusiastic about the potential of community mental health, so the department sent several of its psychologists to Harvard for training. Martin Cohen was one of them. He and his family spent 1965 in Boston. When they returned, he was a zealous proponent of the new approach.

Cohen was assigned to the zone office in Springfield, and he and Ethel bought a house in the city. As deputy zone director, he was responsible for developing a community mental health program for an eighteen-county area. The program included the opening of a new mental health facility in Springfield that would be the administrative hub for community-based services in the region. It would be a radical change from the stereotypical mental institutions of the past.

The McFarland Zone Center opened in April 1967. A 174-bed facility with 300 employees and a yearly budget of $5 million, McFarland offered numerous outpatient programs. In 1968, at the age of 38, Martin Cohen was named superintendent of the facility.

He hired a bright, young, idealistic staff. A feeling of newness and excitement set in. They were going to get rid of the old system and usher in the new. Staff morale was high. It was an opportunity to test their ideas in a brand-new facility with Martin Cohen leading the way.

From the beginning the McFarland Zone Center was a success, receiving numerous certifications and accreditations. The staff at McFarland, though, soon learned that Martin Cohen could be difficult. On some days he was helpful and encouraging, on others he was remote and argumentative. He occasionally lost his temper. He had strong opinions, and he did not hesitate to bring them up, even with his superiors.

Despite the early success and enthusiasm, Cohen did have problems at McFarland—a fire, a suicide, and numerous patients wandering off the grounds. He hired and fired several unit directors. It was a new facility with new ideas, and not all of the people or all of the ideas worked out.

One subordinate remembers: "You either liked Marty or you didn't give a damn for him. There wasn't much of an in-between. He could be a real bastard, but if he liked you, you could do no wrong. He was unafraid of pushing an issue if he felt it was the right thing to do. He'd make a major issue over insignificant things if he was in the mood. I'd say to him, 'Marty, drop it. In the scheme of things it's not worth doing battle.' But Marty would do battle. He could be his own worst enemy.

"On a personal basis he was an excellent human being. Intellectually he was one of the smartest men I ever met, just brilliant. He was extremely loyal and very supportive, too, but Marty had a real problem accepting authority, although he had no problem exercising it."

The Cohen family was happy and close during the late '60s and early '70s. Martin and Ethel lavished affection on their son and showered him with gifts. He even had his own television in his room. He was a handsome child and polite around other adults, but if he didn't get enough attention, he could be a discipline problem.

Ethel found part-time consulting work at several Springfield nursing homes. She was also involved in amateur theatrical groups, and she appeared in numerous plays and musicals. Her life was hectic, but she preferred it to staying home and being a housewife.

Her friends enjoyed her immensely. One says, "Ethel was a delight. Happy-go-lucky. A good sense of humor.

Funny as a crutch. She had a fabulous way with patients. She was a people person. And she was an actress and a singer. Oh, she was marvelous. Ethel wasn't a top-notch housekeeper. She didn't care about keeping house. Charles didn't like eating what she cooked anyway. He wanted fast food. Marty and Ethel were highly intelligent, more or less brilliant, and absolutely fantastic, as friends and individuals. They couldn't do enough for everybody and anybody."

Her weight, well over 200 pounds, was becoming a problem. She was constantly on a diet and joked about it with everyone. Whenever she lost weight, however, she immediately gained it back.

"Martin was worried about her weight, that she might fall and hurt herself," a friend remembers. "But he said, 'I married her when she was a fatty, and she is the most compatible person I've ever met.' Martin would bribe her to diet. He'd say, 'If you lose fifty pounds, I'll take you on a cruise' or 'I'll buy you another diamond.' She'd try, but she'd never succeed. She'd just grin and say, 'I know that he'll buy it for me anyway.' "

Martin Cohen had frequent confrontations with his superiors over political appointments. He simply would not hire a person for political reasons unless he was forced to. In 1975 he got into a heated argument with his boss about a low-level referral. Cohen wouldn't budge. His boss was a quiet and reserved man, but Cohen had him extremely agitated. People in offices down the hall heard them shouting at one another. Cohen finally told his boss to shut up. That ended the argument. Cohen was fired from his position at MacFarland and moved back to the regional office.

Ironically, that office was on the second floor at MacFarland, and his boss ran the regional office, so Cohen simply moved upstairs to work for the man who had fired him. Since the position was technically above that of superintendent, he actually received higher pay as a result of the dismissal.

Cohen was put in charge of "special projects." He was given an office and a paycheck but no responsibilities. He had simply been moved out of the way. For Martin Cohen, that was worse than being fired.

chapter 2

- - - - - - - -

Charmed Life

Martin Cohen was bitter over his firing and unhappy with his job. Tension in the regional office was high. Even though he and Ethel had many friends in Springfield, he decided it would be better to move on.

The superintendent's position at the Galesburg Mental Health Center (GMHC) had been available for several years, so he applied. He got the job, and the Cohen family moved to Galesburg, Illinois, in September 1976.

The Galesburg Mental Health Center, formerly a World War II military hospital, was well past its prime. The facility, which had over 100 buildings on 156 acres, was old and run down. With the state's continuing commitment to community mental health and deinstitutionalization, Cohen knew the institution's future was uncertain. Nevertheless, he was glad to have meaningful work. At 47 he was still relatively young, and GMHC was a new challenge.

A blue-collar community of approximately 30,000 located in the central-western part of Illinois, Galesburg is the largest town in Knox County. The Cohens bought a

two-story brick house on Park Lane, one of the most ex-
clusive locations in Galesburg. It was only one block
long, but Park Lane contained fifteen of the nicest houses
in Galesburg, many of them mansions. The private street
was lined with tall oak trees and guarded at both en-
trances by black wrought-iron gates.

Charlie was 11 when the family moved to Galesburg.
He was well behaved and got good grades, but he was
shy around other kids. It was obvious that he was spoiled,
and the other kids teased him about it.

Summers were extended vacations for young Charlie.
He played tennis and basketball, went swimming, and
spent hours in video arcades. His parents took him on expensive vacations to places like Florida, Hawaii, California, Disney World, and the Virgin Islands. It was a
charmed life.

When Charlie was 13, Martin and Ethel went all out
for his bar mitzvah. Many of their friends from Springfield and Jacksonville came to Galesburg for the weekend. The synagogue was full. The proud parents smiled
radiantly. A big reception was held afterward at a local
hotel with plenty of food, music, and dancing. Charlie received stacks of gifts and checks.

He soon became an avid tennis player. He played five
or six hours a day during the summer and two or three
hours per day during the rest of the year. His parents paid
for lessons and memberships at private clubs and saw that
he had the finest equipment.

Charlie's tennis skills were a source of great pride for
Martin and Ethel. They attended all of his meets, even the
minor ones. During the summer, they took him to youth
tournaments throughout the state. Within a few years
Charlie was one of the best players in his age group in
town.

When Charlie was in tenth grade, he made the high
school tennis team. He was the top sophomore player on

a very successful team and sometimes played with the varsity. During each match Martin Cohen stood by a fence in a suit and thick dark glasses intently watching his son play.

One of Charlie's tennis partners remembers Martin Cohen: "Dr. Cohen was very serious, very professional. He wanted Charlie to be the same. He wanted him to work hard at tennis and keep improving. Charlie had natural ability, but there wasn't that much practice and work for him. He was never that serious about it."

A classmate recalls: "His parents were very doting toward him, but he wasn't spoiled. He was very mature. He had a strong conscience about how he treated people. He was a genuinely nice person. He was very reserved, extremely polite, and very intelligent. Always got high grades.

"Charlie was treated very much like an only child. They were very protective of him. He was their pride and joy. The local paper did a story on his mom, Ethel, and she called him, 'The light of my life.' People would joke with him about that, but that was really how they felt about him. He probably felt a lot of pressure to succeed because they expected a lot out of him, but usually that wasn't a problem. Usually he did succeed."

Another friend adds: "When he was at our house, his mom would call every five minutes to see how Charlie was doing. She was obsessed with him. He was always her baby. She treated him like he was still in diapers. 'Charlie this and Charlie that. Charlie's my baby, my only son.' He always had good shoes, good clothes, good tennis equipment. He had the best of everything.

"His dad expected perfection from him. I stayed over his house a few times in ninth and tenth grade. His dad wouldn't like us clowning around or nothing. He was demanding. When he asked Charlie to do something, Charlie would just do it, immediately, military style.

"Charlie was a different person away from his parents. He was funner to be with, more relaxed. He didn't complain about his parents all the time, but you could tell he was frustrated with them. His parents drove him up the wall."

Martin Cohen made many changes at the Galesburg Mental Health Center. He reorganized the staff, instituted modern techniques and programs, and got several wards certified and accredited. Most of the employees at GMHC respected him, but he had his share of problems there.

Cohen had a rough time with the unions, which were very strong at GMHC. He wasn't used to abiding by a union contract. He also wasn't used to employees berating him at labor-management meetings.

One of them says: "I had a lot of contact with him through my union duties. He was just as bullheaded and stubborn as the day is long. A hard ass. I could tell how mad he was by how hard he puffed on his cigar. He always wanted to get his way. He was very much *the* manager and very much *the* boss. When he said something, he wanted it done his way immediately, if not sooner. It was definitely an ego thing. He had an ego as big as a horse. The other thing he liked to do was patronize you, compliment you. So we had many, many disagreements and many bitter battles."

Cohen was attacked by an alternative newspaper, *Free Voice,* and its editor, Mike Richardson, on several occasions. Richardson once wrote that Cohen was considered "witty, well educated, gifted with a large vocabulary, polished, polite, proper ... But those who know him better realize the charming facade conceals another person.... Martin Cohen is conceited, crude, cruel, cowardly, conniving, and contemptible. The real self is as far removed from the exterior personality as night is from day.... He does not talk to people, he talks down to them."

Cohen responded by denouncing *Free Voice* as "yellow journalism." Richardson also followed Cohen around town taking pictures of him, which once prompted Cohen to challenge him to a fistfight.

In addition, for several years Cohen had a nasty dispute with the city council over fire protection for the mental health center. It wasn't resolved until the state threatened the city with a lawsuit in federal court.

The late '70s were a busy yet happy time for Ethel. Her son was doing well in school and on the tennis court. Her husband had a well-paying, prestigious job. She had plenty of consulting work, and she was involved with numerous community organizations. She also did a number of one-person theatrical presentations for ladies' groups. She wanted to someday write about her life, but she wasn't in any hurry. She planned to live to be 100 years old.

Her weight continued to cause problems. She was developing arthritis in her knees and had to crawl up the stairs to get to the second floor of the house. She took classes at Nutri/System to get her weight under control, but she was never successful.

A friend remembers that Martin and Ethel weren't particularly popular: "They were accepted, but they didn't socialize a lot. I don't think there were a lot of people of their intellectual level in town. They were both quite brilliant. They didn't run into many people who had their same interests. Ethel was not the best dresser in town, and the people they would be socializing with were the upper echelon in town, and they possibly looked down on the way she dressed. In a way, they were kind of eccentric. They were loners, reclusive."

Ethel soon turned her favorite hobby, collecting antiques and junk, into a commercial enterprise. In 1978 she opened a small consignment shop in Galesburg called the

White Elephant. She advertised the shop as "More than a garage sale! Less than a shopping center! Gifts, gadgets, garments, and goodies from the finest homes in Galesburg." She sold used clothing, jewelry, paintings, knickknacks, dishes, and minks, among other things.

"They had a very bizarre family life, to say the least," one of Charlie's friends recalls. "Home-cooked meals were rare. Their home was full of boxes because Ethel would never throw anything away. It always looked like they had just moved in, but the boxes were never going to be put away. There was nowhere to put them. It was just tons of stuff."

Another friend has this to say: "Ethel was very eccentric. All she ever wore were these big colorful mu-mus. She was very motherly. You'd walk into their house and she'd go, 'Oh, Charlie, Charlie,' and squeeze his cheeks and give him a big kiss and talk baby talk, which embarrassed him. I was embarrassed at first until I got to know her, and then she'd do the same thing to me. She also had these little dogs. They were always in her lap. They were the most precious things in her life—after Charlie, of course.

"She was just so flamboyant. She would save Martin's cigar tubes and make sculptures out of them. She would collect anything she could get her hands on. She would make a display of herself. Most people thought she was friendly and funny, but some people were like, 'Whoa, calm down.' She just turned some people off because she was a little out there.

"I think Charlie resented that his parents were strange. He told me he hated his parents on a few occasions, but at the time I thought it was common teenage rebellion."

chapter 3

- - - - - - - -

Shock Value

Charlie Cohen was quiet and well behaved until his junior and senior years in high school, when he came out of his shell. He became outgoing and began pulling outrageous stunts. He would do almost anything for a laugh, and he was recognized as the class clown.

He went to the homecoming dance dressed as a woman in a full-length dress. He and a few friends dressed up as cheerleaders for a pep rally and led the student body through several cheers. He pulled numerous antics in the school hallways as well—dancing and singing or doing somersaults, cartwheels, or handstands. Mooning people became his trademark. He even mooned one of his friend's mothers. Once he poured water down the front of his pants as if he had urinated on himself before going into a fast-food restaurant.

He became the unofficial mascot at basketball games. He dressed in a black and silver outfit and ran around the gym with the cheerleaders carrying a flag to the accompaniment of the Lone Ranger theme song. On several occasions, he did a strip tease down to gym shorts while the band played stripper music. The crowd loved it, but the principal banned him from stripping during games.

He changed his appearance during his senior year as well. He let his hair grow, wore worn-out, ripped clothing, and painted his shirts and shoes. The school had dress-up days, and Charlie usually dressed wrong just to be different. He sometimes went to school in his "Superfly" outfit, which included a cape, sunglasses, and blue tights with a large S on the chest.

Almost everyone laughed at Charlie's antics, which encouraged him, and he became very popular. A few kids at school thought he was an immature show-off, but he didn't care. Many of his teachers and coaches thought some of the things he did were disrespectful. The stunts weren't dangerous or nasty, so for the most part the school administration tolerated him. Despite his antics, Charlie continued to do well in school. He maintained a 3.2 grade point average and made the National Honor Society.

As a friend remembers: "Junior year he started coming out. We'd egg him on. 'Charlie, wear some pajamas to school' or 'Do a headstand against that locker,' and he'd do it. Then he started doing it on his own. We were like, 'Oh, no. We don't even have to tell him to do it. He just does it now.'

"One time a friend and I were hanging around at the Dairy Queen, and here comes Charlie and Dan. They declared it Gay Night. They had shirts tied up on their stomachs. They were wearing makeup. They had tight pants on. Charlie had a roll of socks in his pants. Real colorful clothes, flowers, pastels, acting like gay people. They walked out in the middle of Henderson Street on the median dancing around. We were just dying. Charlie was fun to be with for the simple fact that you didn't know what he was going to do next. It was spontaneous, just to get a reaction from people."

He also got his hair cut in a particularly outrageous style. "One time I cut Charlie's hair at my parents' house," a friend recalls. "Shaved half of it off, just to the middle, and left the rest alone. Then we went to McDonald's, and when he ordered he stood sideways so the person taking his order would see the shaved side of his head. When the person turned around, Charlie turned to the side with the hair. His dad was real unhappy. He called over here and asked my mom why she let it happen. We eventually shaved the other side, too."

By his senior year Charlie was one of the top players on the high school tennis team. However, his longtime coach had left the school, and most of his friends on the team had quit or graduated. He had been playing tennis almost daily since he was twelve, and he was burned out. A few weeks into the season Charlie quit the team. Martin and Ethel had difficulty understanding.

As his senior year progressed, Charlie became more irresponsible and rebellious. He decided that religions were responsible for many of the world's problems, so he renounced his Jewish faith and became an atheist. In a friend's yearbook he wrote, "Dear Jesus, Fuck you in the ass and your dad, too." He and his friends told Jewish jokes, often at the expense of his parents.

He started smoking pot, and he stayed out late and ignored his studies. Charlie and his friends had demeaning names for one another. Charlie was "Jewboy." They also made fun of one another's mothers. Ethel was an easy target. At a party Charlie had while his parents were away, several of his friends got into Ethel's clothes and paraded around the house in her huge mu-mus and bras.

His parents were disturbed and confused by the sudden change in his personality. Martin had a respected position in the community, and Charlie's antics were embarrassing him. Word was getting around town that the psychologist who ran the mental institution couldn't keep his son under control. While Charlie saw his parents as being overly conservative, Martin and Ethel singled out certain of Charlie's friends and blamed them for leading him astray.

Martin expected him to go to college, but Charlie wasn't sure what he wanted to do. He had no serious academic interests and no long-term plans aside from some vague ideas about becoming a comedian, an artist, or a rock star. Martin, however, wouldn't take no for an answer. Charlie felt that his father had his life planned out for him and was trying to squash his independence. His father didn't seem willing to let him find his own way. Ethel wanted him to go to college, too, but she frequently said, "I don't want my baby to grow up and leave home."

Almost all of his friends were making plans for college, so Charlie finally relented. His parents sent in an application to the University of Illinois, and he was accepted.

The summer after graduation several of Charlie's friends planned a cycling vacation through Wisconsin. Charlie wanted to go, but his parents wouldn't allow it. They thought it would be too dangerous. Much to Charlie's chagrin, Martin and Ethel took him on a two-week vacation to New York City instead.

One classmate remembers his home life: "He started resenting a few things about his parents early on. For example, if he was visiting my house he would be invited to dinner, and he would fit right in, and we would all sit around and talk and laugh. If I were at his house at dinnertime, I would have to go to a different room. For a long time, up until his junior year in high school, he just accepted that as the way it was. When he started seeing how other people's family lived, he started thinking, 'Maybe it doesn't have to be this way.' That's when he started rebelling.

"They wouldn't allow him to work either. I was working at a gas station. Dan was working at an ice cream stand right next door, and he had an opportunity to come and work. It would've been a lot of fun. He really wanted to work, but they just refused to let him. He wanted to do other things besides just go home after school. They were really reluctant to let him try other things."

Another friend recalls similar problems in the Cohen household: "Charlie never had much freedom in high school. Early curfew. Restricted friends in the house. Restricted phone calls. None of his friends were treated like that. There were times when we'd get done playing tennis, and he didn't want to go home. He got really depressed because he knew what he had to go home to. It bothered him. You could see it.

"Dr. Cohen always let us know that he was the boss. His word was the law in that household. His mom would say, 'He's the light of my life,' but his dad wouldn't. When Charlie and his mom were together, they got along good. When Martin was around, it wasn't any good."

One former classmate has a theory regarding Charlie's rebelliousness: "All of a sudden there was something inside him that needed to get out. He would do anything to get a laugh, for shock value. I think he was trying to free himself from a lot of the pressure. I know smoking pot relaxed him and made him feel good.

"His parents didn't like the fact that he was doing a lot of these stupid things and wanted him to settle down, and they didn't like his friends. All we did was help him come out of the shell he was in because he was so protected by his parents.

"All his life he was overshadowed by his parents. They always did everything for him, and he had a tendency to fall back on them. They made him feel like he couldn't do a lot of things himself. They made him feel incompetent. I think that's one of the reasons he tried so hard to do so many crazy things, to show that he could do things by himself."

Charlie was anything but violent during his high school years. "He was real compassionate and real sensitive," a fellow student recalls. "He was the most loving person. In high school I would've trusted Charlie with my life. I'm not kidding. I would've done anything for him, and I know he would've done anything for me. It was something unique. It's hard to explain. He was real mellow. He would avoid a fight at all costs. He was the most nonviolent person you would ever meet in your life."

chapter 4

- - - - - - - -

Son-Out-of-the-Nest Syndrome

Charlie started college at the University of Illinois at Champaign–Urbana, which is in the eastern part of Illinois, in the fall of 1982. He and several friends from Galesburg roomed in the same dorm. For the first time in his life, his parents weren't around to tell him what to do.

Martin and Ethel gave Charlie plenty of spending money, so he didn't have to work. He went to concerts, hung out in video and pinball arcades, and watched lots of TV. He smoked pot regularly and experimented with other drugs. When he was bored, he heckled evangelical preachers ministering to students on campus. On nice days he spent hours playing hackeysack. Hackeysack had few rules, no one kept score, and he could play even when he was stoned.

Martin and Ethel visited him on campus many times. In October they attended a mental health conference in Kentucky, and they stopped in Champaign–Urbana on the way there and on the way back. They also traveled to the campus to attend several football games with him.

He didn't want them visiting so often, but he tolerated

them. They always talked about his future, what he planned to major in, and his grades. His father talked about graduate school. Charlie didn't even want to be in college. He wanted to party and have fun. He had no plans for the future. Attending classes and studying were annoyances. He ended up with a C average his first semester, and his parents were not satisfied.

A fellow freshman from Galesburg recalls: "During his first year his parents wanted him to write home a lot, and he hadn't done it. They wanted to know what he was doing all the time. So Ethel sent him a card. I happened to be there when he picked up his mail. It just said, 'Look up the word *ingrate*. Mom.' It was a joke, but I'm sure they would've liked to've had a little camera spying on him all the time. They were so worried he was going to do something wrong that, you know, he did. It was self-fulfilling prophecy.

"They had a different path in life for him, and when he wasn't going through it, they started worrying a lot. Subtle ways of pressuring him, making him feel bad, feel guilty. The more he pulled, the more they pulled the other way. He just didn't accept them or their values. I thought that if they could just step away and look at it objectively, they could see that they were doing exactly the opposite of what they needed to do."

Each year between Thanksgiving and Christmas, Ethel wrote a newsletter describing the family's activities during the previous year and distributed it to friends and relatives. In her 1982 holiday newsletter she explained that she was not having a particularly good year. She had fallen and hurt her arthritic knee while they were vacationing in New York, and her father had died during the summer.

"I have had a rather teary time of son-out-of-the-nest syndrome," she wrote about Charlie living away from home for the first time. "I miss him like I would never have believed. Which shouldn't really happen because I manage to keep very busy and have little time to brood. . . .

"This has been Charlie's year to seek some sort of independence and creativity. I never experienced the terrible 2's or the fearsome 4's or any of the other age problems Dr. Spock or Gesell may have mentioned. But the 'startling 17's' for sure exists! I think we've survived. He talks of playing tennis again; his hair has grown back beautifully from the Mohawk haircut in July! He expresses interest in learning to play drums, sculpting, art, acting. Still has no idea in what direction his interests and skills will take him."

Martin and Ethel took Charlie on vacation to Acapulco during spring break of his second semester. On their first day in Acapulco he met a young man named Pete. Pete was a high school senior from Moline, Illinois, who was vacationing with his Spanish class. Charlie and Pete purchased some pot on the street in Acapulco and spent much of their time partying. Charlie avoided his parents as much as possible. They weren't happy that he was ignoring them, but he had a wonderful time.

Charlie's parents had also promised to buy him a new stereo if he got better grades his second semester, but he didn't care about owning a stereo. They were completely hung up on material possessions, he thought, and he refused to be like them in any way. He loved the partying on campus too much to take his classes seriously. He scored some acid late in the semester and tripped for the first time. "It was fantastic!" he wrote to Pete. "I love Lucy in the sky with diamonds!"

His grades weren't any better his second semester. In fact, they were worse.

* * *

Charlie returned to Galesburg and moved back in with his parents in May. His relationship with them quickly worsened. He smoked pot in his bedroom and stayed out late partying. Martin got him a job on a state road crew, but he lasted only two days. He quarreled with his parents more and more frequently.

Pete had a motorcycle, so Charlie wanted to use his bar mitzvah money for a motorcycle. Martin and Ethel tried to stop him. They wanted him to save the money for college. He threatened to run away and never come back if they didn't give him the money. Martin and Ethel panicked and got the money out of the bank for him, and he bought a large, fast motorcycle. He also bought a black leather jacket and got an earring.

Charlie continued to play hackeysack and to haunt the video arcades. He tooled around Galesburg and up to Moline to visit Pete. He used a variety of drugs, and he turned a few of his friends onto LSD. As an act of defiance he gave away possessions his parents had given him.

When Charlie needed money, he got it from Ethel, although she suspected that he spent much of it on dope. When she refused to give him money, he got mad and threatened her. On several occasions he yelled at her and shoved her around. He also started hitting her, but only when his father wasn't around, and she didn't tell Martin. He left her with bruises, usually on her arms, and once he gave her a black eye. Ethel was frightened of him, and he usually got the money he wanted.

Martin and Ethel were at their wit's end. They were afraid he was ruining his life. The more they did to try to help him, the worse their relationship with him got. They didn't understand where they had gone wrong, and they were angry that he was making them so unhappy. Ethel cried frequently. They suspected that the drugs and his irresponsibility were symptoms of mental illness, so they sent him to a psychiatrist in Peoria. The psychiatrist told them he was fine.

Pete recalls: "He would ask permission to go up to Moline for the evening and stay overnight. They'd always say no. I felt like saying, 'Why not? What responsibility does he have here? You don't make him do anything. He doesn't even have to clean his room.' His room was a pigsty.

"They were cold about the whole situation. They'd be polite about it, but they were cruel. Underhanded comments. Guilt trips. His mom was always ready to cry because Charlie was such a big disappointment. They would speak as if he were eight years old and not in the room. Charlie would be standing right in front of them, and they would say, 'Well, Charlie really does have some problems.'"

Charlie complained to his friends that he hated his parents. They were always ragging on him, trying to control him and push him into things he didn't want. He told an acquaintance that Ethel was worthless and said, "I'll kill her."

Ethel wrote a friend about Charlie, whom she no longer referred to as "the light of my life." "Charlie has become a very strange young man—difficult for Martin and me to comprehend. Selfish, willful, impulsive, very immature. Sleeps late, out with friends *every* night till the wee hours. No communication with us."

His friend, Troy, however, saw Charlie in a different light. "He had a fun way of doing stuff, and you wanted to do stuff with him. He was just a great person. Magnetic, hilarious, just incredibly fun. I was fascinated with him. Never lift a hand to hurt you. He's left an impression on me that few people have. Most people are average, but he wasn't."

The arguing with his parents got so bad that Charlie

moved in with Troy, a young man Martin and Ethel disapproved of.

"They put so much pressure on him at an early age to respond as an adult, it was gross," says Pete. "He didn't want to deal with responsibilities. He just wanted to do wild things and have a good time. They continually tried to analyze and diagnose him. They tried to pin every sickness on him they could think of. They wanted him to be like a 30-year-old professional yuppie. Go to college immediately after high school, slip right into the Ph.D. program. He was just a teenage kid who didn't know what he wanted to do.

"They just kept pushing him and putting him down and picking on him. Mentally it was child abuse. Nothing was ever good enough. They just completely dominated him. Everything he did had to go through them. He would've been fine if they would've just backed off and left him alone.

"He always tried to live up to their dreams. Continually. Then he would fall short and come crashing down hard. They had such high expectations, and there was no way at his age he could achieve them. Sure, he could've been a psychologist, but they wanted it right away and couldn't understand why he couldn't produce. What they didn't understand was that the drugs were part of his escape from them."

By June of 1983, Martin Cohen knew that the Galesburg Mental Health Center would soon be closed. The state of Illinois was slowly but steadily shutting down old psychiatric institutions to make better use of newer ones. Galesburg was one of the state's older mental health facilities, and the state didn't want to continue spending money on the aging buildings.

Cohen knew that within two years he'd need a new job and would probably have to relocate. The first thing he did was sell the house on Park Lane. For several years

Ethel had been having problems getting up the stairs to the second floor, and after having surgery on one of her knees, it was almost impossible. In September they moved to a one-story house on Irwin Street.

The new neighborhood was neat and tidy and the rent was only $375 per month, but it was a big step down from Park Lane. Their neighbors on Park Lane weren't sorry to see them go because Martin had been so argumentative at the neighborhood meetings over the years.

Charlie didn't want to go back to school in the fall, although he hadn't told his parents. Pete had enlisted in the Marines, so Charlie decided to join as well. His parents were devastated. Martin was sure he wouldn't last in the Marines, and Ethel was afraid he'd get hurt. They couldn't imagine why he didn't want to go back to college.

Several of Charlie's friends tried to talk him out of it. They knew the Marines was no place for him. He was a free spirit, not a tough guy. "Look, Charlie, you've always gotten everything you wanted," said his high school buddy Mick, "but in the Marines you're not going to get anything you want."

Charlie wouldn't listen. He had made up his mind. He thought it would be neat to be a Marine. Plus, the Marine Corps was a sure way to get away from his parents.

Charlie's recruiter, Sergeant Andre Thompson, and Charlie went to the Galesburg Mental Health Center one afternoon to speak with Martin Cohen about Charlie's enlistment. Martin yelled at Thompson and told him exactly what he thought of the Marines. Charlie was terribly embarrassed.

Pete was insulted: "You'd think that if your son was going into the Marines that you'd be kind of supportive because it was really the first solid decision he had ever made on his own, but they criticized him over and over about it. 'Oh, Charlie, you're always hurting us. Don't join the Marines. It's going to kill us.' That kind of crap. In their eyes the worst thing he could've done was join the Marine Corps. I think he considered it a punishment for his parents, like 'I'm going to get back at them no matter what.' "

Charlie and Pete were scheduled to go in the Marines just before Christmas. Charlie wanted to get away from his parents at all costs, so in September he moved up to Moline. Martin and Ethel were crushed. They were losing their son.

Pete's parents had a carpet cleaning and furniture reupholstering business, and they gave Charlie lots of odd jobs. He swept, cleaned, ran errands, and helped refurbish furniture. Charlie had done almost no physical labor in his life, so Pete and his father had to show him how to do even the simplest tasks, like mowing the lawn.

Charlie liked Pete's parents, Maryn and David. They weren't critical of his lifestyle, but they tried to instill some discipline and a sense of responsibility. As Maryn remembers: "Charlie came into our lives, and we thought he was weirder than hell, but we loved him, and he was a good kid. He liked it here. He was relieved to be away from his parents. There was a degree of normalcy in his life here that he never knew before. We insisted on it. You got up in the morning, you worked, you had dinner with us, and you went to church on Sunday morning. We made him conform in a loving way, and he knew that we cared. We probably rode him harder than anybody, but it was probably one of the better times in Charlie's life.

"If we could've done anything for Charlie, we would've done it, but Charlie really didn't want help. He wanted to be this rebel, this maniac. He'd try to do things to shock us and say goofy things. We just said, 'Knock it off, Charlie, that's not the way it is around here.' We never knew where he was coming from. You couldn't read him."

Charlie didn't hear much from his parents, and the fun-loving and goofy aspects of his personality reemerged. He and Pete frequented the bars in Iowa, where the drinking age was nineteen. Pete paid Charlie's way most of the time, but Pete didn't mind. They got high almost every day. Pete introduced him to numerous girls, and they had lots of dates and got laid frequently. They traded girlfriends a time or two, and one evening they both had sex with the same young woman.

Maryn kept in touch with Martin and Ethel. She could see how much pain Charlie was causing them. His parents occasionally sent her money toward Charlie's room and board. Just after Thanksgiving, Maryn invited them to Moline for a visit. She also suggested to Charlie that he spend a few weeks with his parents before going into the Marines.

Maryn recalls Charlie's feelings about his parents: "Charlie was disappointed in his parents, but he didn't seem angry at them. They were a joke to him. He didn't seem to love his parents. Charlie was a very shallow person. He didn't know how to have in-depth feelings for people. He had a hard time showing any real emotion, but we never saw him angry either."

Martin and Ethel came to Moline and had a pleasant evening with Pete's family. Charlie returned to Galesburg with his parents that night. A few days later Ethel took Charlie to Florida for a vacation. He spent his nineteenth birthday in Fort Lauderdale.

Charlie arrived in San Diego for recruit training on December 20, 1983. Pete was to start one week later. His first few days in San Diego were intense. He stood in long lines and filled out innumerable forms. The receiving drill instructors screamed in his face. The recruits were awakened at 4:30 A.M. and had to be dressed and outside in formation in just a few minutes. There were strict rules on when they could go to the bathroom, and they got very little sleep. The marching drills were endless. Charlie couldn't handle it.

After a week, Charlie and the other 600 recruits were taken to the "Room of Truth." This was the final opportunity for the recruits to come clean about any lies on their enlistment applications. Drill instructors screamed about telling the truth. Any falsehoods discovered later would result in expulsion from the Marines. The recruits might get a second chance if they told the truth now.

Charlie's recruiter had specifically warned him about the Room of Truth. "Don't talk about anything," he'd said. "Just shut your damn mouth."

Charlie didn't think he could hack three months of boot camp, and he was worried that he would flunk the urine test. He didn't want to go through any more Marine harassment if they were just going to kick him out later, so he stood up and said he had a problem.

He was brought before a staff sergeant and a colonel, who reviewed his enlistment application. The sergeant walked around him while Charlie stood at attention. "What do you have to say for yourself?"

Charlie admitted he had lied on his enlistment application about drugs. He said he had used pot, LSD, Valium, cocaine, hash, and speed. He said he had even tried heroin and ecstasy. He mentioned specifically how many times he had used each drug, as if he had been keeping a running count.

The sergeant screamed, "Why, you piece of shit. How dare you lie to the Marine Corps! Fraudulent enlistment! Failure to report preenlistment drug use!"

The colonel was less demonstrative. "I see that you were a good student in high school, Mr. Cohen. A good athlete. High aptitude test scores. A year of college. Since you've voluntarily come forward, we might be able to salvage your career in the Marines."

Charlie was shocked. "But, sir, you don't know how many drugs I did. There were a lot. I'm not exaggerating."

"We can work around that," said the colonel, "as long as you swear to stay off drugs."

The sergeant screamed in his face, "Do you want to be a Marine?!"

"Uh-uh—"

"We're giving you another chance, Private," said the colonel. "We think you've got potential. Do you understand?"

"Goddamnit, do you want to be a Marine?!"

"Sir," Charlie said calmly, "I'd rather flip hamburgers than be a Marine."

They looked at him in astonishment. Charlie was almost as surprised as they were. A vein bulged on the side of the sergeant's neck. His face shook and turned red. "You filthy piece of shit! You maggot!"

"Get him out of my face," the colonel said.

"A bus ticket back to Mommy! But first, ten days Casual Company!"

Charlie was given a pink T-shirt and assigned to Casual Company, a special unit for recruits the Marines planned to ship out. They had a separate barracks and were given tasks such as sweeping streets, painting rocks, mowing grass, picking up cigarette butts, and pulling weeds. It was humiliating work, especially since they were paraded around in front of the other recruits.

Three days later Charlie pleaded with his drill instructor to let him stay, but it was too late. On January 6, 1984, he was processed out. He was given $119 for the two weeks of his time and put on a bus headed for the Midwest. Martin and Ethel were delighted.

chapter 5

- - - - - - - -

The Year of Lost and Found Events

After returning home from his aborted stay in the Marines, Charlie admitted that he'd been a screw-up and promised to get his act together. He immediately enrolled at Carl Sandburg College, a small two-year college on the outskirts of Galesburg.

His relationship with his parents remained tense. He was polite to them when they left him alone. When they nagged, he lost his temper. They complained to their friends about him, and he complained to his friends about them. He had to report in a lot. When he went out, Martin and Ethel wanted to know where he was going, who would be there, and when he was coming home. He hated living with his parents and constantly thought of getting away from them.

Martin wasn't satisfied with him attending a small junior college, so that winter he sent in an application for Charlie to Knox College. Also located in Galesburg, Knox is a prestigious liberal arts college with high academic standards. It is also very expensive. Even though Charlie had done poorly at the University of Illinois, his father was a prominent member of the community, so he was accepted. He enrolled at Knox in March for the spring trimester and got a room in the dorms.

Charlie made lots of new friends at Knox. He told everyone about his stay in the Marines and what he'd told the colonel. He pledged the TKE fraternity. The TKE brothers smoked lots of pot, so Charlie fit right in. LSD could also be found on campus, so he began tripping frequently. On Flunk Day, a day when the school administration unexpectedly canceled classes, he did a "double dip"—two hits of acid.

An acquaintance from Knox remembers him from that semester: "Charlie would say something bizarre, something extreme, and open his eyes real wide and look at you like he was nuts. He'd tilt his head back a little, raise his eyebrows, and look at you to see what your reaction was. I always thought there was a little more to that look than just a joke."

Another friend says that Charlie "was a great guy. For me there was nobody better to talk to. He helped me out. He was one of the most understanding people. We talked about everything—life, what we wanted to do. He was just as confused as anyone else, but he helped me straighten out a lot of my problems."

The term ended in June. Charlie's highest grade was a C–, and he flunked one class. He was placed on academic probation, and he informed his parents that he wouldn't be continuing at Knox.

Ethel tried to put a good face on Charlie's troubles. "Oh, poor Charlie," she told some neighbors. "He's had such a hard time in college. He just can't figure out what he wants to do. We'll eventually put him in another college and maybe things will work out."

Charlie got a room in the TKE house for the summer and found a part-time job as a lifeguard. In a letter to Pete he referred to himself as a "civilian, lunatic, child-molester, anarchist, atheist punk." He also received a letter from his father. Martin was "willing to make further investment in the education-exploration area," but only if Charlie swore off pot. Marijuana was "destructive to a degree that makes repair improbable," he wrote. "You are my flesh and blood—I've lived with you many years longer than others—I believe I know you better! . . . Can you possibly accept my judgment about marijuana? If it weren't for the fact that I love you very much I wouldn't even be trying to write these things."

In June, one of Charlie's friends from the TKE house, Tony, told him about a condo near San Francisco owned by a friend of his who was away on business. The condo was available to them for the entire summer. Charlie immediately agreed to go.

Martin and Ethel were against the idea. They wanted him to work through the summer and go to school in the fall. Charlie promised to get a job on the West Coast to pay for his expenses, but they suspected that the trip would be a waste of time and money. They were also afraid he'd get himself in some kind of trouble out there. They offered to take him on vacation to California, but he refused to take any more vacations with them.

Despite their objections, Charlie was not to be denied. As Ethel told her friends, "What Charlie wants, Charlie gets." In early July, Charlie and Tony drove to Mountain View, California, which is 40 miles south of San Francisco. Charlie found part-time work in a fast-food restaurant, but he hated the job. "Flippin' burgers sucks the horse with a passion you would not believe," he wrote to Pete. He went to San Francisco numerous times, mostly to the Haight-Ashbury neighborhood, where he scored some acid and Thai stick.

Charlie had to ask his parents for money several times during his stay on the West Coast, and by August they'd had enough. They bought him a plane ticket home, and he returned to Galesburg. He was furious with them for ruining his trip, and they were just as angry with him.

Charlie ran into Dan, a high school buddy, back in Galesburg. Dan was a student at the University of Illinois, and he suggested that Charlie come back to college with him for the fall semester.

Charlie didn't have any other plans, so he agreed. His parents were delighted. After some last-minute letter writing by his father, Charlie was reinstated at the U of I. He promised to study hard. In late August he and Dan moved to Champaign–Urbana. Naturally, Martin and Ethel paid all of his expenses.

Charlie and Dan rented a small two-bedroom apartment. Early in the semester, Dan became involved with an Asian coed named Li, and after a few weeks she, too, moved into the apartment.

Charlie, Dan, and Li became very close. The three of them went everywhere together. They shared food and money and sometimes stayed up all night studying or partying. They had many odd friends and many parties.

By September 1984 the closure of the Galesburg Mental Health Center was well under way. Approximately half of the employees had been transferred or laid off, and half of the patients had been moved to other facilities or released. The target date for the final closing was January 1986.

There was a tremendous amount of community opposition to the closure. The Galesburg Mental Health Center was the third largest employer in the city, and it put over $20 million into the local economy every year. Galesburg's economic survival was at stake.

Community leaders, local politicians, and the unions banded together to fight the closure. They demonstrated, held press conferences, and collected 20,000 signatures on a petition. They railed against the governor, claiming that he didn't care about the mentally ill or communities like Galesburg, but all of their efforts were fruitless.

Before the closing was announced, Martin Cohen was told by his superiors, Mike Belletire, secretary of the department, and Don Hart, regional director, that if he managed the GMHC closure smoothly, he would be given a significant position at the Zeller Mental Health Center in Peoria. Cohen was 55 years old and making $57,000 per year. He had 31 years with the state, just four years short of full retirement benefits. Finishing his career at Zeller, which was only 45 miles from Galesburg, appealed to him. They weren't sure what position he would get, perhaps one as assistant superintendent, but they promised he would be well taken care of.

However, in the spring of 1984, James Dalzell, the superintendent at Zeller, announced that he had taken a job elsewhere. The superintendency at Zeller was one of the premier positions in the department. There wasn't another opening like it in the department, and there wasn't likely to be another anytime soon.

Cohen wanted the job badly. He contacted Belletire and Hart and made his interest known. He had more seniority than almost anyone in the department and the longest tenure of any superintendent in the state. The top post at Zeller would be the crowning achievement in his illustrious career. It would dispel any doubts that had arisen after his firing at McFarland.

Before leaving the area, Dalzell recommended Cohen for the job, but Hart and Belletire balked. Instead, they put together a committee, which initiated a nationwide search for candidates. Cohen was insulted. He couldn't remember the department ever conducting a nationwide search.

Hart and Belletire reminded Cohen of his earlier agreement to go through with the closing without making

waves, but Cohen wouldn't let the matter drop. He submitted an application for the position and felt confident
he would get the job.

In September he was told he had not been chosen for
the Zeller position. A candidate with no superintendency
experience got the job. Cohen was angry and humiliated.

On September 20, 1984, Martin Cohen submitted his
resignation. He gave 60 days' notice. He also held a news
conference to announce the decision, during which he
complained bitterly about the selection process for the
position at Zeller. Belletire was furious.

That same night Cohen called James Drake, a Springfield lawyer, and told him what had transpired. "Goddamn it, Marty," said Drake, "withdraw the resignation
immediately."

Cohen tried to withdraw his resignation the next day,
but it was too late. Belletire wouldn't allow it. A day later
Cohen received a phone call from Springfield. He was
told to leave the facility immediately. He was not to clean
out his office or speak with any of his employees. He no
longer had a job.

On October 30, Cohen filed a lawsuit for $375,000 in
damages in Sangamon County Court in Springfield, Illinois, against Donald Hart, Mike Belletire, and the Department of Mental Health and Developmental Disabilities.

Martin was in shock over what had transpired. Almost
overnight his entire career was in shambles. Everything
he had worked to achieve had fallen apart. He became reclusive and despondent. He moped around the house in
his pajamas, so full of rage and despair he could barely
speak. He often sat and stared, not focusing on anything,
lost in anger and grief. He wouldn't speak on the phone
or meet with old friends.

Ethel was deeply affected as well. One day their future
had seemed secure, and the next day their lives were in
ruin. Ethel tried to cheer him up, but Martin snarled at

her or simply ignored her. No matter what she did or said, it didn't help. She was so worried she was afraid he might try to harm himself. To make matters worse, Ethel had a compressed vertebra caused by her weight, a painful condition that severely limited her mobility. Her confidence and good humor quickly deserted her.

Charlie was having problems of his own at Champaign–Urbana. Despite what he had promised his parents, he hadn't buckled down. He partied more than he studied. He did a bong hit almost every morning when he woke up. He missed classes. He tripped whenever he got some acid, and he kept some Knox College friends back in Galesburg supplied with LSD as well. He complained to his parents about school, and he frequently threatened to quit.

He met lots of girls, but he was shy and awkward with them and didn't develop any serious relationships. He hadn't had sex for so long, Charlie told friends, that he wasn't sure he remembered how it was done. He claimed he was beating off so much his balls had turned blue.

His parents' trouble took its toll on him. He didn't know whether to be angry with his father or to feel sorry for him. Sometimes their problems depressed him. Other times he was ashamed of his parents and complained bitterly to his roommates about them.

"I think I'll beat off three times a day, take some bullshit classes, get a bullshit degree, and support my parents for the rest of their lives," he wrote to Pete.

His grades were as poor as ever. He got two D's, two C's, and an A in scuba diving.

In her 1984 holiday letter, which she entitled, "The Year of Lost and Found Events," Ethel wrote, "I've delayed as long as I can, short of not writing at all, because this is ending up a largely wretched year and I don't want to share anything so dismal. You all deserve better at this happy season, but so do we. I figure I've shared the good over the years and likely you'll be interested in the less than good. So here goes."

She wrote about Charlie's endeavors and her and Martin's various health problems before addressing Martin's firing. "Shafted royally" was the term she used to describe the state's treatment of Martin. "We still can't believe it," she wrote.

She was worried about their future. "Martin hopefully will seek new employment and find something worthy of his fine credentials. Likely it will be out of Illinois. Only time will tell. . . . Next year has just got to be cheerier than this one."

chapter 6

- - - - - - - -

There Is No Pain, You Are Receding

Martin Cohen soon became bored. Ethel had the White Elephant. It didn't make any money, but at least it got her out of the house. Charlie was away at school. Martin found himself alone much of the time. He was gaining weight and smoking too much. He wasn't old enough to receive a pension, although he did receive a $20,000 annuity from the state. He and Ethel had some savings, but it wouldn't last forever. He needed to generate some income and overcome his depression, so he opened a private practice.

He rented an office on Main Street, put up a sign, and installed a phone and some furniture. Ethel was happy to see him doing something. Martin got up and went to his office everyday, but no one showed up, and the phone didn't ring. Galesburg is a small town, and everyone had heard about his firing and his depression. They knew he couldn't control Charlie. Nobody wanted to go to a psychologist who couldn't keep his own life in order. Ethel felt terrible for him. She called each day to make sure he got at least one phone call and sent him cards so he got some mail.

An old friend encouraged him to come to Chicago and look for a job. His friend assured him that he wouldn't have any problem finding work there, but Cohen wouldn't even try. He said he didn't like large cities.

As the winter term of 1985 got under way at the University of Illinois, Charlie Cohen began seeing a young woman named Becky. They spent a few nights together, and he fell deeply in love with her.

Becky was on a health food diet, so Charlie went on one, too. He ate nothing but rice, granola, raw vegetables, and wheat toast. He boiled the granola to remove the fat and rinsed the rice to remove all traces of salt. He drank lots of water to flush out his system. He started exercising, too, doing hundreds of sit-ups on the floor in the apartment. His weight dropped. His parents considered the health food diet just a phase and took him to Burger King when they visited.

Charlie and Becky spent about three weeks seeing one another, but she wasn't seriously interested in him. Soon she started seeing other young men. Charlie was deeply hurt. He couldn't accept the fact that she didn't love him.

As the weeks rolled by he became morbid and introverted. He couldn't bring himself to study. It seemed pointless. After a few weeks, he stopped attending classes altogether.

He spent much of his time alone. Some days he didn't get out of bed. For weeks he didn't want anyone to see him. He spent hours fantasizing about forcing Becky to have sex with him. He took whatever drugs he could get his hands on, but he wasn't enjoying dope anymore. Being high just made his unhappiness more intense and intolerable. In March he scored some powerful "white blotter," a form of LSD. He swallowed two tabs and felt

like he had lost his mind for the next twelve hours. He
wept and couldn't stop.

One day he suddenly gave up the health food diet and
began bingeing on junk food. He ate a gallon of ice cream
in one sitting. Another night he consumed several containers of raw cookie dough. He resumed the health food
diet occasionally, but it always ended after a few days
with another binge. Over the course of two months he
gained 50 pounds.

Dan was busy and didn't have time to deal with his
roommate's problems. Charlie wasn't the same friend he
had grown up with. He had gotten unpredictable and
strange. He even seemed to distrust Dan. Li was depressed and melancholy as well. She and Charlie often
discussed the philosophical implications of suicide. Dan
felt like a baby-sitter. Both Charlie and Li were going off
the deep end, and he had no intention of going off with
them. He began pulling back from them. The mood in the
apartment became tense.

That winter and spring Charlie developed an infatua-
tion with Jim Morrison of the Doors. He wanted to look
like his creative, indulgent idol, so he let his hair grow
like Morrison's. He read *No One Here Gets Out Alive,* a
biography of Morrison, several times and carried the
book around with him. He studied Morrison's song lyrics
and sometimes adopted the dark, morbid attitudes of the
music.

Charlie was also interested in *The Wall,* a movie based
on the Pink Floyd album of the same name. In the movie,
the main character loses his mind and crudely shaves off
his eyebrows. Inspired, Charlie got very high and shaved
all the hair off his body except his eyebrows. It took several hours.

The stunt had the desired effect of shocking everyone,
but for Charlie it was more than a joke. It was a state-

ment. He wanted to shed his skin like a snake or a lizard. He had picked up the metaphor from Morrison. The rock singer had worn a snakeskin suit, referred to himself as the Lizard King, and used images of lizards and snakes in several songs to evoke darkness and evil.

Charlie felt constricted and wanted to rip out of his skin so he could start a new life, but he knew it was impossible. His life was a trap, a problem with no solution, and shaving his entire body didn't help. The next day the same problems were still there, and an uncomfortable, itchy stubble grew back all over his body.

Dan went home for a weekend in early spring, leaving Charlie alone in the apartment with Li. They got high, listened to some music, and Charlie suggested they go to bed together. She refused, but Charlie made several more attempts to get her into bed. When Dan returned, Li complained to him about Charlie's advances.

Dan felt betrayed and confronted Charlie, who was extremely embarrassed. He broke down and sobbed, apologizing profusely. He told Dan that everything about his life had gone wrong. His parents were both wrecks, and he didn't know what he was going to do. Dan told him to forget about it, but things weren't the same between them.

Charlie called his parents and admitted that he'd dropped out of school. They wanted him to move back home. He agreed on the condition they buy him an electric guitar and an amplifier. They refused. He held to his demand, and they finally gave in.

Things weren't any better at home. Martin and Ethel mulled about the house like two overweight blobs. They vegetated in varying degrees of depression. They slept until they woke up. They stayed up late watching *The Tonight Show* and played Scrabble and gin rummy in the middle of the day. Charlie couldn't stand being in the little house with them. He worked on learning to play the

guitar for a few weeks, but he soon grew bored and gave
it up.

In May, Kevin, a friend from high school, called from
Houston. He had a two-bedroom apartment for the summer, and he invited Charlie to come to Houston and
spend the summer with him.

"Don't worry about the money," Kevin said. "I'll cover
you until you find a job. C'mon, we'll have a lot of fun
together."

Charlie immediately agreed. As with his California
trip, his parents were not happy with the idea. They complained that he didn't have direction. He was drifting
aimlessly and costing them lots of money. As always,
they eventually gave in.

Charlie was still in an emotional funk when he got to
Houston. He told Kevin about his troubles at the U of I.
Kevin tried to cheer him up. He took him on several tours
of the city. They went to bars, saw some local bands, and
went to museums. They also played lots of basketball and
tennis, and Charlie's disposition slowly improved.

Charlie found a full-time job as a lifeguard. Martin and
Ethel had been sending him money, but after a few pay-
checks Charlie actually started repaying them. They were
amazed. Charlie resumed his no-fat health food diet and
started losing weight. Kevin wasn't into drugs, so Charlie
managed to stay drug-free as well. Soon Charlie was
down to his normal weight of 160 pounds. He was finally
getting his act together.

As the summer ended, Kevin began to prepare for his
fall classes at Rice University and moved to an apartment
closer to campus. Charlie felt deserted. He could've continued with his job and kept the apartment, but living
alone in a strange city didn't appeal to him. He abruptly
left and returned to Galesburg.

* * *

Charlie moved back in with his parents. Ethel had closed the White Elephant, her seven-year business venture, the previous spring. She couldn't sell it, so it simply went out of business. Her health was getting worse. She had high blood pressure, and her back and legs ached. She had a hard time getting from one room to another. She gave up her consulting work and devoted most of her attention to her small dogs and her new hobby—contests.

Martin was applying for work all over the country but having no luck at all. His lawsuit against the state was tied up, and he wasn't sure it would ever get resolved. His self-esteem was at an all-time low. In August, he and Ethel went for a cruise, which temporarily lifted their spirits, but once they returned to Galesburg the monotony of forced retirement enveloped them again.

Charlie's situation was just as bleak. He had no job, no school, no money, no girlfriend, and no idea what he wanted to do with his life. He hung out with his friends Rick and Jonathan occasionally, but he stayed in the house much of the time in a self-imposed exile from the world. Seeing other people depressed him, and his parents' situation made him feel even worse.

Martin was making strange comments. "I need to have you here, son," he told Charlie. "You're my pillar of strength." In his lowest moments, he talked about his life insurance policies and made vague references to suicide. One time he said, "You know, Charlie, maybe you and your mother would be better off if I wasn't around."

Such comments unnerved and demoralized Charlie. He told his father that some LSD or cocaine might make him feel better, and he offered to procure the drugs for him. Martin declined the offer.

Charlie found a part-time job at McDonald's for minimum wage, which he hated. Martin and Ethel sneered at such a job. They also demanded that he stop using drugs, but he wouldn't. Martin gave up on him. Ethel cried a lot.

"Suffice it to say it's not been a productive year for us," she wrote in her yearly newsletter. Charlie left before the year was out.

He moved into a room with Tom, a friend who was attending Knox College and living near campus. Tom had a large waterbed and thick shag carpeting in his room. Charlie slept on the floor in a sleeping bag. Tom was a body builder and a successful student. He had spending money and lots of dates. Charlie had virtually no money and no dates. Whenever Tom brought a young woman to his room, Charlie had to get lost. The one thing they had in common was partying.

Charlie thought about saving some money and moving back to Houston, but he couldn't save much on his salary. He put himself on another of his extreme diets, but dropped it after a few weeks and binged on pizza, chips, and snack food.

Tom encouraged Charlie to reconcile with his parents, but Charlie refused to even try. He claimed that he constantly tried to please his parents but nothing he did satisfied them. He felt he had never been accepted by them.

After a few months Charlie became desperate for money. He suggested to Tom that they rob someone at knife-point outside a liquor store, restaurant, or ATM.

"Charlie, I know you need money, but that's not the answer," Tom said. "It's not worth it. You'll get caught. Look for another job or something."

Charlie brought up the idea again several more times over the next two weeks. He had specific locations picked out. He thought the stickups would be easy, and he wanted Tom to help.

Finally, Tom said, "Look, I have a better idea how we can make money. I know somebody I can get coke from. I'll buy it, you sell it, and we split the profits. Nobody will know I have anything to do with it."

Charlie was thrilled with the plan. It was February 1986. A few days later Tom withdrew his student loan money from the bank and took a train to Chicago. He bought an ounce of cocaine from a friend and returned to Galesburg.

The coke came in rock form. It was 92 percent pure. They ground it up and added twelve grams of Inositol, a tasteless, odorless dietary supplement, which they bought at a health food store. That gave them 40 grams. If Charlie sold all 40 grams for $100 a pop, they'd have $2,000 profit to split between them.

Most of the students at Knox College came from wealthy families, and they had lots of spending money. Cocaine was in high demand on campus, so Charlie had little problem finding buyers. He sold the first ounce in a week. He and Tom couldn't believe how easy it was. Tom immediately made another trip to Chicago. Charlie quit his job at McDonald's.

Almost every evening Charlie and Tom snorted a huge line or two of coke, cranked a few tunes, and went to the campus game room to play pinball. Each night they tried to do a larger line than the night before. Once they each snorted a one-gram line. Tom's heart was beating so rapidly he thought he was having a heart attack.

There was a party in Tom and Charlie's room almost every night. Customers knocked on their door at all hours. Tom and Charlie began staying up all night and sleeping all day. The hangovers were painful. Charlie would get depressed and go off by himself for hours. Everybody in the campus drug scene knew Charlie was selling coke, and rumors of his dealing started getting around town, too.

Tom was still going to classes and studying whenever he could. He was trying to keep the situation from getting out of control. Charlie, however, didn't seem to care if it got out of control. If Tom didn't want to party, Charlie found someone who did. When his customers couldn't afford cocaine, he pulled out his own stash. He was getting several of his friends high regularly, and he didn't ask them for money.

Whatever coke Charlie and Tom snorted came out of their profits. Tom was clearing about $800 per week. He bought new clothes, took his girlfriends to expensive hotels in limousines, and bought the most expensive stereo system he could find in Galesburg. Charlie started out with profits as high as Tom's, but soon he was making no more than $150 to $200 per ounce. He complained to Tom about it.

"You're making all this money, and I'm doing all the work," he said.

"You're snorting your profits," said Tom. "What do you expect?"

The situation got progressively worse. Tom suspected that Charlie was dipping into his stash surreptitiously. They started arguing. By the end of the spring term, Charlie couldn't break even. Tom had to come up with the difference out of his profits to pay off the coke.

"Charlie, you've got to chill out," said Tom, but Charlie wouldn't chill out. He passed out frequently and couldn't hold up his end of a conversation. He was extremely thin, and his face was drawn and pale. More and more people were staying away from him.

Martin and Ethel moved to Peoria in April. They thought Charlie was still working at McDonald's.

"I saw him once when I came back to Galesburg for a weekend," a friend remembers. "He had really changed. The cocaine had definitely started to affect him. I just wanted to get together with him and do something. We were driving some place, but on the way he stopped off at this place and then stopped off at that place to see if anyone wanted to buy some coke. I wasn't into it at all.

I wanted to see him, but I didn't really want to be dragged along on a business trip.

"Another time he called me at U of I. Dan and I were living together. He said he wanted to come visit. We said, 'Great, you can stay with us.' Then the conversation turned to, 'Well, why don't you guys talk to some people and see if they want to buy some coke.' We were both like, 'Why don't you just come down for a visit? Just forget about the coke.' Leave that at home.' But he still wanted to bring the coke. That seemed to be the most important thing—setting up business deals. We didn't want to be middlemen for some drug deals. By the end of the conversation we didn't want him to come, and he ended up not visiting."

Another friend from Knox recalls: "Charlie became really dependent on using cocaine to meet people and socialize instead of using his social skills. What he gave away he did to make himself popular, which is a very easy way to get people to like you. You become the center of attention. When the coke dries up, your popularity dries up, too. That's the lie of cocaine. It's extremely shallow.

"He used coke several times a day. He just became more and more dependent on cocaine. He was starting to lose himself in it at that point. It got to the point where it scared me. He was really fucking himself up."

In late May 1986, Charlie helped Tom move his belongings to his parents' house in suburban Chicago. When they got there, they discovered that Tom's parents were on vacation. Tom suggested that Charlie spend a few days visiting, so Charlie stayed. Tom got another ounce fronted to him, and the two immediately lapsed into another coke bender. The coke hadn't been cut yet, and they stayed up doing lines for three days.

Charlie became paranoid. He heard strange sounds. He

thought people were watching him. At one point he felt like he was having an out-of-body experience. Everything was so surreal it was like living in a cartoon. When they recovered, Tom assessed the damage. They had snorted ten grams of almost pure cocaine.

After a few days, Tom's parents returned, and Tom took Charlie to the local train station. Charlie was to return to Galesburg with the remaining coke, cut it, and sell it. If everything went as planned, they would be able to repay the $2,000 Tom owed to the supplier.

"Now just take it easy, Charlie," said Tom. "You can't be doing as much as you were or we're screwed."

Charlie sold some of Tom's coke back in Galesburg, but he used and gave much of it away. He mailed a few grams to a friend across the country with the note, "Here, dude, this is for being a good friend." He gave a gram to a friend and returned a day later and bought it back for $100. He blew another gram off a table and onto the floor for a joke.

Tom's coke was gone within a few days, so Charlie began hanging out with Stan, another dealer on campus. He soon convinced Stan to front him a few grams.

He couldn't come up with the $2,000 for Tom, and he knew he had only a few days before Tom would come looking for him. He didn't know what to do. Troy was home on leave from the Marines, and Charlie told him about the situation.

"How much are you into them for?" Troy asked.

"Two thousand."

"Two thousand! Fuckin'—A. I'm scared for you, man. Galesburg can be a violent place. There are plenty of murders in this town over drugs. You got to get the fuck out of here."

Charlie started telling everyone that he was going to Chicago to score an ounce of coke, which he was going to sell immediately for a huge profit. "It's either gonna make me rich, or it's gonna get me killed," he said.

He borrowed $400 from a friend named Gary. He also borrowed Rick's car and promised to pay him $200 when he returned. He dropped by Stan's room and asked him to front him another gram for his trip to Chicago. By then he owed Stan about $300. Charlie promised to pay him back as soon as he returned. He showed Stan a wad of cash, and Stan asked Charlie to pay him right then.

"I need the money to cop, man," said Charlie. "Let me cop, and then I'll give you the money. I'll take care of you. I'll give you the money plus I'll give you some out of my stash."

Stan's car was broken down near Peoria, so he agreed to front Charlie another gram if he gave him a ride to his car. They drove to Peoria in Rick's car, doing lines of Stan's coke along the way. Stan had been up for several days on a coke bender of his own.

Stan worked on his car for about an hour. Charlie did a few lines while he waited. Stan couldn't get his car started, so Charlie had to take Stan with him. Charlie had planned to simply take off in the car, but now he was stuck with Stan, and he didn't know how to get rid of him. Before they got to the highway for Chicago, Charlie turned south for Springfield.

"I thought we were going to Chicago," said Stan.

"I was just saying that," said Charlie. "I had to keep this thing quiet. We're going to Springfield."

They got to Springfield at 4 P.M. They snorted more of Stan's coke along the way. They drove around Springfield while Charlie stalled for time. At first, Charlie said he was supposed to meet the supplier at 5:30 at a particular hotel. At 5:30 he claimed that he was supposed to meet the guy at a different hotel at 8 P.M., so they drove around town for another couple of hours. Stan was getting very tense. Things weren't adding up. He just wanted the money Charlie owed him, and he wanted to go home.

At 8 P.M. they checked into the hotel where the deal was supposed to go down. Charlie told him that they might have to spend the night.

"Then I've got to get some different clothes and a toothbrush," said Stan. They had both been up for several days, and their clothing was filthy. Charlie gave Stan $100 and told him to take a taxi to a clothing store and to buy them both some clothing.

Stan left with the $100, but he had a hunch that Charlie would split, leaving him stranded in Springfield. He went back to the room a few minutes later to see if Charlie was trying to sneak out. Charlie stepped out of the bathroom just as Stan walked in the room.

"I thought you were going to get the clothes," said Charlie.

"I forgot my cigarettes," Stan mumbled.

"You better hurry up before the stores close," said Charlie.

Temporarily pacified, Stan left. He took a taxi to a nearby clothing store, bought T-shirts and jeans for both of them, and returned. He was gone no more than thirty minutes. When he got back, Charlie was gone. He had left the car keys and the car. Stan waited around the hotel room for a few hours. He assumed that Charlie was out scoring the coke, but he never came back.

On June 16, 1986, Charlie found himself in Phoenix. He didn't really know what was going on. The past few days were a fog. He remembered panicking in Springfield. He had been certain that Tom, Stan, and Gary were coming after him and that they would kill him if they found him.

He had thrown out his wallet in Springfield to avoid being identified and had taken a taxi to St. Louis, several hundred miles away. It had cost over $200, but he hadn't cared. He remembered buying some clothing in St. Louis to disguise himself, including knee-high moccasin-style boots. He had gone to the airport in St. Louis and hopped the first flight out. It was headed for Phoenix.

He had been wandering around Phoenix in a daze for hours. Every part of his body ached. He was desperately hungry but didn't have any money. He wasn't sure where it had all gone—over a thousand dollars lost, stolen, or spent along the way. Even when he'd had the money he had known he wouldn't be able to hang onto it. He had been spiraling out of control, yet he felt incapable of stopping.

His head hurt. He was dirty and smelly and hadn't shaved for a week. He walked into a Dairy Queen and asked a clerk to accept his $90 Vuarnet sunglasses, which was his prized possession, in exchange for some food. The clerk wasn't interested, so he wandered off.

He came back to the counter a few minutes later. He said that someone had given him some money, and he ordered a chicken sandwich. The clerk put the sandwich on the counter and rang up $2.45. Charlie admitted that he couldn't pay for it. The clerk turned to call the manager. Charlie leaned over the counter, grabbed the sandwich, and ran out the door. The clerk called the cops.

Charlie ate the sandwich and walked to a 7–11 a block away. He went in and said to the clerk, "Hey, you want to buy a pair of sunglasses?"

"No thanks," said the clerk.

He offered to sell him some cassette tapes instead. The clerk turned him down again. While the clerk waited on another customer, Charlie grabbed a sandwich and started eating it.

The clerk yelled, "Hey, are you going to pay for that sandwich?"

"Yeah, sure. Don't worry about it."

He picked up a burrito, a Danish, and an ice cream cone and suddenly threw his sunglasses on the counter. "This should more than cover it," he shouted and ran from the store. The clerk called the police.

The police found him in a shopping center less than a block away from the 7–11. He was taken to the 7–11 and the Dairy Queen, where both clerks identified him, and booked on two counts of theft.

The next day he called his parents collect from the Phoenix jail and told them what had happened. He also made a collect call to Jonathan and Rick's apartment. Jonathan accepted the charges.

"I'm in jail in Los Angeles," he said, afraid to tell anyone in Galesburg where he was.

"What are you doing in Los Angeles?" Jonathan asked.

"I got picked up for shoplifting some food. I was so stupid."

"I thought you were going to Chicago."

"That didn't work out."

"What about all the money you had when you left?"

"It's all gone. I don't know what happened to it."

"People have been coming around looking for you, man. They're really pissed off."

"I don't care. I don't care about anything anymore."

His parents hired a lawyer in Phoenix, who quickly arranged for Charlie to plead guilty, pay a fine, and be placed on probation. He was released the next day. The lawyer picked him up, drove him to the airport, and saw that he boarded a plane for Illinois.

Tom, Gary, and Stan never got the money Charlie owed them. Jonathan didn't realize that Charlie had called from Phoenix, not Los Angeles, until he got his next phone bill.

chapter 7

- - - - - - - -

The Force of Love

Martin and Ethel had moved to Peoria for no particular reason other than it was larger than Galesburg and offered more employment opportunities. They rented a large ranch-style home. They took 400 boxes with them, which Ethel considered their life treasures. She continued her "sweepstaking" hobby and fantasized about winning trips and cruises, although she usually won prizes such as discount coupons and sunglasses instead.

After returning from Phoenix, Charlie moved in with his parents in Peoria. He told Martin and Ethel he needed several thousand dollars to pay off his drug debts or else dealers from Chicago would kill him. He parents refused. Martin and Ethel did, however, write checks to the Dairy Queen and the 7–11 in Phoenix for a total of $6.65. The fines, air fare from Phoenix, and lawyer fees set them back another $1,500.

Charlie spent the first few months in Peoria in hiding for fear of his life. He hardly ever went out of the house. He stopped using drugs altogether, and he didn't call his friends in Galesburg. He was afraid that Tom, Stan, or Gary would find out where he was and come looking for him. He had no friends in Peoria and very little to do. Once again, he felt like a total failure. He had never been happy and didn't deserve to be happy.

Naturally, Martin and Ethel were unhappy with him. Their only child, their pride and joy, had become a drug user, a thief, and a vagrant. He had betrayed everything they had done for him. He had cost them dearly in money and emotional duress. Martin urged Charlie to get some counseling, but Charlie refused. He wouldn't admit that he had a problem. As a last resort, Martin decided to treat him himself.

"Something good always comes of something bad," Martin told a friend. "Maybe this will give me some time to really get to know him."

They went for long walks, and he tried to get Charlie to talk about his feelings, but it was useless. His father was the last person Charlie would open up to. Martin became frustrated. If he couldn't help his son, he might as well give up his profession because he couldn't help anyone.

A friend of Ethel and Martin's remembers the situation well: "He hated Marty with a purple passion. His father tried to help Charles, and the more he did the more Charles hated him. He wouldn't hear of his father counseling or anybody else counseling. That's why he hated him.

"Ethel wouldn't acknowledge that Charles had mental health problems. She made excuses for what he did. Martin didn't make excuses. His father was ready to kick him out and let him go on his own, but Ethel wouldn't have any part of it."

To make matters worse, a Springfield judge dismissed Martin's lawsuit against the state. The state argued that since Martin Cohen had resigned his position at the Galesburg Mental Health Center, he couldn't sue the state. The judge agreed.

In July, Martin got a job with an outpatient clinic in Peoria. It didn't pay well, but it was better than nothing. As Ethel wrote in her yearly newsletter: "[Martin's] old skills are still very much there and part of the time he enthuses over his work. The other part he complains about the heavy work load, small salary, impersonal work environment, etc. Martin's welcome to the world of private enterprise!"

Ethel got a part-time consultant's job on the mental health unit at a local hospital. In her typically self-deprecating manner she wrote, "Just a few hours a week but to my liking. Gives me an excuse to put on panty hose and wear different earrings everyday! And me putting on panty hose is like a wrestling match with me as my opponent! Makes for a brisk morning."

She again got involved in the theater. "I auditioned for and got the role of Yente in *Fiddler on the Roof*," she wrote. "My third time in the Yente role. Guess I'll keep doing it till I get it right!"

Hoping to get Charlie out of the house, Martin and Ethel bought a family membership at the Landmark Racquet and Health Club, which was not far from their home. Landmark had a workout room, racquetball courts, bowling alley, snack shop, off-track betting lounge, restaurant, movie theater, and video game arcade. Charlie started going to the video arcade at Landmark in the evenings, and he soon felt safe enough to go to the gym. He used his middle name, Mark, to hide his identity. After a few weeks he began lifting weights. He was very ambitious about the weight lifting and even used dietary supplements.

He ran into Eric, a friend from Galesburg, who was also living in Peoria and out of work. They decided to look for work together. Every morning for several months Eric and Charlie went out and applied for jobs. Eric even-

tually found work, but Charlie didn't. He had no job
skills and little work experience.

Charlie met a friend of Eric's named Helen, and the
three of them hung out together frequently. They went to
movies and played cards. Charlie remained alcohol- and
drug-free.

Martin and Ethel watched him very closely. They gave
him a strict allowance and demanded he get permission
from them for everything he did. They let him use the
family cars occasionally, but they scrupulously checked
the mileage.

Helen remembers the continuing problems he had with
his parents: "He would get moody with his parents, and
he wouldn't speak with them, or they'd get into a fight
about something. He said they picked on him, harassed
him, and wanted too much from him. They had a lot of
arguments about jobs, about going to school. His dad
would get on him about getting out and doing more
things instead of depending on them so much. They'd
shout at one another, and Charlie would isolate himself in
his room for a day or two."

He ran into Ed and Pete, two Galesburg friends, at
Landmark that fall. They asked him for his phone
number, but he wouldn't give it to them because he still
was paranoid. Ed and Pete gave him their phone numbers,
and he said he'd call them if he ever wanted to talk, but
he never did.

That fall Martin's lawyer, James Drake, petitioned the
judge to reconsider Cohen's case. He argued that although Cohen had resigned his position at the Galesburg
Mental Health Center, he had been forced out when the
state refused to give him the superintendent's position at
Zeller. The judge took Drake's motion under advisement
and ruled that the lawsuit should go to trial. The case

went before a Sangamon County jury in Springfield on December 16, 1986.

During the three-day proceeding, one of the members of the selection committee for the Zeller position testified that he had been coerced to vote against Cohen. Drake also subpoenaed the selection committee results, which revealed that Cohen had actually received the highest ranking. On Friday, December 19, the jury decided in favor of Martin Cohen. He was awarded a judgment of $249,000. For him, the victory on principle was more important than the money.

That winter Martin and Ethel gave Charlie an ultimatum—either get a job or go back to college. Charlie hadn't been able to find a job, so he went back to college. In January 1987, he registered for two classes at Illinois Central College in Peoria. It was his fourth college in 4½ years.

In April, Martin Cohen was laid off from his job. The lease on the large house ran out at the same time, and the state was threatening to appeal the $249,000 judgment. Martin and Ethel had no idea when they would get the money, if ever, so they quickly moved to a small, two-bedroom apartment. By then all three of Ethel's lap dogs had died or been put to sleep. "It saddens me to even mention this," she wrote in her yearly newsletter. "I miss all three dogs more than I can express."

One of Charlie's friends from the health club was with the Cohens when they moved. "I remember them having to pack up everything. It came on pretty sudden, and they had a couple of days to move. It was a tough time. I was there to help them move. Mark was really upset about it. He threw something and yelled at his dad. That was the first time I ever saw him throw a fit. Then his mom got real upset. She started crying. I felt bad for her."

* * *

In May 1987, Charlie met a young woman named Katie Adams. The two had worked together at McDonald's in Galesburg, although Charlie didn't remember her. Katie remembered him, however, because of his drug problems, but he seemed different. When he was dealing, he always came to work jumpy and wild-eyed. Now he wasn't as skittish, and she found him much more agreeable.

Katie was thin, five foot three inches tall, with big brown eyes and short hair. She was also four years younger than Charlie. They met at a party in Peoria and spent the next several hours talking. He told her about his cocaine binges and his arrest in Phoenix. Katie told him about the last few years of her life, much of which she had spent getting high and drinking. He hadn't gotten high for almost a year, and she had gone clean just three weeks ago. They each admitted that at their lowest points they had felt suicidal. They were surprised at how much they were telling one another.

They began dating almost immediately. He borrowed one of his parents' cars and drove to Galesburg to see her even though he was still very afraid of being seen in the area. Neither of them had much money, so they did things that didn't cost much. They went out to parks and listened to music and read. They went hiking and took long drives in the country. They managed to get together almost every weekend.

Charlie received A's in both of his classes that winter. He took two more classes at Illinois Central College during the summer session. He was enjoying his classes. He was working out quite a bit, and he was feeling confident. Katie was attending Alcoholics Anonymous meetings in Galesburg, and he attended a few meetings with her. Soon he was attending Narcotics Anonymous meetings in Peoria on his own.

Charlie also got in touch with two of his Galesburg

friends, Rick and Jonathan, whom he hadn't spoken with in almost a year. They weren't holding any grudges against him, and he felt that he was finally recovering from that fiasco.

On June 16, 1987, he celebrated his anniversary—a year off drugs. Helen and Eric took him out to dinner. He reminisced about his cocaine abuse. He admitted he had been hooked on coke and had acted like a fool, but he maintained that he was beating cocaine.

"I've whipped this," he said, "and I did it on my own."

He was very proud of himself. He even thought about going to local high schools and telling his story to the students. He had messed up his life, he claimed, but he was putting it back together.

Katie had grown very fond of Charlie, but she wasn't sure she was in love with him. Charlie had no such doubts about Katie. He had been unhappy for a long time, but since they'd met his depression had gone away. She was the key to his salvation, he decided.

Katie was bowled over by the intensity of his affection. In just two months she had come to mean everything to him. She'd never had a boyfriend who was as gentle, polite, and concerned with what she thought and felt.

Katie frequently visited Charlie in Peoria and came to know his parents. Katie felt very comfortable with Ethel. She was funny and intelligent, and it was obvious that she loved Charlie very much.

Martin liked Katie immediately, and he spoke with her whenever she was there. He had read a lot of the same books she had read, and he seemed capable of intelligently discussing almost any subject. Katie immediately noticed, however, that Charlie reacted very differently with his father.

"There was no question of his respect for his mother," she says. "He'd laugh and talk with her, but there was a cold distance, a silence, between Dr. Cohen and Charlie. It was very tense between them. When he was with his father, he was incredibly flustered and claustrophobic."

She and Charlie often went to dinner with his parents. For the most part the meals were lighthearted and casual, but the conversation often turned to Charlie and school. "Dr. Cohen was critical of Charlie, and school was a sore spot between them. Dr. Cohen was very ambitious and aggressive, which heightened the tensions. His father knew that the problems Charlie had in school were because of drugs. There was some incredible resentment that hadn't been dealt with. There were grudges being held over his head.

"Dr. Cohen knew he was bright and put him down for not being in a good school. He was supportive, but there was this undertone of disapproval, like, 'I'll accept you, but you're not quite cutting it.'

"Most of the time Charlie would just sit there and ride it out. It embarrassed him, but he didn't want to make a scene. Sometimes he got frustrated and retaliated. He'd say, 'Why do you have to keep harping on me?' "

Katie had just finished her first year of college and had gotten good grades. Martin held her up as an example to Charlie. "It made me cringe," she says. "Dr. Cohen was using me as a weapon. It was almost like the father was competing with the son. He was egging Charlie on, baiting him. 'The more I can put you down, the better I will feel.' It was more than concern. His father was extreme. Charlie just didn't want to play the psychological game with his dad. He was tired of it. He had doubts about everything, and that competitive pressure just added to his doubts."

The last couple of times Katie saw Charlie, though, she saw a side of him that troubled her. "By the end of the summer the amount of tension, anger, and frustration that he was putting a lid on, especially in the company of his father, was incredible. It was scary. I knew he wasn't aware of how much anger he had inside. It was physically visible. His father was oblivious. He just kept pushing the buttons. Charlie was a time bomb waiting to go off. I knew that if he were on coke again, that would be the end of it. He'd freak out. He wouldn't care what he did. All of that anger and frustration would just explode."

By the end of July, Charlie was getting serious about Katie. Although he hadn't proposed marriage, he frequently mentioned their future together. He talked about settling down with her and raising a family.

Katie wasn't so sure about their future together. She was going back to college in the fall, and she knew she wouldn't see much of Charlie. She wasn't willing to make any long-term commitments, and this talk of raising a family was making her nervous. After all, they had been dating less than three months.

The two had another problem as well. She wasn't willing to have sex with him, and he was pressuring her. In a group of friends he constantly made jokes about sex, and some of his jokes had a violent edge to them that disturbed her.

In early August she began to withdraw from the relationship. She put off visits and didn't return his phone calls. It all was too intense for her. She had enough of her own problems, and she couldn't handle his. She was going back to school in a few weeks, and she wanted to focus on her classes.

Charlie was confused and distraught. He didn't know why she had suddenly cut him off. When he got her on the phone, she mumbled something about needing more time and space. At the end of August she left for college. He wrote to her.

8/23/87

Dear Katie,

Don't doubt the force of love. I secluded myself from the people who cared for a long time. I dwelled in thoughts of self-pity, self-doubt, distrustfulness of others and myself. I then resolved myself to not caring about anyone's needs or feelings but my own. I wanted to destroy everything and everyone that lasts forever. I thought about killing my parents a lot. I wanted nuclear war to come so I could rape the nearest 13-year-old girl. During this time I also feared that my parents might try to kill me. I felt they would be justified somehow. I wanted to be dead. Cocaine. Bulimia. Phoenix jail.

Nothing has changed. The world is essentially the same—headed for destruction or salvation. . . . I still think about stealing my parents' car and taking off. Just going on a rampage of real hardcore destruction. I'd love to rape and kill. I would fucking love to keep people at gunpoint or slit somebody's throat. I'd love to fuck you up the ass. I fantasize about raping you.

I feel like God and the devil are having a tug of war with my soul—right now at this very moment. It happened yesterday and the day before. This will always be—till I die. God's winning.

Love, Charlie

The letter scared the hell out of her and confirmed her worst fear: he was dangerous. She decided to stay away from him.

Charles Cohen as Superfly during his senior year in high school.

Cohen during the summer of 1988, a few months before he murdered his parents.
(Jerry Lehane III)

Cohen in September 1988, when he was forming a punk rock band sometimes called John Hinckley's Kids.
(Joe Ferrara)

Ethel, Charles, and Martin Cohen in 1976. *(Robert Huddle)*

The townhouse in Hockessin, Delaware,
where Martin and Ethel Cohen were murdered.

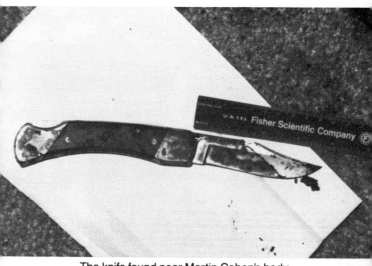

The knife found near Martin Cohen's body.

One of the barbells Charles Cohen used
to kill his parents.

CRIME INFO BULLETIN

SAN FRANCISCO POLICE DEPARTMENT

89-06   03/21/89

On Saturday, February 25, 1989 at 1030 hours, the above depicted suspect
was photographed while attempting to use a homicide victim's stolen credit
card at an ATM machine in Berkeley, California.

The victim, Conrad Lutz, was found stabbed to death in his Twin Peaks
apartment at 3649 Market Street, #503. The murder occurred at that location
on Friday, February 24, 1989, at approximately 2250 hours. The victim's
wallet and credit cards were stolen. The victim was known to bring men
home from United Nations Plaza and Civic Center Plaza in San Francisco.

Refer any information to:

Inspector James Crowley or
Inspector Ora Guinther
Homicide Section 553-1145 (Days)
Operations Center 553-1071 (Nights)

                                              FRANK M. JORDAN
Case No. 890-260-496   CHIEF OF POLICE

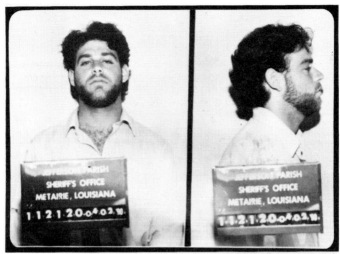

Cohen being booked on charges of attempted theft and assault, under the alias James McDowell, in a New Orleans suburb on April 2, 1990.

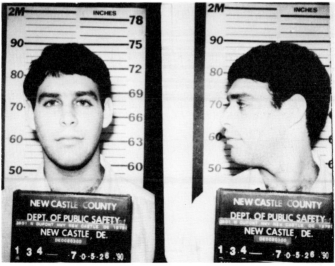

Cohen being booked for the murders of his parents in Delaware on May 26, 1990.

J. Dallas Winslow, Jr., one of Cohen's
public defenders in Wilmington, Delaware.

Prosecutors Steve Walther and Bobby O'Neill.

Dr. Robert Sadoff, one of the defense's mental health experts, who testified that Cohen was mentally ill.

Dr. David Raskin just after his dramatic testimony that Cohen was a paranoid schizophrenic.

Detective John Downs of the New Castle County Police Department, the chief investigating officer in the Martin and Ethel Cohen murder case.

Katie Adams speaking with reporters after testifying for the prosecution in Wilmington, Delaware, in April 1992. She dated Cohen in 1987 in Peoria, Illinois, and received a threatening letter from him after they broke up.

Diane met Charles Cohen in Peoria in 1987. She fell in love with him when he was in a Wilmington jail in 1990.

Charles Cohen being led into a Wilmington courthouse on July 2, 1992, two months after being sentenced to life imprisonment for the murders of his parents.

chapter 8

- - - - - - - -

Hardcore

During the fall of 1987, Charlie worked part-time as a clerk in the diet office at St. Francis Hospital in Peoria and took an algebra class at Illinois Central College. He didn't know if he was stable enough to handle a busy schedule, but he was going to try. He had messed up so many times before, but this time he couldn't let it fall apart.

His mind was raging with thoughts of Katie. Sometimes he felt inadequate and vulnerable, and other times he thought he would explode with rage and hatred. He didn't understand what had happened. He had offered her his unconditional love, and she had thrown it back in his face. He would've done anything for Katie, but evidently that wasn't good enough for her. He felt like such a fool.

She was like the other girls in his life. Each one had hurt him, but this time was the absolute worst. She wouldn't even respond to his letters. Couldn't she see how much pain she had caused? Was she really that heartless?

He hadn't realized it at first, but now he understood

that she was evil. He was seeing everything so much more clearly. She shouldn't be allowed to get away with it. He had cried over her, but now it was her turn to cry. If he killed her, he realized, the pain would go away. He visualized raping and killing her. He would drag it out, making her suffer as he had. She would beg for mercy and forgiveness. She would regret everything she had done to him, every transgression. He would forgive her, of course, just before he wasted her.

He would be more careful in the future. He wouldn't trust people. They might say they were his friends, but he wouldn't believe them until they proved themselves. Every time he had been kind to someone, that person had turned on him. Kindness had brought him nothing but pain. He had to be cruel and rude, or people would walk all over him. He would keep to himself, become a loner, avoid his friends.

He spent a lot of time locked in his bedroom away from his parents, who thought he was studying. He didn't care what they thought. He felt like a caged animal. He couldn't bear to even look at them. He tried to ignore his father, but it wasn't possible. Once he had to tell him, "Fucking leave me alone!" Another conversation erupted into a shoving match.

He remembered the arguments his father had started with him in front of Katie. That was probably why she had dumped him. Everything that had gone wrong in his life could be traced back to his parents. They were the root of all of his problems. For so long he had just wanted to be left alone. They had ruined his life, and he couldn't help fantasizing about ruining theirs.

The state of Illinois threatened to appeal Martin Cohen's jury award, which would have tied up the money for several more years, so that fall Martin Cohen and the state of Illinois settled out of court. Cohen got $110,000 after the lawyer's fee.

Ethel was getting treatment for her arthritis once or twice a week, and she had high blood pressure, but she was in another musical that fall. She wrote in her 1987 holiday letter, "I really ached almost too much to have participated in the play, but I want so desperately to stay in the mainstream of activity. Now that it's over I ache even more."

Charlie had become a regular at Narcotics Anonymous meetings in Peoria. The meetings gave him a chance to talk about his problems with Katie and his father. The other participants discussed their problems, and he was fascinated by their stories. He eventually chaired a few NA meetings.

One member recalls him vividly: "From the way he talked about his past he just felt that he really got screwed. He felt like he hadn't been treated fairly. He had a vendetta against just about everything and everybody. Very bitter about life in general. I teased him about it. I'd say, 'Mark, you've got it made. You're living at home. You don't have to have a job. Your parents are helping you. You don't have to pay for anything. What's your complaint?' He always had something to complain about. Nothing was ever the way it should be, but he did it in a funny way. It was always a joke. He was always trying to be the happy-go-lucky guy. You never really knew where he was coming from, whether he was joking or what he was feeling. I think he was really depressed and lonely at times. He had a lot of things going on inside that people didn't see."

Helen experienced Charlie's bitterness firsthand: "Charlie had mood swings where he would be a fine, nice, typical person, and then something would snap in him and he'd get verbally abusive and really cut people down, and then he'd go off by himself and not want to be around anybody for four or five days. Then you would hear from Charlie, and he'd want to be with people again. But he had to have periods of solitude. Sometimes the best thing was to leave Charlie alone. You could tell by the way he said hello on the phone whether it was one of those times."

One cold, windy November evening, Charlie stormed out of the apartment and walked to a nearby phone booth. He couldn't take living with his parents in the tiny apartment another day. He knew if he didn't get away from them soon, something bad would happen. He called Jonathan in Galesburg, who was sharing a house with Rick. Charlie asked Jonathan if he could move into the house with them.

"I don't think that's a very good idea, Charlie, for my own state of mind," Jonathan said. "I talked to Rick about it, and he isn't comfortable with it either."

Charlie didn't say anything.

"I consider you a really good friend, Charlie, but I'm just afraid having you move in with us would be disruptive," Jonathan went on. "You hit rock bottom every six months, and I don't see any reason to believe you're not going to do it again. I want to finish school, and I need a stable environment."

Charlie started to cry. First Katie and now this. "Sometimes I feel like I could kill someone, and it wouldn't even matter," he said.

"See," said Jonathan, "that's a perfect example of what I'm talking about."

"I always thought we knew where each other's head was at."

"That can't possibly be true, Charlie, because I never seriously considered killing anyone. I don't have any idea where your head is at."

The two didn't speak to one another again for several months.

Charlie found a one-room apartment in Peoria in a rundown apartment building in a bad section of town. He didn't have any furniture. He put his clothing in the kitchen cabinets. There were cockroaches and mice in the building. Helen and Eric came by a few times, but they were afraid to be in the neighborhood at night. The lock on the apartment door didn't work, so he had to lock it with a padlock. He wasn't making much money at the hospital, so he applied for and received food stamps.

Charlie's apartment was cold and lonely. His life bored him. Too often he thought about Katie. Each night he turned up the music on his boombox and wallowed in self-pity as the hours rolled by. He hated memories of her.

He wasn't sure what to believe anymore. His perceptions were often clouded. One thing he understood was that he missed Katie. He wanted her to hold him. He wanted to touch her smooth, soft skin, but he wasn't sure he could control himself around her. He couldn't always suppress his anger. He realized that it was part of his nature to be destructive. He had to fight against his destructive nature to remain sane, yet he had to yield to it or he would go crazy.

He had met a young woman named Diane at the hospital, and they became good friends. She had told him about her anorexia, and he told her about his drug abuse. She seemed to care, and he was attracted to her, but she was seeing someone else.

In November he stopped attending his algebra class. He just couldn't take it. He had fallen behind. It was all too much—moving, working, school, his parents, Katie.

On December 1 he decided to write a letter to her. He had to choose his words carefully. It was a sensitive area.

He didn't know what she was feeling. Only one word came to him—"Goodbye." He mailed the letter.

At the end of the year he quit his job at the hospital, and a month later he moved back in with his parents.

On June 22, 1976, Roger Re attacked and killed his estranged wife Jayne in her Wilmington, Delaware, home. He shot her with a .38-caliber revolver three times in the back and shot her in the head with a shotgun. Two years later a judge ruled that Re was mentally incompetent to stand trial, and he was placed in a maximum security building at Delaware State Hospital.

During the next six years Roger Re gained the confidence of the hospital administration and obtained numerous privileges. He ran an auto repair business at the hospital, had keys to numerous buildings, and left the hospital grounds frequently. He also had a private room in one of the buildings and became involved in at least one sexual relationship with a female employee.

Word of Re's activities got back to the state attorney general, who launched an investigation. On March 20, 1985, three hospital administrators, including Robert Feeney, the hospital director, were suspended for repeatedly allowing Re to violate hospital policies. Two other employees who were implicated in the scandal resigned as well.

The next day Roger Re disappeared from the grounds of the hospital. The police searched the area using scores of patrolmen, patrol dogs, spotlights, and helicopters, but they couldn't find him. Two days later, he gave himself up at an apartment on the hospital grounds. Within a month Re was found competent to stand trial for the murder of his wife. He was later found guilty of murder and sentenced to life in prison.

During the next two years, Delaware State Hospital went through two more directors, and by late 1987 the hospital was in bad shape. Employee morale, after numerous management changes and reorganizations, was abysmal. The facility was understaffed, especially in nursing, and staff turnover was high. Patient treatment and quality control were lax. Patients were leaving the hospital without authorization, and there were numerous charges of patient abuse. Critical accreditations and certifications had fallen behind, and the aging facility was in poor repair.

In 1987 the state hired a private consulting firm, MGT of America, Inc., to conduct a comprehensive review of the hospital. MGT found a host of problems, many of them stemming from a leadership vacuum. Neil Meisler, the newly hired director of the Division of Alcoholism, Drug Abuse, and Mental Health, knew the hospital was in critical condition. One of his first actions was to conduct a nationwide search for a permanent director.

In January 1988, Martin Cohen heard about the opening at Delaware State Hospital and applied. In February he was invited to Wilmington for two days of interviews.

That winter Charlie gradually alienated his closest friends in Peoria. He played a tape for Eric and, with a weird smile on his face, insisted that the singer was the devil. Eric was at the end of his rope with Charlie. He had become progressively more bizarre. Eric told him to leave, and Charlie left and never came back.

Charlie was also pressuring Helen, who had become a close friend, to become more seriously involved. She was seeing another guy and told Charlie she just wanted to remain friends. Charlie persisted and made a few more passes at her. She rebuffed each of his advances, hoping he would get the message.

One night he asked her to give him a ride to downtown Peoria. She agreed. On the way Charlie told her he loved her. She again told him she wasn't interested. Charlie suddenly became furious and started yelling at her. Helen pulled the car over. It was cold and raining.

"Get out," she said. "I can't listen to this bullshit any-more."

She had never abandoned anyone in the rain before in her life. Charlie got out, and she sped off. They never spoke again.

Dr. Martin Cohen was hired as director of Delaware State Hospital and started at his new job on March 28, 1988. He and Ethel were overjoyed. After working only nine months during the past 3½ years and spending much of that time in deep depression, he was getting a chance to start a new life. He would spend the remainder of his career doing meaningful work in an environment where he was needed and appreciated. He was 58, and he agreed to stay at the post until his retirement.

The hospital had a press conference on his first day. The secretary of the Department of Health and Social Services cited Cohen's strong administrative skills as well as his background in institutional and community mental health services. He was the hospital's hope for the future.

Cohen also spoke with the press. "The biggest problem we face is stigma," he said. "People seem to think of themselves as invulnerable to mental illness, when actually, I think ... we're all vulnerable. Everyone has a breaking point."

When asked about the seemingly endless list of problems facing the hospital, which had over 360 patients and a $22 million budget, he said, "I love this stuff. I like problem-solving. I like to be in the middle of the action. I guess I like crises."

Martin Cohen took Val Starcher, the deputy director of the hospital, out to dinner his first day on the job. Cohen talked about his son, whom he referred to as "the apple of my eye" and "my boy, Charlie." He admitted, how-ever, that Charlie had problems. He was a perennial college student, he didn't know what to do with his life, and he couldn't hold a job.

The conversation shifted to work. They talked about different types of patients. Starcher said she had the hardest time working with geriatric patients.

"What do you think would be the toughest type of patient for me to work with?" Cohen asked her.

"Adolescent patients?" she guessed because of his problems with his son.

"That's very perceptive of you," he said. "That's the population that I'd rather not work with. I don't relate well with them."

In the meantime, Jonathan was putting together a band in Galesburg. The band, which was called Bourbon and Clorox, consisted of a few Knox students. They needed a singer, but not a traditional one. They needed someone with more intensity, urgency, and desperation than talent. Jonathan immediately thought of Charlie. He had always wanted to be in a band.

"Look, you don't particularly want to deal with me, and I don't particularly want to deal with you," said Jonathan, "but if you want to be in this band, you can. I think you could do it."

Charlie was still suspicious of Jonathan, but he agreed, and he began coming to Galesburg for practice every week or so.

Their first gig was at a Knox fraternity house on Good Friday. Charlie dressed in a hooded coat. The music was raucous, fast, and loud. Charlie howled and shrieked in a deep monotone. He glared at the audience, never changing expression. His voice was full of power and pain. The lyrics were like death to him. He felt no emotion except hatred. The effect was eerie and chilling. The audience was spellbound. He laughed with the final guitar blast, and the audience chanted his name.

He and the other members of Bourbon and Clorox suddenly were very excited about the prospects for the band. Charlie felt he had found his calling. The band members talked about making a go of it. If they had come this far in such a short time, imagine how far they could go if they put their minds to it.

Charlie stayed in the house rented by Jonathan and Rick for about a week. It had been almost two years since he had taken off from Galesburg. Tom and Stan had both left Knox, so Charlie wasn't worried about running into either of them. However, one afternoon Charlie bumped into Gary on campus. He had borrowed $400 from Gary before running off in June 1986.

"I'm really sorry about the money, man," said Charlie. "I'm still trying to pay you back."

"Look, Charlie, forget about the money," said Gary. "Just do me a favor. Get your life together."

Martin Cohen stayed in a room on the grounds of the hospital during his first few weeks on the job. Ethel came to Delaware in April, and they got a motel room near the hospital and searched for a house. They wanted to buy a one-story house because of Ethel's arthritis.

Martin sent in an application for Charlie to the University of Delaware. He and Ethel hoped that Charlie would come to Delaware with them. They didn't want to leave him in Illinois. He wasn't stable enough to live on his own. He'd probably get himself in trouble again. They wanted to get him into a new environment where he, too, could start over.

By the end of April, Ethel and Martin had found a place that suited them. It was a modern two-story town house for rent in a new development in Hockessin called Gateway Townhomes. Everything that Ethel needed— bedroom, living room, dining room, kitchen, laundry room—was on the first floor. The second floor had two bedrooms, a bathroom, and a small loft, which would be perfect for Charlie. They took possession of 532 Beech Tree Lane on May 1, 1988.

Despite their problems over the past 3½ years, Martin and Ethel were in good financial shape. They still had money in numerous stocks, retirement accounts, CDs, savings accounts, and life insurance policies. They also had over $100,000 from their settlement with the state of Illinois, which they invested in a life and health insurance policy for Ethel.

Val Starcher remembers an odd incident, though: "I walked into Marty's office one day not long after he started, and he was on the phone with Charlie. This was before Ethel and Charlie moved to Delaware. He motioned for me to sit down, and I overheard the conversation. Marty said, 'Well, son, I can't wait till you get here. We'll have good times together, I promise you. We'll take long walks together.' My impression was that he was talking to a young child, maybe a child of Boy Scout age. The thought even entered my mind that maybe the child was a slow learner. The first time I heard how old Charlie was, I was really shocked. I truly didn't think he was talking to a young adult."

The band members' enthusiasm soon waned. First of all, the drummer was going home for the summer. Second, there wasn't much interest in Galesburg for a band like Bourbon and Clorox. Their only gigs would be the occasional fraternity party.

Nonetheless, Charlie didn't want to move to Delaware with his parents. He wanted to stay in Illinois and devote himself to Bourbon & Clorox, but he didn't have a job, a place to stay, or any money. His parents weren't willing to give him money to live in Illinois on his own, so he had no choice. He reluctantly moved to Delaware in May.

chapter 9

- - - - - - - -

Heading for a Fall

Charlie was bored, sullen, and lonely during his first months in Delaware. Once again, he was living in a place where he didn't know anyone, and he blamed his parents for his unhappiness. He walked around Hockessin occasionally, but there wasn't much to the small, quiet village. He had no one to talk to besides his parents.

He spent hours on the deck behind the town house or in his room fantasizing. His life was a wreck. He was going nowhere. Everyone else had plans and a future and girlfriends and friends. But what did he have? Nothing except two old people who had nothing better to do than abuse the control they had over him. Their relationship had always been a psychological battle. If only he were free of them. The pressure was too much. Something had to give. They were heading for a fall.

A landscaper observed the tense home life: "We worked at Gateway for about two months that spring. I would see them come and go all the time, often her and the son, and she would be driving a big blue car.

"On one particular afternoon we were working right in front of their house, and she came flying in there driving kind of fast. No sooner did she have the car parked than the son was out of the car, up the stairs to the front door, and slammed the door. The lady wasn't even out of the car yet, and she was screaming about something or other. She hobbled up the steps with a cane.

"Later we were working out back. He would be home all the time. There was one old chair on the back patio, and he would sit out there hour after hour, five or six hours at a time. He would just smoke cigarettes and stare off into the yonder. He didn't seem to do anything.

"A couple times we heard them raising their voices inside. You couldn't make out actual words, but you could hear them yelling, going on and on. Guys would talk about it, how all he does is come home, argue, and doesn't do anything. It was really strange."

One day Charlie noticed that a good-looking young woman lived next door. He went over and introduced himself. Her name was Stacey, and she lived with her father. They chatted in a friendly manner while he paced her living room.

Charlie asked her if she had a boyfriend. She did. He paused in front of the fireplace and picked up the fireplace poker. He waved the fireplace poker like a sword, smiled oddly, and said, "So much for the boyfriend."

She could tell he was trying to be funny, but he was making her uneasy. She wanted him out of the house.

"Well," she said, "it was nice meeting you, but I've got to go."

In May Charlie received a letter from the University of Delaware stating that he had not been accepted. Charlie didn't care particularly because he didn't want to go back to school. The application had been his parents' idea. He knew they wanted him in college just to keep him out of trouble.

Martin Cohen wrote a letter to the dean at the University of Delaware in Charlie's name asking them to reconsider. He pointed out that Charlie's father was the newly hired director of Delaware State Hospital.

In the meantime, Martin and Ethel convinced Charlie to register for summer classes at the university. At least he would meet some new people and get out of the house.

Martin Cohen planned to attend a mental health conference in New Orleans in late May, and Ethel was going with him. Charlie didn't want to go. He wanted to spend a few days away from his parents, but they insisted he come along. They didn't trust him enough to leave him on his own.

Martin attended the conference during the day, and Ethel relaxed in the hotel. Charlie went out into New Orleans occasionally, but he was in a dour, surly mood.

A therapist recalls a conversation she had with Ethel at the conference: "She said something like, 'We can't always be responsible for what our kids do.' She was trying to be at peace with herself and not blame herself and feel guilty that they had done something wrong. I think that as a parent we begin telling ourselves that before we really believe it."

The conference ended on Friday, but the Cohens stayed until Sunday. That gave Martin and Ethel two days to entertain Charlie, but Charlie was not to be entertained. He was sullen and uncommunicative. Both sides came home very dissatisfied with one another.

The Cohens had problems concerning the use of the family cars. Martin usually took one of the cars to work. Ethel took swimming lessons at the local YMCA two or three times a week for her arthritis, and she saw a Wilmington doctor frequently, so she needed the other car on most days. That left Charlie without transportation. They let him use a car occasionally, but not without asking him where he was going and when he would be back. They wouldn't give him any money unless they knew what he planned to spend it on. He was totally dependent on them.

Martin's older brother came from New York to visit the Cohens one evening that summer. Charlie exchanged greetings with his uncle, whom he hadn't seen in years, but then went up to his room, where he remained the rest of the evening.

Charlie started summer classes in June. He took an art history and a drawing class. In July, he received a letter from the University of Delaware stating that he was formally accepted. Charlie decided he wanted to live in the campus dorms in Newark that fall. He didn't want to live with his parents. Martin and Ethel were already facing a $7,000 out-of-state tuition bill, and they weren't willing to fork over room and board money as well. Besides, they knew he would have easy access to drugs in the dorms. He threatened to move out, but they refused to give him any money if he did, so he stayed.

Martin Cohen was getting along well at the hospital. He was the first person with any clinical experience to run the hospital in over a dozen years, so he was sensitive to the needs and problems of the staff, who responded well to him.

In July, Charlie got a part-time job at a gas station in Hockessin. He was paid $4 per hour and usually worked the 3 P.M. to 9 P.M. shift. It was his responsibility to take care of the pumps and to answer the phone in the office, but Charlie had problems from his first day on the job. If he didn't answer the office phone in five rings, the call was transferred to the owner's house. The owner, Ken, got numerous calls during Charlie's shifts. Eventually, Ken called Charlie and gave him hell.

One day Charlie left for lunch and never came back. When he showed up for work the next day he couldn't explain why he hadn't returned the previous day. Another time he missed an entire shift. He often asked other employees to cover for him if he had something to do, but he wouldn't cover for anyone else when they wanted time off. Elizabeth, the gas island manager, cursed him out over it, and he cursed her back.

"He gave me the creeps," says Elizabeth. "He was the type who would stare. At times he could be quite open and friendly, but he had an incredible temper. He would get really pissed off about little things. I decided to keep my distance from him."

Charlie met many young women in his summer art classes, and he asked several to go out on dates, but for the most part they weren't interested. He dated a young woman named Ally a few times, and he even sent her a dozen roses, but she felt he was too forward. He acted like she was the only person he could talk to. He whined about his past drug use and his problems with his parents all the time as well, which bored her.

Charlie hadn't made a good impression on his neighbor Stacey either. She knew there was something wrong with him, but she didn't know what it was. For the first couple of months she had the impression he was mildly retarded.

She noticed him watching her from his bedroom window when she was working on the lawn or sunbathing on the back deck. Her father was often away on business, and Stacey was somewhat nervous being in the town house alone because of her odd neighbor.

On one occasion he brought over a small candy dispenser filled with pennies and offered it to her.

"What's this?" she asked.

"I want you to have it in case someone bothers you," he said. "You could put it in your hand and hit someone with it to protect yourself."

"Gee, thanks," she said.

* * *

In July he saw a poster for a compilation of songs by local bands. There was a phone number on the poster. When Charlie called, a young man named Evan answered the phone. He was nineteen and about to start his second year at the University of Delaware. His hobby was copying and distributing recordings of local punk bands. He and Charlie had similar musical tastes, and they both wanted to form a band. The two quickly became friends.

Charlie had a recording of the Bourbon and Clorox show from the previous spring, and he played it for Evan. Evan offered to copy and sell recordings of the tape, and Charlie was delighted with the idea. It would give him immediate stature in Delaware's punk scene. Charlie drew a logo, consisting of an eagle gripping a bourbon bottle in one set of talons and a bottle of bleach in the other for the cassette sleeve.

In the liner notes they wrote, "Look for a studio tape from Bourbon and Clorox this year. Call the band for booking. . . . A special thanx to . . . all of our fans from Illinois and Delaware." They claimed that Bourbon and Clorox was "originally from the Chicago area now in DE!!!!"

They made sixty copies of the tape in July. Evan took copies of the tape to local record stores, and Charlie hawked the tape wherever he went. He sold numerous copies to the kids hanging out on Main Street in Newark.

Charlie's problems at the gas station came to a head on a hot August day. Ken was frantically trying to fix the station's propane tank, which was leaking. He was afraid it would explode. Charlie was in the air-conditioned office. A customer drove up to the full-service island, but Charlie didn't serve the customer.

"It's a full-serve customer," Ken shouted to him.

Charlie nodded, but he stayed in the office. Ken called to Charlie another time, but he still didn't move. Finally,

Ken left the leaking propane tank to serve the customer himself. When he was done he stomped into the office and shouted, "What are you waiting on?"

"Relax, pal," Charlie said.

"You know what?" said Ken. "I'm gonna relax. *You're fired!*"

"I guess you want the shirt right off my back," Charlie said. He was wearing a shirt that belonged to the station.

"You know, you're right," said Ken. Charlie took the shirt off and left.

That same month, Charlie wrote a strange letter to his friend Rick in Galesburg. In it Charlie complained that Jonathan had insulted and humiliated him several times during the past year. He claimed that Jonathan "made friends just to manipulate them."

He asked Rick to tell him everything Jonathan did, everywhere he went, and everyone he met. "He has to pay," Charlie wrote. "He's screwed us. We've got to get him. He shouldn't be allowed to get away with that."

Rick was perplexed by the letter and showed it to Jonathan. He wasn't sure what to make of it either. How was Charlie going to make him pay? And for what? Charlie was going off the deep end, or he was playing some sort of weird practical joke. They hoped it was the latter.

chapter 10

- - - - - - - - -

John Hinckley's Kids

In August Charlie met a young man in Newark named Mark, and they became close friends. Mark had a Mohawk haircut, rows of earrings in his ears and nose, one earring in his left nipple, dozens of silver bracelets, long black painted fingernails, cigarette burns on his arms, and numerous crudely applied tattoos. He was 18 years old and alienated from his parents. Neither Mark nor Charlie knew very many people in Newark, so they began hanging around together.

"He wasn't violent," Mark recalls. "He wasn't really much different than anybody else. He wouldn't go out picking fights or anything like that. Charlie was polite and nice to his parents. They were on speaking terms, but he had a different way of looking at things. He was a big idealist about the way society should be—politics, the military, about the way people should treat each other. If his ideas didn't work out and things didn't go his way, he'd get upset about it.

"He did have rapid mood swings at times. He would be up and happy for a while, and he would get talking about what's going on and how fucked up the world is, and he'd get pretty upset about it."

Charlie told Mark about his plans for starting a band, and Mark wanted to be in on it. They had to recruit a few more guys, so Mark took Charlie to meet Phil and Dan, some friends of his who lived in a rented house on South College Avenue. Both were happy to join the band.

Now Charlie had enough people for a band, but none of them had any musical equipment. He asked his parents for money to buy enough equipment to outfit the entire band. He reminded them that they had made him leave Illinois and quit Bourbon and Clorox. He promised that the band would get paying gigs and eventually pay them off.

His parents had no hopes of him becoming a serious musician, but they begrudgingly agreed. They were just happy that he was willing to apply himself to something, and they hoped he would stick with it. The band would also give him an outlet for his unfocused antagonism, which seemed to be on the rise. So Martin and Ethel put up $1,500, and Charlie purchased several amplifiers, a guitar, a bass, a microphone, and a used drum set. Charlie decided to play the drums, an instrument he had never played before.

As his first semester at the University of Delaware got under way, Charlie and the band began practice sessions in the basement of his parents' town house. They didn't know how to play their instruments, so they tried to figure it out as they went along. The practices usually deteriorated into chaotic noise fests, with each person trying to outdo the others. Charlie had written some song lyrics, but none of the band members liked them, so Phil just screamed. Charlie flailed wildly on the drums. Once they all screamed "Fuck!" into the microphone over and over. They talked about a few names for the band. *John Hinckley's Kids* and *S.D.I.* were two possibilities they discussed.

They planned to have a shocking performance-art aspect to their live shows. They would play almost naked, throw things into the audience, and twitch about as if possessed. They would also stage violent acts, like tying up the lead singer during a song and beating him with chains.

Within a few practice sessions it was obvious that Evan was not working out. He had the wrong attitude. He didn't want to scream and make noise. He wanted to play songs. Charlie's new friends were much more nihilistic than Evan. They had weird haircuts and outlandish clothing, whereas Evan was more clean-cut. Evan noticed that Charlie was growing more negative, too. His drawings were becoming bizarre, and he seemed angry.

"Your outlook is too positive," Charlie told him. "It doesn't work for me. You're blind to what's happening in the world. It'll lead to your downfall."

Then Charlie told Evan he was no longer in the band. For two months he had been Charlie's best friend, but now Charlie didn't want to have anything to do with him.

Martin and Ethel were shocked at the bizarre appearance of Charlie's punk rock friends. Nor had they anticipated how loud the band would be. The din was driving them crazy, and the neighbors were complaining. Martin and Ethel complained to Charlie about the noise and restricted the band to practicing only when they were both gone from the house.

Charlie also met Paul on Main Street in Newark that summer. He was only thirteen years old, but he was tall and lanky and looked older than his age. He had a Mohawk haircut, wore a leather jacket and combat boots, and had been drinking regularly since the age of eleven. Whenever they got together, Paul got Charlie to buy him some vodka in a liquor store. Sometimes Charlie even paid for it. Within a few weeks, he and Charlie were good friends.

One afternoon in early September, Charlie ran into

Paul in Newark. Charlie knew Paul had a pair of electric hair clippers, so he said, "When are you going to cut my hair?"

"I can do it right now if you can give me a ride home," said Paul.

Once at his house, Paul started shaving the sides of Charlie's head. As the clippers buzzed over his head, he thought back to the other Mohawks he had gotten. This was at least the fourth one, but it meant more to him than the others. It symbolized his refusal to conform to his parents' demands. He had done what they wanted for two years. He had gone along with their watchfulness and distrust. He had been drug- and alcohol-free. He had taken classes and gotten good grades, yet still they blamed him for the Phoenix incident. They'd punished him long enough. He wouldn't stand for it any longer.

Guys like Mark, Phil, and Dan inspired him. They led antisocial, nonconformist lives. They knew that the system was corrupt, and they refused to be a part of it. It was a fucking game, and everyone, from the cops, teachers, and businessmen to his parents, played along. You couldn't work for change within a perverse, wicked system. You had to destroy it.

When Paul was done, Charlie looked in the mirror. He would have to go home, and he knew how his parents would react to the Mohawk. His mother would nag and complain, but she had always done that. It was his father he worried about. This would be one more thing his father would use to intimidate and control him. His father hated him, and he hated his father. It was that simple.

Paul could see that Charlie was bumming out. "It's just a haircut, man," he said. "I mean, you're twenty-three. You can do what you want."

Paul was right. To hell with them. He wouldn't listen to them ever again.

Charlie went home, got some money from his mother,

and went shopping. He bought black jeans and a black shirt. A few days later he found an army fatigue jacket in a used clothing store and painted some slogans on the back of it. He bought a pair of black boots and dark glasses. He wanted his skin to look pale and deathly, so he decided to wear long pants and his army jacket to block out the sun even on hot days.

Now the makeover was complete. He'd gone to his first few classes dressed neatly in a sports shirt and khaki pants. He'd blended in. He'd hung out on Main Street in straight clothes. He'd set them up. Now he was going to shock them. He would give them a little taste of anarchy.

In September, Jonathan called Charlie. Ethel answered the phone, and Jonathan asked her how she was doing. She didn't say much and sounded very tense.

Charlie got on the phone. "Why did you call?" he asked. Jonathan knew something was seriously wrong.

"To see how you're doing?" Jonathan said.

"I'm doing really well," said Charlie. He was cool and collected, but his voice was black with hatred. "I'm seeing things much more clearly now. I was aware of your intentions to dump me from the band all along, but I was just playing along with your little charade."

"What are you talking about?"

"I suppose I should thank you for giving me the opportunity to use you. I've sold five hundred copies of the tape, and I'm keeping all the money. I'm the puppet master now."

"I don't care about the money." Jonathan knew there would be no communication with him whatsoever. It didn't matter what he said. Charlie would keep interpreting things however he wanted.

"I'm putting my own band together, and they're going to be much better than Bourbon and Clorox."

"Come off it, man."

"No, you come off it, asshole."
"You're the asshole!!!"

It soon became clear that practicing at Charlie's parents' place wasn't going to work out, so the band moved the equipment to the basement of the house on South College Avenue, where Phil and Dan lived, and held practices there.

Despite practicing regularly for the next month, the band didn't make much progress. They knew only a few parts of a few songs, and they played them over and over. Nevertheless, Charlie had high hopes for the band. He wanted to get paying gigs, so he could pay off his parents for the equipment. He wanted to go on a tour around the country in a van next summer.

The house on South College Avenue was a gathering place for all sorts of people. Roommates came and went. Runaways crashed on the floor when they couldn't find anywhere else to go. People were in and out of the house at all hours. Small impromptu parties with lots of drugs took place several nights a week. The place was full of old broken furniture, and people had spray-painted graffiti on many of the walls.

Charlie hung out at the house frequently with Phil, and they became good friends. Phil's motto was, "All normal people should be shot." He hated society in general and the police in particular, whom he referred to as "fucking pigs." He had a drinking problem and a history of emotional instability. Twice in the previous two years he had committed himself to a mental health facility.

Sometimes when Phil got drunk, which was almost every day, he became suicidal. He said if he ever decided to waste himself, he'd buy a machine gun, go to a mall, and take a dozen or so of the normal people out with him. Phil also had a combative relationship with his girlfriend, Joanne, who was a high school senior and hung out at the house frequently. They fought all the time, screaming and punching one another.

Joanne recalls meeting Charlie: "I met Charles when Phil met him, at a party somewhere in Newark. He was there by himself. He was talking to everybody and being real friendly. He was acting goofy and dancing by himself, and people were talking about him. Everybody thought he was a narc.

"After that he came to the house a lot. Phil liked him. I'd say to Phil, 'Why do you hang out with this guy?' And he'd say, 'Because he thinks like I do. He has the same kind of ideas.' They were both nonconformists, very antisociety. Phil thought society was rotten, and apparently Charles felt the same way."

Charlie began asking people about buying dope, and his new friends became wary of him. With his sudden change in appearance, many of them were suspicious he was a narc. He also had a run-in with a young woman on Main Street. They were kidding around by throwing ice at each other when suddenly Charlie snapped.

"He just flipped out, and he started hitting me," says the young lady. "Then he pushed me really hard into the street in front of a car. The car was moving. It didn't hit me. It swerved out of the way. Then he ran off. After that I didn't hang out with him anymore. He scared me.

"When I met him at first he seemed okay, but he was kind of weird. He tried to act funny, but he wasn't really all that funny. You'd be talking to him, and the next minute he'd just walk away. He'd be nice one time, and the next time he was mean. Sometimes he just didn't want to bother with anybody."

Charlie took four classes that fall—drawing, sculpture, design, and political theory. He had a genuine interest in art. He often sketched little drawings, photocopied them, and handed them out to his friends. He glued a collage of his small drawings together and pasted copies up around campus. One of the drawings on the collage was a nude self-portrait with a knife.

Charlie's drastic change in appearance after the first few classes surprised his classmates and teachers. Most of the instructors and students who got to know him concluded that he was quite odd. He didn't keep up with the class work and didn't seem particularly interested. He seemed preoccupied and often missed class. Claire, a young woman in his drawing class, saw a side of him the other students didn't.

"When I first met him he seemed nice, and I sat next to him in class, but the more I got to know him the stranger he got," she says. "Whenever he would carry on a conversation it would always end the same way. He would either contradict something I said or argue with me or try to make it look like I meant something that had negative connotations. He would just try to turn it around, sort of twist it, just to make me feel badly or make me look bad in his eyes. It made me feel very uncomfortable, and it drew attention to us because sometimes he would raise his voice.

"He didn't like to answer questions about himself. He would get defensive and say, 'Why do you care? Why are you asking so many questions?' And he just shook his head like he was disgusted. He mentioned that he had been institutionalized. That was one thing he was quick to volunteer, but he didn't seem at all ashamed that he had been in an institution. He was bragging or trying to shock me. I didn't know whether to believe him or not. Maybe he was under the impression that he could intimidate me.

"He always seemed to be smiling, so at first he came across as friendly. I noticed that he seemed to be smiling when we would be arguing, so I didn't think the smile was very friendly after I got to know him. It always seemed a bit mocking. I just thought he was a very, very judgmental person. I was a little tentative about going to class because I didn't want to have confrontations with him. I didn't know if he would try to harm me."

Charlie quickly became disillusioned with the art department. He didn't think his instructors knew what they were talking about. He didn't think much of the art students either. They were always chatting and making small talk. Their words were empty, he concluded. They were empty. They hadn't gone to the edge of madness and seen what he'd seen. They didn't know what it was like. They were blind, and they would never make any real art.

He wanted to scream, "Don't lie. Don't pretend. Fuck you. Don't let it go to your head." He wanted to shove all of their conceit and pretension down their throats. One of these days someone would start something with him. It would take just a little spark to ignite it. One of these days someone would set him off, and they would regret it.

chapter 11

- - - - - - - - -

The Greatest Thing You Can Do for Someone

One day Martin Cohen and Val Starcher were returning to their offices from one of the wards. They were walking along a road on the hospital grounds talking about mentally ill adolescents, particularly schizophrenics, and how their parents deal with guilt.

"People have to come to terms with the facts," said Cohen. "They can't blame themselves. They can't wallow in, 'Why me? What did I do wrong?' What if I went around blaming myself for the way Charlie turned out? I'm not about to get into that game, and other people would do well not to get into it either. I've had a lot of problems with Charlie, but I'm not going to tell you it's hereditary. I'm not going to lay that on Ethel."

Cohen was silent for a moment. Starcher had never heard him make such negative comments about Charlie. He had almost always spoken about Charlie with great pride. Cohen then turned to her and asked, "Do you think I'm going to go through the rest of my life blaming myself for the way my son turned out?"

Naomi Wirt recalls another incident that hinted at their estrangement: "Wanamakers was having a sale on sneakers, so one day Martin asked me if I'd take him there on lunch hour. So I took him. He wanted a nice pair of sneakers because he planned to take long walks in the evening with Charlie. He and Charlie liked to do things together, he said. He was looking at sneakers and couldn't decide which brand. I said that I always wore Reeboks, so he bought Reeboks. A couple of months or so after that I asked him how he liked his Reeboks. He just gave me this quizzical look and said, 'I've never had them on.' It made me think that there weren't any walks."

Martin Cohen went through his six-month job review in September with a glowing report. Neil Meisler, Cohen's supervisor, was very happy with his performance.

The major task facing Cohen at the hospital that fall was Medicare certification, which was critical for funding, staff recruiting, and a host of other concerns. During the years following the Roger Re fiasco, the hospital had had trouble keeping up with certification. By the fall of 1988, it had lapsed on all of the hospital units except one, Sussex 1, and there were serious problems on that ward.

Meisler put top priority on certification of the ward. The hospital had been receiving bad press for years, and the constant criticism had crippled staff morale. The hospital needed the certification to begin healing the wounds.

"Marty, you're going to get that unit certified," Meisler said. "We have to pull together the staff on one unit. If we can show that we can get one ward certified—"

"Don't worry," Cohen told him. "I've dealt with these problems before, and we'll get it done."

Cohen met with the staff on Sussex 1 every day. They told him that everything was fine. They were on target. Cohen believed them. That was his style—get people he could trust and give them the support they needed. He wouldn't interfere. If they needed help, he was there to assist.

* * *

Things weren't going well for Charlie. He was having bad thoughts, and he knew they wouldn't soon pass. In fact, he knew they would only get worse. He was afraid everything was going to come crashing down.

On October 8, he called Jonathan in Galesburg and got his answering machine. The machine cut him off before he was able to finish his message, so he called back another three times leaving incoherent, vaguely threatening messages.

On October 9, Charlie phoned his friend Li in Chicago. He had shared an apartment with her at the University of Illinois and had remained friends with her over the years. He called every few months and confided to her. Li had changed since college. She didn't use drugs anymore, she had a job, and she had become very religious.

Charlie told her that he was unhappy and didn't know how much more he could take. He sounded suicidal. Li urged him to go to church and pray to God for strength.

"There is no God," he said indignantly. "I wish I was religious because then I could believe anything anybody told me to believe. It's like what we were taught in school. Be like everybody else. Conform. Don't change. You know what else? I wish I was retarded so I could escape this goddamn living hell, this prison cell of my life. I wish I was old so I could accept my death."

She couldn't stand his despondent ranting, so she got off the phone as soon as she could. There was no point to speaking with him anymore. She couldn't help him.

That same night Charlie decided to get back in touch with Tom. Two and a half years had passed since he'd screwed Tom over an ounce of cocaine, so he couldn't still be pissed off.

Charlie called Tom's parents' house, but Tom no longer lived there. He was going to college in Chicago. Charlie left his phone number. When Tom found out that Charlie had called, he was shocked. He immediately returned the call.

"Tom, look, dude, I'm real sorry about what happened," said Charlie.

"But why did you just run off?" Tom asked. "You didn't have to disappear like that."

Charlie admitted that he had gotten carried away and had gone on a binge. Once he'd realized how much coke he'd gone through, he panicked.

"Charlie, even if you came back to me with eight hundred dollars, we could've made it up on one trip," said Tom.

Charlie again apologized.

"Are you still partying?" Tom asked.

"Not at all. I'm totally clean."

"That's great, man. I don't touch the stuff anymore either."

"I want to repay you. I want to make things straight."

"That sounds fantastic, Charlie. How are you going to do that?

"Why don't you send me another ounce," said Charlie, "and I'll sell it and give you the money I make?"

Tom laughed. "You must be crazy," he said. "How stupid do you think I am? I fell for that once, Charlie, and you're not going to screw me over again."

"C'mon, dude," said Charlie. "I'm not going to screw you over. I said I was sorry about that."

"Charlie, you haven't changed at all. It's time you grew up. Get your life in order, and get off the shit, and call me back in a year. Then we'll talk."

On Tuesday night, October 11, 1988, Martin and Ethel Cohen went to King of Prussia, Pennsylvania, for a mental health conference banquet. Cohen gave the keynote address.

After the banquet he and Ethel met with two old

friends, and they chatted about old times. Martin told them that he and Ethel planned to move back to Galesburg when he retired. One of them asked about Charlie.

"He's starting to come around," Martin answered. "I think he's finally found himself. It takes some kids longer than others." Then he added, "We're going to have to get him a car of his own." Ethel agreed.

In late October Ethel's friend Dorothy from Springfield, Illinois, visited the Cohens for a week.

"Whatever you do, please don't mention his haircut," Ethel said to Dorothy shortly after she arrived. By then Charlie's Mohawk had started to grow in, but it still was a delicate issue around the house. He had taken to wearing a black leather cap much of the time.

The next day Ethel and Dorothy drove to campus to pick up Charlie. While they were waiting for him Ethel said, "Dot, Charlie is not the sweet boy that you remember."

"What's going on?"

"He has changed so much."

Just then Charlie showed up and got in the car. Ethel's demeanor abruptly changed. "Oh, hi, sweetheart," she said. "How was class?"

Ethel and Dorothy didn't talk about Charlie again. He seemed polite but distant and subdued. He spent most of the time in his bedroom and didn't interact with his parents.

"Charlie doesn't have his meals with us," said Ethel. "He's on one of his diets."

Charlie was very interested in his political theory class. The instructor discussed the theories of Marx, Locke, and Machiavelli concerning the individual's struggle against government and society. During the lecture on Marx, Charlie wrote in his notebook that the strong always exploited the weak. During the October 7 class, which focused on John Locke, Charlie noted in large, underlined letters, LIBERTY: FREEDOM TO BE LEFT ALONE.

Charlie wasn't happy with the allowance his parents were giving him. It was just another form of control and humiliation. He harassed his mother into giving him more money occasionally, but still it wasn't enough. Money gave him freedom and independence, and that was the last thing they wanted to give him. He had even taken to stealing cash from them, so they had to hide their money.

Charlie had met Karen in his summer drawing class, and they were taking a sculpture class together that fall. She also lived in Hockessin with her parents, so they occasionally car-pooled to class. Charlie had asked her out during the summer, but she had turned him down because he seemed flirtatious and a little strange.

Karen got to know him better that fall. She noticed that he was always trying to shock people, but the Mohawk, army coat, and combat boots were no big deal to her. She knew the tough-guy look he had suddenly affected wasn't really him. It was just an attention-getting device.

As the semester progressed, she noticed something else about him. He would smirk at her in a strange, eerie way and stare at her. That look wasn't just for attention, she realized. She felt threatened by it, physically and sexually.

One night in October he called her. He invited her to come over and read some of his poetry. She declined, but he read his poetry to her over the phone. Each poem was about despair, hatred, or suicide, and it made her feel very uncomfortable.

When he finished, she told him that she had been depressed, was seeing a counselor, and was on medication for manic-depression. Charlie told her that he had been depressed for years and that he was suicidal.

"Why don't you talk to somebody about it, a psychologist, maybe your father," she said. "Maybe you have a chemical imbalance and need medication. There's nothing wrong with taking medicine for that type of thing."

They talked for a long time, and she tried to be positive about it. "A lot of people get depressed and need help," she said. "It's not that unusual."

She urged him to take the first step, but he was non-committal. When she asked him about it in class a week later, he acted like he didn't want to talk about it. She mentioned it again, but he gave her the look, scaring the hell out of her. She was too afraid to get any more involved.

About ten days after speaking with Tom, Charlie called him again. He asked Tom for the Chicago coke supplier's phone number, so he could contact him directly without involving Tom. Again Tom refused.

"I'll get the money up front," Charlie pleaded.

"I haven't talked to him in two years," said Tom. "I'm totally out of that circle. I'm sorry. It's over."

Charlie started yelling at Tom.

"Goodbye," said Tom as he hung up the phone. "Have a nice life."

One night a group of employees from the hospital, including Ethel, got together to meet with a psychic. Martin decided to stay home. Ethel was working part-time as an occupational therapist at Delaware State Hospital. They all went out to dinner, had a few drinks, and took turns meeting privately with the psychic. When they were through, they talked about what the psychic had told them. Ethel seemed visibly shaken, though, and wouldn't talk about her reading.

The psychic told one of the others that he couldn't read Ethel's future. "I could get nothing where she was concerned," he said. The psychic also told the group that

there would be a sudden change in the administration
in the next few months. They thought he was referring to
the presidential administration.

Charlie's political theory class on October 26 was devoted to Machiavelli. Charlie wrote in his notebook, "as
long as it works (violence and destruction) ... the ends
justify the means." On October 31 he noted, "Use evil
means when absolutely necessary ... violence is always
justified in the final analysis." He also wrote the word AN-
ARCHISM in large letters in his notebook. For the defini-
tion of "authority" he wrote, "to create order—to protect
people—to make people fear."

Charlie and the band were supposed to play their first
gig at a Halloween party in Newark on Friday, October 28. They practiced almost every night during the
week before the gig. Charlie painted the letters 'S.D.I.' on
the back of his army coat.

The mood at the party between the skinheads and the
punk rockers was tense, and several fights broke out.
Mark was attacked by a couple of skinheads who thought
he was gay because of his jewelry and painted fingernails. Someone pulled out a gun, and several skinheads
menacingly waved baseball bats. Charlie dropped a lit
cigarette in a trash can, which caught on fire and smoked
out the room. Because of the chaos, the band didn't get a
chance to play.

The next day Charlie drove to New York City. He
needed a release from the despair, loneliness, and hatred.
A life had to be sacrificed to avenge the pain he had suffered. Killing someone would bring some balance back to
his world. It was the only solution.

He parked near Central Park and hiked though the park
looking for a secluded trail. He found what looked like a
suitable spot and hid in some bushes. He planned to jump
out, rip the life from someone with his knife, and flee. He

was shivering with excitement. His nervous system was overdosing on adrenaline. He craved the raw power of destroying a human life.

He waited a long time. A few people strolled by in couples, but no one came by alone. After several hours he gave up and went home. He knew the urge to kill wouldn't just go away. If he couldn't kill a stranger, he would kill someone he knew.

Charlie scheduled a band practice for the week following the aborted Halloween Party gig, but no one showed up. Phil and Dan had missed several practices. Mike, the new guitarist, showed up about half the time. Mark was the only other band member who showed up regularly, but he was out of town. Charlie was frustrated. The band wasn't making progress. He noticed that someone had damaged one of the drum heads. That was the final straw. He packed up the equipment and took it home.

Darlene, who had run away from home, was staying in Mark's room for a few days while he was gone. One evening Charlie came over to hang out with Darlene. While he was there he decided to redecorate one of the walls in Mark's room, which was covered with posters of rock bands. Charlie tore down all of the posters. He told Darlene that he wanted to use the wall to display his own artwork.

When Mark came home and saw what had been done to his room, he was furious. He confronted Charlie about it. "Darlene told me she loved me," Charlie said, "so I had to destroy something."

That didn't make any sense to Mark. "Look, Charles, until you figure out why you did that," he said, "I don't want to have anything to do with you."

The Medicare certification survey of Sussex 1 was completed on October 26 and 27. On Monday, October 31,

Martin Cohen and his staff were informed that the ward had not been approved for certification. They had 90 days to correct a list of problems, but no one on the unit was confident they could do it.

Cohen was totally unprepared for the setback. He had trusted the unit team too much and faulted himself for not having checked things firsthand. He had been naive about the problems at the hospital.

Things only got worse when a patient, Henry Posner, left the hospital without authorization and did not return. Posner hadn't been violent since 1981 when he had killed his father, but the police were searching for him. The story got front-page coverage in the local paper. The hospital was getting more bad press, the last thing it needed.

At 4:00 on Friday afternoon, November 4, Neil Meisler called the hospital's management team together for a meeting. Meisler calmly told them that he would not accept the loss of certification and that he was holding every one of them personally responsible. If they couldn't put a satisfactory plan in place within a short period of time, they would not be in their positions any longer. Then Meisler got up and walked out.

The department managers were shocked and offended. Cohen was perhaps the most shocked. Meisler hadn't given him any warning about the threat, which applied to his job as well. Everyone silently filed out of the meeting room. Martin Cohen stayed behind and stared out a window.

That night Meisler called Cohen at home. Meisler wanted him to come in the next morning, Saturday, and start on a new plan for the ward. Cohen was so upset, he didn't want to speak with him.

"How could you do that?" he asked Meisler. "You embarrassed me in front of the staff."

"Don't worry about that, Marty," said Meisler. "You

and I should sit down tomorrow and plan how we're going to correct this thing."

"I can't," Cohen said. "I just can't do it."

Darlene, age sixteen, was studying cosmetology at a vo-tech school, and she hung out on Main Street in Newark with the other punk rockers. She had met Charlie on several occasions through Mark and Paul. She knew Charlie was interested in her, but she wasn't sure about him. He seemed strange. Once she, Paul, and Charlie were hanging out in Dougherty Hall, a snack bar and lounge on campus. She and Paul left to go meet someone. They said they'd be back in half an hour. Charlie agreed to wait for them. They didn't get back to Dougherty Hall for almost five hours, but Charlie was exactly where they had left him, sitting in the same chair in the same position.

He once told her, "When they drop the bomb it will be forty minutes of complete anarchy. People will be running around raping and killing one another." He said it as if he were looking forward to it. She didn't know how to take him.

Charlie called a band practice at his house for Sunday night, November 6. Charlie had asked Paul to take Phil's place as lead singer. Mike, the guitarist, showed up for practice, as did Darlene, to watch. Mark wouldn't come to practice because he was still mad at Charlie about his posters.

After practice Darlene and Paul decided to hang out and watch a movie with Charlie. They watched *Blue Velvet,* which Charlie had rented several times. It was one of his favorite movies. The strange violence and bleakness of the movie excited him. Charlie particularly liked Frank, the violent, twisted character played by Dennis Hopper.

Blue Velvet opens with several shots of an all-American

town, with robins fluttering about and people working on their perfect lawns. "They're probably starting with this real hokey beginning to show you that everything isn't really nice. Underneath everything is really fucked up," said Paul.

"Exactly," said Charlie.

Afterward they went upstairs to Charlie's bedroom. He showed them his knife. It was a folding knife with a wooden handle and a four-inch blade. He began playing with it, throwing it in the air and catching it. He ran it across his neck as if he were cutting his throat. He swung it around and struck poses like a ninja warrior. They laughed, but he was making them nervous.

He told them about the psychopath who had escaped from Delaware State Hospital. He said that his parents were worried that he might come to the house and attack them. Paul and Darlene noticed that Charlie was subdued when he was with a group of people, but when he was alone with them he got really weird.

As usual, he steered the conversation to death. He talked about killing himself as if it were some kind of a power trip. "Sometimes I just want to end it all," he said. "I wonder what it would be like to die."

"Why are you always talking about suicide?" Darlene asked. "That's stupid. If you can get through life you can do anything you want."

"Death is better than life," he said. "Death is best."

Charlie added that he wouldn't kill anyone because that would be showing them mercy. "The greatest thing you can do for someone is kill them," he said. "Why don't you make them live in this world and be miserable."

Soon Charlie was humping up and down on the bed, moaning as if he were having sex with someone. He pulled out his penis and pretended he was masturbating.

"You are so perverted," said Paul.

"But I'm not queer," he said. "I hate homos."

Charlie gave Paul a ride home, and Darlene came along. During the ride Charlie bragged about his cocaine dealing experiences.

"I've got connections in Illinois," he said. "I can get an ounce of coke fronted to me. It's a cinch to get rid of, and you make good money. You want to go in on it with me? We'll split the profits on whatever you sell." Paul and Darlene weren't so sure they wanted to get involved.

Darlene didn't have anywhere to go, so Charlie told her she could stay at his place. On the ride back to Hockessin he said that he wanted to get the skinhead who had beat up Mark. "Do you know where I could get a gun?" he asked. "One with a silencer on it."

"Oh, sure," she said, "like people are always offering to sell me guns."

When they got back to the house they went up to his room and lay down on the floor and began making out. After a while he looked at her and said, "Why are you being so nice to me?"

"I'm just being friendly."

"You're not supposed to be nice. That shows weakness. You're supposed to be strong and mean."

"I don't believe that."

"I'll tell you something about myself, if you can keep this quiet."

"Okay."

"I have an idea I'm going to get in trouble with the law," he said. "I'm going to end up in jail."

"How do you know?"

"I've just got a feeling."

They went back to making out. He shoved his hands under her shirt. She pushed his hands away. He tried to unzip her jeans, but she pushed his hands away again. He kept getting rougher and more insistent. He was on top of her, grinding his pelvis into hers. She wanted him to stop, but he wouldn't.

He moved his hands up to her neck and squeezed. She started gasping. She didn't know what he was doing. She kept thinking that he would stop. She finally pushed his hands away.

"Don't you think that's a little rough, you bastard?" she said and stomped out of the room. She went outside and paced in the parking lot, crying. She had expected him to follow her, but he hadn't. She wiped her eyes and her nose on her T-shirt. It was a cold night. She didn't know what to do. The only way she could get back to Newark would be to hitchhike, but there was very little traffic that late. Even if she made it to Newark, she didn't have any place to go.

She finally went back inside. He was awake, but he didn't say anything. She slept on the couch in the loft. He gave her a ride into Newark the next morning.

During the next week Charlie bragged to Mark, Paul, and several others that he'd made it with Darlene. She told them that he had tried to rape her. She saw Charlie from a distance on Main Street several times that week, and she was sure he was following her.

On Monday night, November 7, Charlie ran into a young woman from school at a coffee shop on campus. Her name was Marie. He knew her from the art department.

He usually had his Mohawk combed down under a cap, but that night he was wearing it up. He was dressed in black with a large silver pendant of a dragon on a chain around his neck.

"Hi," she said.

"Oh, wow, I didn't think you'd recognize me," he said. "I'm in disguise today."

"Well, it's not a very good disguise."

"Obviously not," he said dejectedly.

They chatted for a little while. She said she liked the dragon.

"In China only royalty get to wear dragons," he said.

"I guess that doesn't hold anymore since there is no more royalty in China."

He seemed confused and disappointed by the comment. After a few more minutes of conversation, she left and walked home to her apartment. About half an hour later she heard a knock at the door. It was Charlie.

"I know I've only just met you, but you seem pretty cool, and I think I can trust you," he said. "If it's not too much bother, can I come in and talk?"

She was somewhat wary of him. It was late, she was alone, and she didn't know him that well, but she let him in anyway. They sat in the living room on the floor. She turned on all the lights so she would feel safer.

He told her that his best friend, who had been in his band in Illinois, had committed suicide. He didn't know why. His friend had seemed happy and well-adjusted. He was very intelligent and had a lot going for him. They had been best friends for a long time, he said, and they had done lots of outrageous things together.

"That person was a part of my life, and now he's gone," he said. "I feel I should be upset, but I can't bring myself to feel any emotion."

"You're going through a tough time," she said. "It's hard to know what to feel."

"I want to go out and do something radical or destructive in honor of my friend."

"Why don't you go to the funeral if you feel you should do something?"

"I really don't have the money to go to Illinois right now. I just don't feel as bad as I should."

"That's to be expected," she said. "Sometimes when people's parents die, they don't think they're sad enough, and they get freaked out and end up seeing a psychiatrist about it."

"That's just parents," he said indignantly. "This is my best friend who was always going to be there for me, and that's more important."

She didn't agree, but there was so much urgency and conviction in his voice that she didn't challenge him. Although they were approximately the same age, she felt as though she were speaking to someone much younger. He seemed like an adolescent who hadn't grown out of an aggressive stage.

Before he left, he said he felt alone in Delaware. As much as he didn't like Illinois, he wished he were back there.

On Wednesday evening, November 9, Charlie managed to score a half gram of cocaine. He went to the house on South College Avenue to hang out with Phil. They sat down in Phil's bedroom and did some lines.

"I haven't done coke for 2½ years," said Charlie. "It's the only drug that gets me off."

Phil asked him where he had gotten the money for the coke. Charlie told him that his grandfather had died and left him a lot of money.

They did several more lines, and Charlie became increasingly depressed. He said that nothing was going well for him. He hated school, living with his parents was fucked up, and he was sick of girls. He said he thought about quitting school and going back to Illinois, but that was a bogus scene, too. He told Phil he had gone to Texas once when things weren't going well for hm, but he wasn't sure what he would do this time. He just didn't think he could deal with it anymore. He wasn't sure he wanted to go on living.

As the coke was running low Charlie got desperate for

more. It was close to midnight, and Phil didn't know where he could get any.

"You got to hook me up," said Charlie.

"I would if I could," said Phil.

"You got to make this last effort for me. You might not see me again."

"Come on, man. Don't say that. Snap out of it."

Charlie asked the other people in the house if they could help him get some coke, but nobody had any or knew where to get it. "Can't you think of somebody you bought some off of?" he asked several people. He was speaking very fast and starting to annoy people. No one in the house had ever seen him use coke before, and suddenly he was acting like an addict.

Phil had to work the next morning, so he went to bed, leaving Charlie alone in the living room with his roommate Keith. Keith had seen Charlie around the house with Phil, but he didn't know him very well. Keith could see that Charlie was very high. It was late, but Keith was willing to talk with Charlie until he came down enough to drive home. They listened to a few records and talked about Charlie's band.

Charlie still wanted more coke, and he convinced Keith to go with him to the apartment where he had bought the half gram earlier that evening. Charlie drove. It was a short drive, but Charlie drifted into the wrong lane several times, and Keith had to shout to keep him from passing out at the wheel. When they got to the apartment complex, Charlie admitted that he didn't know the apartment number. Keith was annoyed and regretted leaving the house with him.

Charlie was eventually able to locate the dealer's apartment. Once in the apartment, however, he admitted that he didn't have any money. He wanted to pay by check. The dealer refused to accept a check, so Keith and Charlie went back to the house on South College Avenue.

It was 3 A.M., and Keith went to bed, but Charlie still wouldn't leave. He stood in the hallway knocking on Phil's bedroom door, trying to wake him up. A different roommate woke up instead and told Charlie to go home, which he did.

Employees at Delaware State Hospital had Friday, November 11, 1988, off for Veteran's Day. On Thursday, Martin Cohen was presented with a memo from several department heads formally protesting Neil Meisler's treatment of them the previous week. They argued that Meisler's threat to fire them was unfair. They were doing all they could in a very difficult environment, and they felt unappreciated. Everyone was blaming one another, and Martin Cohen was in the middle. He hadn't realized how deep the problems were.

On Saturday, November 12, he sat around the house reading the newspaper and watching television, trying to forget about the situation at the hospital. Ethel went grocery shopping. She also ordered some Christmas presents for a few old friends. It was a leisurely Saturday.

Charlie spent most of the day in his room. He had made a promise to himself, and he intended to keep it. The time had come. Justice would be his. He visualized it over and over. He was so close. He could feel it in his blood. His heart was pounding with pain and fear, but the pain made him strong and the fear set him free.

The world was in chaos, and he was slowly being destroyed by it. There was no love or trust, only lies and betrayal. It was always the same. Nothing ever changed. Words meant nothing, absolutely nothing. His parents were symbols of that world, and he would strike back at it. Anarchy was the only answer.

There was no hope for them. They couldn't change. From the day he was born they had lied to him. His parents didn't love him. They were frauds. They were slowly killing him, especially his father, using intimidation to control him. They had made him feel worthless, and he would show them what it felt like. He would avenge the pain, rejection, and humiliation. They were evil, and he would bring them down. Violence was justified. Evil means were necessary. They had shattered his world, and now he would shatter theirs.

He thought about poisoning them, but that was cowardly. He would do it courageously, with his own two hands. He would be relentless, unyielding, and merciless. He would feel the raw power as their lives slipped away.

He had worked out all the details. It wouldn't take long. He had everything ready, right where he needed it. He knew *exactly* what he would say and how they would respond. It was over for them, over. He would string them along like puppets in a play of his contriving.

He went to the loft and looked down into the living room. His father was watching television. He could hear his mother in the kitchen. So close now. Fear and pain. They'd never know what hit them. Merciless. No hope for them. Evil means. Anarchy. Nothing ever changed. He called out to his father.

part III

Love and Madness

chapter 1

- - - - - - - -

In Jesus' Name

On Thursday, May 24, 1990, Charles Cohen was taken to
the Jefferson County Courthouse in Gretna, Louisiana, a
suburb of New Orleans, to be arraigned on charges of
simple battery and attempted simple robbery. He was
shackled to six other prisoners at the foot and wrist and
led into the courtroom of 24th District Court Judge Er-
nest V. Richards IV. Richards's courtroom was at the end
of the courthouse, overlooking the Mississippi River.

Richards was presiding over the "call of the court cal-
endar." His court had started at nine and had gone
through numerous arraignments. Those who hadn't made
bail, like Cohen, were transported to court from the
prison in sheriff's vans.

Cohen and the other inmates, dressed in orange overalls, were ushered to seats in the jury box. Charlie was at
the end of the group and seated nearest the judge. He was
clean-shaven, and his hair was neatly cut and trimmed. He
looked more like a college student than a prison inmate.

Scott Brannon was in the courtroom. He was prepared
to testify on behalf of who he thought was James

McDowell, if necessary. He was sitting in the front row of the courtroom.

When Cohen saw Scott in the courtroom, he said softly, "I'm sorry."

"What for?" Scott asked. "You're going to get out of here. Just shut up."

Cohen kept whispering, "I'm sorry. I'm sorry."

At ten the clerk called the name James McDowell. He stood. He had enough loose chain to stand without disturbing the inmate next to him.

"Do you have a lawyer, Mr. McDowell?" the judge asked.

"No, I don't," he said.

"He has two records," said the clerk.

A representative from the Indigent Defender's Bureau, Lawrence Biri, Jr., was present to represent him. Biri didn't know much about the case and hadn't spoken with him before. He introduced himself to Cohen, quietly explained the procedure, and told him to plead "not guilty" when asked. As Biri turned away, Cohen started talking.

"With all due respect, your honor, ladies and gentlemen of the court, I'd like to make a confession—"

Biri interrupted him. "Your honor, at this time I would advise the defendant not to make any statements. I don't know what he's about to say."

Biri turned to Cohen and said, "Sit down, man!"

But Charlie continued. "Your honor, I—"

"Sit. Sit down," Biri repeated.

"No, sir. Excuse me, I'd like to make—"

"He's been advised, your honor," said Biri.

"All right, Mr. McDowell," said Judge Richards. "I want to tell you that anything you say can be used against you in a criminal prosecution. Your lawyer has given you good advice, but if you want to make a statement you can do so."

"I realize that, sir," said Cohen. "Uh, I'm guilty of the

charge here today and not the least, not the least of which, uh, three, three murders. I'm—my name—my real name is not James McDowell. My real name is Charles Cohen, and I'm one of America's most wanted criminals. I make this confession in Jesus' name."

Everyone in the courtroom stared at him. No one said anything or moved except the short, thin inmate to his left, who looked at him with huge eyes and leaned away from him.

Brannon thought the confession was a bad joke. He'd worked very hard to get him out, and now he had pulled this stunt. What was he trying to do, get attention? If he wasn't careful, he was going to get himself in even bigger trouble.

Charlie felt dizzy. It was a catastrophic moment. He hadn't anticipated so much objection to his confession. He had thought they would believe him and do something about it, but they weren't doing anything. They were just staring at him like he was nuts or high on something.

"I'm going to order that a plea of not guilty be entered on behalf of the defendant," Judge Richards said. "I grant this attorney fifteen days to file special pleadings. I set his trial date for September the tenth. Mr. McDowell, are you able to afford to hire a lawyer to represent you?"

He didn't answer.

"How long have you been in jail?" the judge asked.

"Uh, since April second, something like that."

"I'm going to appoint the IDB to represent you in connection with this charge."

He sat down and the court proceeded with other arraignments.

Martha Duley, Judge Richards's court reporter, had never heard anything so bizarre in her fourteen years of work at the courthouse. People just didn't stand up in open court and confess to murder. She couldn't wait to

call *America's Most Wanted*, but the other court officers
and clerks told her the guy was just crazy and not to
waste her time.

"I don't care," Duley said. "I'm calling anyway." She
was too excited not to at least check. Maybe there was
some reward money.

When Richards's court broke for lunch, she got *America's Most Wanted*'s phone number from one of the secretaries in the building who knew the number from
watching the show. She called and asked, "You all looking for a Charles Cohen?"

"Just a minute," a man said. "I'll check."

She was put on hold. The man from *America's Most
Wanted* got back on the line soon and said, "We sure are."

"I know where he is," she said.

She told him what had happened. He asked for a description of the person. Duley described him, and he put
her on hold again. When he came back on the line, he
asked her to describe him again, and she did.

"We don't know if it's him or not," he said, "so please
don't tell anyone until we confirm it one way or the
other."

Cohen sat in court until the arraignments for the other
inmates were completed. Like Duley, Biri couldn't believe what he had just heard. The guy was up on minor
charges, so he probably would've been released when his
trial came up. As Cohen and the other inmates were being
escorted from the courtroom, Biri urged him not to say
anything to the police until someone from the IDB met
with him.

While the court was taking lunch break, Judge Richards called the Indigent Defender's Bureau and suggested
that someone speak with James McDowell as soon as
possible. All of the IDB's other lawyers were out of the

office, so Richard Tompson, head of the IDB, went over
to the Jefferson Parish Correctional Center to see him.

Tompson didn't know all of the details of the guy's
statement, just that he had stood up and confessed to murder. Tompson wanted to see him before the police got to
him. He knew he had some time while the police attempted to verify his claim—at least a couple of hours, if
not a couple of days. The police probably weren't taking
his confession very seriously at this point. Tompson
didn't know whether to take it seriously himself. Once he
got the straight story from him, he could give him some
sound legal advice.

The first thing he had to do was shut him up. Some defendants had a natural urge to incriminate themselves.
Tompson got to the prison at about 1:20 and met with Cohen in a holding cell.

Lieutenant Walter Amstutz, age 38, sat in his office
at the Jefferson Parish Correctional Center. He was a
fifteen-year veteran of the Jefferson Parish Sheriff's Office, but he didn't have much to show for it. As far as he
was concerned, being Commander of Intake Booking at
the prison was one of the worst positions in the sheriff's
office. He'd been transferred from platoon commander to
the prison two months ago. It was a demeaning transfer,
an obvious demotion. The prison was a miserable place to
work. It was hot, and he had to break up fights every hour
or so.

Amstutz had spent fifteen years doing real police work.
At one time he'd supervised twenty officers. He'd occasionally gone undercover. He'd been the department's
hostage negotiator for four years and had saved numerous
people in crisis situations. In fact, he was one of the most
decorated officers in Jefferson Parish history, with a total
of nine medals from the sheriff's office and several commendations from community organizations.

He knew why he had been exiled to the jail—politics. His father-in-law, Jerry Chatelain, had run against the incumbent sheriff of Jefferson Parish, Harry Lee, and lost in 1987. Amstutz wasn't interested in politics, and he hadn't supported either campaign. He wouldn't hang up signs for Lee's reelection or buy tickets to Lee's fundraisers. Lee claimed that Amstutz had been transferred to the prison because he had a skin condition that prevented him from firing the department's new automatic handguns. Amstutz knew that was a crock. He had a skin condition, but he could've easily continued using the old service revolver. Lee just wanted to punish him.

Amstutz had seen the writing on the wall several years ago. His days in the department were numbered. All the plaques, commendations, and medals meant diddly, so he'd started taking law classes in the evenings at Loyola. In another year or so he'd be a lawyer, but every day in the prison was hell. He desperately missed real police work.

At noon Amstutz got a call from the warden's secretary. She had a guy from *America's Most Wanted* on the line. He was calling about an inmate who had apparently made a confession in court that morning. She didn't know what the guy was talking about and asked Amstutz to handle it. Amstutz told her to put him through.

The caller from *America's Most Wanted*, Anthony Batson, told him he'd called several people within the sheriff's office, but no one had been able to help him. They didn't know what was going on. Amstutz was his last resort.

"What can I do for you, Mr. Batson?" Amstutz asked.

"First of all," said Batson, "do you have an inmate by the name of James McDowell in your custody?"

"I'd have to check," said Amstutz. "Could you give me a few more details about what's going on."

Batson told him that an inmate at Jefferson Parish Correctional Center allegedly had confessed in open court to being Charles Cohen, a fugitive wanted in Delaware for the murder of his parents. Cohen had been profiled on *America's Most Wanted* over a year ago. Batson said the suspect was jailed under the name James McDowell and was being held on battery and theft charges.

Amstutz checked the jail sheet and the court docket. James McDowell was on both. He was an inmate in the prison and had been in court that morning. Batson gave him a phone number for the New Castle County Police in Delaware, and Amstutz said he'd look into it.

Amstutz pulled McDowell's file and read through it. It contained mug shots, prints, and an arrest report from April 2. He called the New Castle County Police in Delaware and spoke to Detective Allen Ruth. Amstutz told him about the courtroom confession. Ruth verified that Charles Cohen was wanted in Delaware for murdering his parents, but he was skeptical about the confession. They'd gotten hundreds of false leads on Cohen over the past eighteen months. Ruth gave him some information about Cohen, and Amstutz said he'd call back if things looked promising.

Amstutz compared the physical description of Cohen from the Delaware police with the physical description of McDowell from the Metairie arrest report. They both had brown hair, blue eyes, and were five foot ten inches tall. Cohen weighed 165 lbs., and McDowell weighed 160 lbs. That was interesting.

Amstutz then checked the Social Security numbers and the dates of birth. He wrote them down on a piece of paper to compare them.

McDowell's date of birth: 1/14/64
Cohens date of birth: 12/6/64

McDowell's Social Security number: 531-09-7394
Cohen's Social Security number: 349-50-0194

They were similar, especially the Social Security number. It was almost as if someone had switched some of the numbers around to disguise them.

Amstutz called Ruth back. "We could very well have something here," he said. "Could you fax me some pictures?"

Ruth faxed him a picture of Cohen from his University of Delaware student ID. Amstutz got the photo at 1:30 P.M. He compared it to the mug shot of James McDowell taken on April 2, and he couldn't believe what he saw. The hair on the mug shot was a little longer, but the beard, the tilt of the head, the smile, and the eyes were identical. He had never seen a closer match. Amstutz was getting excited. This was the first interesting case he'd worked on in months.

He called Ruth again. "This is him," he said. "There's not a doubt in my mind that this is the guy."

Ruth faxed a copy of Cohen's fingerprints to Amstutz, who got a Jefferson Parish print expert to compare the faxed prints with McDowell's. The print expert felt reasonably certain that the prints matched, but because of the poor quality of the faxed prints he couldn't be positive.

John Downs had been in court all day testifying in a different murder case. Ruth called the courthouse and got Downs on the phone. Ruth told him what was going on. Downs thought it sounded promising, but he tried not to get too excited. He told Ruth he'd call him back from court the next chance he got.

Ruth called Amstutz and suggested that he speak with McDowell. Maybe he could get some information out of him that would clear things up. Amstutz decided to give it a try. Before he went any further, Amstutz called his boss, Chief Louis Vedros, the prison warden. He didn't want to call Vedros because he knew what the warden would say, but he knew he'd better if he cared about his job. He told Vedros what had transpired. It was 2:30 P.M.

"Drop what you're doing," Vedros said. "Don't handle it. Call homicide." Amstutz was disgusted. They wouldn't let him handle a good case. Politics was biting him on the ass again.

Amstutz called the detective bureau, and they sent two homicide officers to the prison. When they arrived, Amstutz showed them the faxes and explained what was going on. The three of them decided to speak with whoever he was, McDowell or Cohen. They went upstairs to the holding cell where he was meeting with Tompson.

Cohen and Tompson had been talking for over two hours. Charlie told him about the murders and his eighteen months on the run. He wept several times as he told the story and seemed very confused to Tompson.

Tompson told him not to speak with anyone but him. "If you open your mouth and tell the police anything," Tompson said, "I will personally come back here and cut out your goddamn tongue. If you want to confess to anything, we'll get you a minister. Just keep your mouth shut until you get a lawyer in Delaware, or you'll regret it."

When Amstutz and the two homicide detectives got to the holding cell, they were met at the door by Tompson. "How can I help you, gentlemen?" he asked.

"We'd like to ask Mr. McDowell a few questions," said Amstutz.

"I've advised my client not to speak with the police," Tompson said. "Mr. McDowell has nothing to say."

"Okay, but would your client be willing to provide additional information, so we can fill out the arrest report correctly? He gave one name in April and a different one today."

"I'm telling you, don't ask my client any questions. It's his constitutional right not to speak with you."

The homicide detectives and Amstutz went back to Amstutz's office. "Walt, it doesn't look like there's much to do here but write up a report, and we'll leave that to

you." With that the detectives left, but Amstutz didn't
mind writing a report. The case was finally his.

Ruth called and asked Amstutz to fax McDowell's
prints to Delaware. Amstutz faxed the prints, and Ruth
called back a little while later. They had a positive ID.
The New Castle County Police fingerprint expert had
compared McDowell's prints to Cohen's and was certain
they were the same.

"We're sending you our warrant," said Ruth. "Book
him for murder."

Amstutz had Cohen brought to the booking area. By
then several other attorneys had approached Cohen. One
had suggested an insanity plea, but Charlie didn't like
that idea. He was insulted that anyone would suggest that
he was mentally ill.

Amstutz instructed all of the booking officers not to
ask the defendant any questions. He didn't want anyone
initiating a conversation that a tricky lawyer could use to
argue that his Miranda rights had been violated. A seemingly innocent conversation could screw up an entire
case.

Amstutz went to see Cohen at four. Before he could
say anything, Cohen said, "You know you can't question
me. My lawyer has advised me not to answer any questions."

"Mr. McDowell, I don't intend to question you," said
Amstutz. "This is strictly a booking formality. We're going to take your fingerprints and your mug shot. At this
time I have reason to believe you are Charles Cohen, a
fugitive from Delaware. Therefore, I'm booking you
under the NCIC warrants on two counts of first-degree
murder and two counts of possession of a dangerous
weapon during the commission of a felony."

Charlie said he understood. After he was fingerprinted,
the booking officer handed him a pen and asked him to

sign the fingerprint cards in the space designated. He signed each card Charles *Mark* Cohen.

Amstutz was shocked. Not only had he admitted that he was Cohen with the signature, but he had used a middle name. Amstutz ran to a computer terminal and pulled up the NCIC record for Charles Cohen. There it was on the screen. Charles *Mark* Cohen. No one had told him Cohen's middle name. Finally, he had the verification he'd been looking for all day. The mystery man had told the truth in court. He wasn't James McDowell. He was Charles Cohen, and he was wanted for the murders of his parents. Amstutz had been a police officer for fifteen years, but nothing this unusual had ever panned out.

Amstutz called Delaware and spoke to John Downs. He told him about the middle name, and Downs was elated. "We'll be on the first flight out of here," said Downs.

chapter 2

- - - - - - - -

He Made Me Laugh

Assistant State Prosecutor Steve Walther was at home in Hockessin mowing his lawn on Thursday afternoon, May 24, 1990, when he got a call from his boss, Attorney General Charlie Oberly.

"Steve, Cohen popped up in a courtroom in New Orleans," said Oberly. "I want you to fly down there and take care of things."

Ninety minutes later Walther was on a plane with John Downs and Allen Ruth headed for New Orleans. Walther would handle the legal proceedings in New Orleans, such as the extradition. Downs and Ruth would investigate Cohen's activities in New Orleans and escort him back to Delaware.

They were 99 percent sure that Cohen was McDowell, but they still had a nagging feeling that it could be a screw-up. No one had compared two good sets of prints, and they wouldn't know for sure until then.

Amstutz met Downs, Ruth, and Walther at New Orleans International Airport at 10:45 P.M. He gave them a ride to a hotel near the courthouse, where they went over the case details. Amstutz showed them McDowell's mug shot. Downs, Ruth, and Walther were getting giddy. It sure looked like Cohen.

Downs had a set of Cohen's fingerprints with him, and Amstutz had a set of McDowell's. Downs compared them. He wasn't a fingerprint expert, but he had seen enough prints in the past eight years to recognize matches. The two sets were the same. His last doubt was gone. After eighteen long months they finally had him.

"It's him," he exclaimed. "It's him."

The four middle-aged men jumped about the hotel room, slapping high-fives and whooping and hollering.

Amstutz picked up Downs, Ruth, and Walther early the next morning and took them to the Jefferson Parish Correctional Center. A fingerprint expert from the sheriff's office compared the two sets of prints and confirmed the match.

A public information officer from the sheriff's office came by Amstutz's office and congratulated the four of them on behalf of the sheriff. Amstutz knew something was wrong. The guy was being too nice. He was blowing smoke.

"We want you all to be there when we move the guy," he said. "We'll get TV cameras, newspaper photographers, and we'll have you all in the pictures with Sheriff Lee and our boy Cohen."

Downs, Ruth, and Walther cringed. They didn't want any publicity. They wanted to get Cohen back to Delaware as quickly and as quietly as possible.

Cohen's vague declaration that he had killed three people prompted investigations in New Orleans and Jefferson Parish. If two of the victims were his parents, who was the third? The New Orleans and Jefferson Parish authorities didn't want to let him go until they were relatively certain that he hadn't been involved in any murders in the area. They compared his prints with unidentified prints obtained from the scenes of several unsolved murders in the area. Downs wondered if Cohen thought he'd hit and killed the parking lot attendant when he'd absconded with his parents' LTD from the Los Angeles impound lot.

Tompson pointed out to the media that Cohen hadn't specifically mentioned any names in his courtroom statement. Technically, therefore, he hadn't confessed to murdering his parents, the only murders with which he was charged.

Walther immediately began extradition proceedings. He didn't want the case tied up in the Jefferson Parish courts. By midmorning the police departments in New Orleans and Jefferson Parish hadn't been able to tie Cohen to any local murders, so the Jefferson Parish district attorney decided to release him. An extradition hearing was scheduled for that morning.

Amstutz took Downs, Ruth and Walther to the courthouse at ten. Tompson didn't know that the Jefferson Parish authorities would schedule an extradition hearing so quickly. He hadn't even come into work that Friday. Someone from his office called him about the hastily scheduled hearing, and he rushed to the courthouse.

Cohen had already been brought over from the prison, and he was sitting handcuffed on a bench in the hallway. Tompson spoke with him briefly and advised him to waive extradition. "Under the circumstances," he told him, "by not waiving you're just delaying the inevitable."

At ten-thirty that morning Charles Cohen appeared in 24th District Court and waived his rights to an extradition hearing. The theft and assault charges were dropped in deference to the Delaware murder charges.

Downs, Ruth, and Walther were delighted. They'd assumed they wouldn't get Cohen out of New Orleans until Monday. They had a few things to look into before leaving, but they could finish up that afternoon, leave the next day, and spend Memorial Day with their families. Before Walther left the courthouse, he asked Tompson for permission to interview Cohen, but Tompson told him his client would not speak with the police.

Amstutz got a phone call at the courthouse during the extradition hearing. It was Sheriff Lee, and he was furious. He started shouting at Amstutz so loud and so fast that Amstutz couldn't understand a thing he said, but he knew why he was mad. A booking cop from the prison and the son-in-law of his chief political rival had resolved the Cohen case, which was generating a lot of publicity, and the sheriff's boys hadn't.

"Nobody in the prison can make a case like this," the sheriff shouted.

"Sheriff, I beg to differ with you. I'm certainly qualified to make any kind of case, especially one like this."

"You're not a homicide detective, and this is a homicide case. I don't want somebody in the jail handling a homicide."

"Sheriff, this is not a homicide. This is a warrant. Homicide had been contacted, and they told me to handle it."

The sheriff started ranting and raving into the phone again. The only words Amstutz could make out were, "Somebody in homicide is going to pay for this."

The lambasting continued unabated until Amstutz managed to interject, "Look, Sheriff, I think I saved your behind on this. If I hadn't made the case, this guy might've been cut loose. Then what would've happened?"

The sheriff responded with more yelling.

"Then I made you look good again by picking up these Delaware people at the airport," said Amstutz. This last comment sent the sheriff into orbit. He was yelling so loud Amstutz thought he might have a heart attack.

"What right did you have to pick up those people at the airport?" the sheriff bellowed.

"Sheriff, nobody else made any plans to pick those folks up, so I did."

"You work in the prison, and you're to stay there until I tell you otherwise."

"Sheriff, I was off duty and I chose to go to the airport to pick them up."

At that point the sheriff hung up. Amstutz knew right then that his career as a police officer was coming to an end. He'd never get transferred out of the prison. He'd be lucky if he wasn't busted down to the typing pool.

Downs, Ruth, and Walther met with the sheriff after lunch. The sheriff was cordial, but he clearly wanted to blame Amstutz for some imagined screw-up. Amstutz volunteered to help Downs, Ruth, and Walther that afternoon, but Sheriff Lee assigned two detectives from homicide, Maggie Pernia and Les Jones, to assist the Delaware authorities during the remainder of their stay. Amstutz returned to the prison.

Downs, Ruth, Walther, and the two Jefferson Parish detectives went to find Charles Cohen's New Orleans hideout. Cohen had given 2127 Carondelet as his address when he was arrested on April 2, so that was their first stop. They learned that Cohen had lived in Apartment 5 with Greg Fitch, but he wasn't there.

Fitch had spent the previous evening at his girlfriend's apartment and hadn't watched the TV news or read a newspaper in over a day. When he came into the ACORN office on Friday afternoon his boss, Beth, immediately approached him and said, "Come with me, Greg." He followed her into her office.

"Have you see today's newspaper?" she asked.

"No, why?"

"Greg, I don't know how to say this."

"How to say what?"

"James killed his parents."

"God almighty, what?"

"And his name isn't James."

"Huh? Excuse me?"

She showed him the story about his roommate's court-room confession in the morning paper. McDowell was a wanted killer and his name was Charles Cohen. Fitch was speechless. He'd been living with a person who had killed three people, and he could've been next. McDowell had told Scott Brannon that Greg was a vampire who fed off the psychic energy of those around him. Had he some-how become McDowell's enemy? Would his buddy James have killed him too?

"I knew you were naive, Greg," said Beth, "but I didn't realize you were this naive."

"Oh, man, this is so weird," Fitch mumbled several times. His stomach started turning. He couldn't believe it. It was happening too fast. He had been living with one of America's most wanted criminals.

The police had already called the office several times looking for Fitch. "Don't talk to the police," Beth said. "Don't say anything to anybody. Get a lawyer."

"Wait a minute," he said. "I didn't do anything wrong. I don't need a lawyer. I don't want to have anything to do with this."

Fitch called the Jefferson Parish Sheriff's Office. He was told to stay where he was. Someone would contact him shortly. The dispatcher contacted Pernia, Jones, and the Delaware authorities just as they were leaving Fitch's apartment and gave them the phone number for ACORN.

A few minutes later Downs called Fitch at ACORN. They agreed to meet at an intersection near the office.

"How will I know it's you?" Fitch asked.

"Don't worry," said Downs. "You'll know. We'll look like cops."

At 3 P.M. Greg Fitch stood on a busy corner and watched as five cops walked toward him. They ushered him to a police cruiser. Fitch sat in the backseat between

the two burly detectives from Delaware. They drove to
his apartment. Downs asked him where he was from.

"I'm from from Canton, a small town in central Illinois."

"Greg, you ever been to Galesburg?" Downs asked.

"Yeah, sure. It's about forty-five miles from where I
grew up. Why?"

Downs didn't answer, but he and Ruth smiled at one
another from either side of Fitch. He had no idea what
they were smiling about.

When they got to 2127 Carondelet, they ushered Fitch
to his apartment door. A reporter from a New Orleans
television station was interviewing one of Fitch's neighbors on the sidewalk in front of his apartment. A newspaper reporter was interviewing his landlord. Several other
neighbors watched as he was led to his apartment. Fitch
almost fainted from embarrassment.

Downs asked Fitch to write a note granting them permission to search the apartment. Fitch wrote the note,
signed it, and dated it. They went inside and closed the
door behind them.

The apartment was almost empty. Most of Fitch's belongings had already been moved. All that remained was
some trash, a few pieces of old furniture, and Cohen's belongings. The cops started looking through everything.
One of them pulled a duffel bag of Cohen's belongings
out of the closet and dumped it in the middle of the room.
Downs confiscated three drawing manuals, several notes
on small pieces of paper, and a 1978 appointment book
filled with drawings and poems.

When they finished looking through everything, they
sat down and told Fitch to describe how and when he had
met Cohen and what they had done together. Fitch told
them about meeting McDowell during Mardi Gras. He
told them about helping him get a job and living with
him. He explained how he'd heard that McDowell had

been arrested and how he and Brannon had tried to get him released.

They peppered him with questions as he told his story. Why did he help him? Had he ever met him before? What did he tell you about his parents? What did he tell you about his past? Were you ever suspicious of him? Did he use drugs?

Fitch calmly answered each question and said, "I'm not involved in this. I didn't know who he was until I heard about it this afternoon."

All five looked at him skeptically. Fitch was seated on the couch. "Don't you believe me?" he asked.

"Greg, people lie to us all the time," Downs said, getting up and pacing in front of him.

"Just tell us the truth, son," said Ruth.

"After a while we can tell when people lie," said Downs, his voice getting louder.

"Greg, let's get this cleared up once and for all," said Ruth.

"He had a New York ID card with his picture," said Fitch. "Everything seemed legit."

"We don't have all day, son."

"What is this all about?" he said. "I've already told you everything I know."

Downs paused in front of him and said, "Did you know Charles Cohen was from Galesburg, Illinois?"

Fitch experienced his second serious shock of the day. Cohen was from Galesburg? He knew lots of people from Galesburg, but he had never met Cohen. It was too much of a coincidence. Things were getting hairy. The cops would never believe him. They were already convinced that he'd harbored a fugitive. Aiding and abetting. He was heading for a fall—hard time in the house of correction.

Fitch stood and headed for the door. "I'm not answering another question until I get a lawyer," he said.

One of the Jefferson Parish detectives leaned against the door. Fitch couldn't open it.

"Why do you need a lawyer?" said Downs. "You haven't been charged with anything."

Fitch sat back down on the couch.

One of the Jefferson Parish detectives contacted the station with a portable police radio and requested an NCIC search on Gregory Fitch.

"The typical sentence for harboring a federal fugitive is ten to fifteen years, sometimes more," Walther chimed in.

"Let's start over," said Downs.

"Take it slowly," said Ruth.

Fitch went through it all again, and they grilled him as he went along. They pointed out minor inconsistencies and demanded explanations. Fitch felt weak. They were wearing him down, but he tried to remain calm.

"I realize you're just doing your jobs," he said, "and if I were in your situation I probably wouldn't believe my story either, but I'm innocent. I didn't do anything."

"Why did you help him out so much if you didn't know him?"

"He was a nice guy, the kind of guy you wouldn't think would harm a flea. None of us imagined he was an axe murderer. He came off as a perfect gentleman."

"Weren't you suspicious?"

"No, I never suspected him of anything. He was just happy-go-lucky."

"Why did you become friends?"

"He was funny. He was always doing crazy stuff. He made me laugh."

"Were you guys on LSD?"

"Give me a break."

It was obvious they weren't going to get anything else out of him. Either he was telling the truth or he was a good liar. The NCIC check hadn't turned up anything. Fitch gave them his girlfriend's phone number.

"We'll be in touch," said Downs as they left.

Fitch wandered outside. He felt like he had been through a wringer. The newspaper reporters and TV crews came running toward him. What the heck, he thought. He'd survived two months with a murderer and an afternoon with the cops. The media couldn't be much worse.

chapter 3

- - - - - - - -

A Lot of Heartache

Downs, Ruth, and Walther felt reasonably certain that they had done everything they had to do in New Orleans, so they made reservations for a 6:30 A.M. Saturday flight out of New Orleans. Cohen's dramatic courtroom confession had generated a great deal of media coverage in New Orleans, and they wanted to leave as early as possible to avoid any more publicity.

Charlie had become somewhat of a celebrity within the Jefferson Parish Correctional Center. All day Friday inmates and guards stopped by his cell asking him questions and giving him advice. He read the Bible for guidance. He was scheduled to be baptized on Saturday, but he would be gone by then, so his baptism would have to wait. Nevertheless, he was relieved to be going back to Delaware. His long, tiring sojourn was finally coming to an end.

Amstutz met Downs, Ruth, and Walther at the Jefferson Parish Correctional Center at five on Saturday. Cohen was released to the custody of the Delaware authorities and loaded him into a police cruiser. He was dressed in a dirty and torn light blue shirt, green pants, white socks, and boat shoes. They were the same clothes he had been wearing when he was arrested in Metairie two months earlier.

Pernia and Jones drove them to the airport. There weren't any photographers or reporters to greet them. Downs read Cohen his Miranda rights and officially arrested him. The airline wouldn't allow them to bring him through the airport or onto a commercial flight in handcuffs, so his handcuffs were removed, and he was seated in a wheelchair. They placed an orthopedic brace on his knee to immobilize him.

They were a little early for the first leg of their flight, so they wheeled Charlie into a waiting room. An awkward, strained moment followed. One of the detectives mentioned that it was a lot colder in Delaware than in New Orleans.

"I'm not worried about the weather," Charlie said. "I could be content anywhere. God will take care of me wherever I go."

Their first flight left New Orleans for Atlanta. Walther was seated near the front of the plane. Downs and Ruth sat in the back with Charlie between them. No one on the plane knew that Charlie was in custody except the crew.

At first Downs, Ruth, and Cohen didn't say much, but after a short time they were engaged in a friendly conversation. They talked about New Orleans and the French Quarter. Downs and Ruth called him "Charlie." All three tried to foster a relaxed atmosphere. Downs and Ruth didn't want him getting nervous and freaking out on the plane. Charlie didn't want to appear threatening to them or to anyone else.

They also talked about Charlie's conversion to Christianity. Ruth told him that Downs had been a minister before becoming a police officer. Charlie was encouraged by the news and automatically trusted Downs. He still felt very unsure of himself and his new religion, but here was another Christian, a minister no less, who could guide him.

Charlie asked Downs a few questions about Christianity. Downs enjoyed the opportunity to speak with a recent convert. The discussion was an extension of his training as a minister.

Ruth talked about some of the men he had arrested who had turned to God in prison. He also added, "You'll be going to jail for the rest of your life, Charlie, but you might be able to spread the word of Jesus in jail. That might give you some comfort, and you might be able to help some of the other inmates."

They landed in Atlanta for a short layover. On the second flight, they talked about Downs's search for Charlie. Downs said he had received over a thousand leads concerning his whereabouts. Charlie asked Downs where he had gone to look for him, and Downs told him about his trip to California. He said that he had met some punk rockers in Hollywood who had remembered seeing Charlie in the area.

Downs told him that he had hit the attendant as he had gunned the Ford out of the impound lot. Charlie didn't know he had hit the attendant, and he asked if he was okay. Downs told Charlie that he had suffered very minor injuries.

Charlie asked Downs about his relatives. Downs told him that one of his cousins had died from cancer while he was on the run. Charlie got choked up. He asked for a few moments by himself. News of his cousin's death triggered all of his guilt, which he realized he would never overcome. Charlie asked Downs to contact an ex-girlfriend in New York and a few of his friends in Galesburg to tell them he was okay.

Charlie was thinking about confessing to the third murder. He felt compelled to clear that up. Conrad Lutz's family had undoubtedly suffered not knowing what had happened. Perhaps he could end some of their misery.

The plane landed in Philadelphia at noon. A New Castle County Police cruiser was waiting for them on the tarmac. Cohen was taken off the plane, cuffed, and put in the police car. He was relieved to find out he wouldn't be brought through the airport. He dreaded having cameras shoved in his face.

They arrived at New Castle County Police headquarters in Minquadale, just south of Wilmington, and he was taken to the processing area where he was booked. An *America's Most Wanted* camera crew was at the police station. They came into the building and were able to get a shot of Charlie being booked through a window at the front desk. When a police officer saw them, he ushered them out of the building.

At one o'clock Cohen was put in a holding cell. He was nervous, exhausted, and hungry. The entire day had been mentally draining. He did some exercises to loosen up and decided to go through with the confession. He didn't care about his rights, the strategy for his defense, or saving his skin. He had to come clean with his sins to be saved. Downs was a minister, and he would understand.

At two-fifteen Downs and Ruth took Charlie to an interview room. They had a sense that he might talk. His lawyer in New Orleans had asserted Cohen's right to remain silent, so they weren't allowed to question him about the crimes. However, if he expressed an interest in talking, they could listen as long as they read him his Miranda rights and he understood them. They had asked an officer to watch through the one-way mirror and to turn on the videotape camera if Cohen started talking.

Downs asked Charlie some questions to fill out the pedigree form—date of birth, place of birth, height, weight, etc. They gave Charlie a box lunch of chicken from a fast-food restaurant.

Charlie asked, "What happens next?"

Downs explained that he would be arraigned and taken to Gander Hill Prison.

"When am I going to be interrogated by the FBI?" he asked.

He was told he wouldn't be interrogated. No one would ask him any questions unless he volunteered to speak with them.

"Will the FBI come to the prison to interview me?"

At that point Downs and Ruth knew he might talk. The cop behind the one-way mirror turned on the video camera. It was 2:25.

"After today, basically you go to jail," said Ruth. "We never talk to you. That's what I tried to tell you before."

"Uh-hum," said Charlie.

". . . Believe it or not, the whole thing is not like you would picture it," said Ruth. "You would think . . . that they would, you know, jump up and down."

"Or announce now that this is a formal interrogation," Downs added. "We don't do that."

"Yeah. You guys are being cool," said Cohen. "I just don't understand exactly, you know, I mean . . . from what I understand they don't even know about the third murder. I mean to me that seems like an important thing I should tell someone, and I don't know who to tell it to so that all that can be taken care of."

"Right here," said Ruth.

"Right here?"

". . . It's totally up to you," said Ruth, "but like you said, you thought it would be a good idea to clear that other one up."

"Yeah."

"I think that's an outstanding idea, 'cause like I told you, there's a lot of heartache that goes around."

Charlie asked to eat his lunch, and Downs and Ruth left the interview room. When he was finished, they came back, and Downs read him the Miranda warning. Downs didn't want to have any legal problems with Cohen's statement later on. Almost every confession was challenged in court, and he knew this one would be challenged, too. He asked Charlie if he understood his rights. He said he did, but he had one question.

"My question is, what would you guys recommend I do in terms of a defender, lawyer, or what would you recommend would be in my best interest at this point? I just want your personal opinion."

"The lawyer decision is totally up to you," said Ruth, "depending on what you're trying to accomplish."

Charlie asked if the victim's relatives would be notified. Downs assured him that they would be contacted before the story hit the press. Charlie then agreed to make a statement.

Ruth warned him that if he told them about a third murder, "We're obligated to pass that information along, as far as toward the courts."

"I'm just surprised that no one has even mentioned it until, you know, I had to come out with it myself and say, 'Hey, let's do something,' " said Cohen. "To me that's something wrong there."

Downs gave Charlie the rights waiver form to fill out. He checked "yes" that he understood and was waiving each of the Miranda rights. He signed and dated the form.

For the next 25 minutes, Charlie told them in detail about the Conrad Lutz murder. He explained how he met Lutz, that he spent a night with him before the murder, how he promised to "take care" of Lutz the next night, and that he had him close his eyes before stabbing him. He described the bloody struggle that ensued and how Lutz died trying to make it to the alarm near the front door. He also told them how the police came, but he remained perfectly silent, and they left.

"Why kill someone?" Downs asked.

"I don't know," Cohen answered.

"Why not just mug some old lady or roll somebody?"

"The thought of doing that entered my mind, but ... I could never mug anyone. I could never just hit someone, take their money, or grab their purse. I don't know, for some reason, in my makeup, I could never do that."

Charlie also assured them that he hadn't committed any other murders during his eighteen months on the run, but he declined to tell them anything about his travels.

"See, I don't want to tell the whole story. . . . I want to reserve some time for myself to think things out and think about getting the facts right. I don't want to just pour out my confession at one time like this because I just don't feel right about doing that. . . . I would prefer it if you tried not to dig deeper just because I'm going to try not to let you, okay?"

When Downs asked Charlie how the Nissan ended up in Chester, Pennsylvania, Charlie proceeded to tell the following story about the events immediately following the murder of his mother and father.*

After packing the LTD with his guitar and amp, clothing, cassettes, boombox, and a map, Charlie went to see a coke dealer he'd met a few weeks earlier in Newark. He wanted to get high and stay high until he had driven thousands of miles away. The dealer and his girlfriend were at home.

"He said he didn't have very much in his apartment at the time," Charlie told Downs and Ruth, "so I showed him some money and said, 'Look, I want a lot.' So he

---

*Some of the quotations were rearranged and some phrases were deleted to make the story more readable.

said, 'Well, I have to go to the projects to get it.' And I said, 'That's all right. Let's go.'

"This guy knew nothing about it except that he had a guy with money, a guy he really didn't know, but the money talked. I convinced him to take me. . . . I really had to talk him into it because he didn't want to. I think he could tell there was something fishy about it, but the money overwhelmed that and he took me."

Charlie drove. It took about half an hour to get to Chester. Charlie followed the guy's directions to the projects, which were only a few blocks from I–95. The guy made a call from a pay phone and a man came out of one of the buildings. They were completing the deal when another man ran up to Charlie.

"We were standing outside the place, and another guy comes up and goes right to me, of course, puts a pistol to my head and says, 'Give me your money.' Here I am a white boy going in there. And I was like, 'No, I'm not going to do it,' and he just said, 'Where is it?' I said, 'In my pocket.' And he took it. I had a bunch, wads in both pockets. He took one of them. And he just left.

"I don't think I was thinking too clearly to go into an all-black neighborhood at night. It's not smart. After I was stuck up [the dealer] said, 'Go sit in the car and let me do this.' Then we came back to Delaware together."

They snorted some of the coke on the ride back to Newark, and Charlie gave the guy some coke for his troubles. After dropping the guy off, he realized that most of the coke was gone. He wanted more, so Charlie went back to Chester by himself. He drove around the projects looking for the fellow who had robbed him, but to no avail.

"I met a different guy. I figured he'd want money, too. I said, 'Hey, man, you want to help me sell some stolen merchandise. I got a nice color TV, a VCR, all kinds of good stuff. Help me sell it, and I'll give you half the money.' I think he saw an easy hustle coming his way. Rather than just take me out directly, you know, hit me and take my money, he was somewhat sympathetic. Plus, he helped me get more cocaine, which I smoked and snorted with him.

"So I got him real high, and we went back to my parents' house. It was the same night, the twelfth. It might have been the morning of the thirteenth by the time I got back. We parked behind the house, by the post office. Then I said, 'Wait here. I'm gonna get us some merchandise.' He was nervous, too. He could tell something was wrong, too, but greed is a big factor. This must've been very late, maybe midnight or one A.M. There were no lights on in our complex that I recall. I cut across the ditch and the field and went in the back door. I snorted some more cocaine there in the kitchen on the table. I was nervous, but cocaine has a way of relieving tension, so I did more cocaine and tried to get myself numb." He went up to the second floor to look quickly at what he had done before gathering some of his parents' possessions to sell.

"I got as much stuff as I could, and then the thought occurred to me, 'Why not sell the car?' I decided that I could trust this guy to sell the Nissan for me and get big money off of that, so I could go on the lam and run away from the scene of the crime. This part was never premeditated. It was just spur-of-the-moment stupidity. It all happened real quick. I never intended [to go back]. I intended to leave as soon as I got cocaine for the road. I was just gonna take off. It would help me stay awake all night and drive.

"So I take the Nissan and pull it around and say, 'Hey, man, you drive in this car, and I'm going to follow you back there. We're going to just sell the car, forget the TV, that's too bulky. Let's just sell this car and just give me a grand and I'm happy, you know, I'm out of here.' He reluctantly agreed, and I followed him, but I lost him on the way back, or he lost me, whatever, I'm not sure which, and I couldn't find him in the projects."

Downs asked Charlie if he had stolen any of his parents' bank cards. "I wasn't that smart," Cohen said. "I didn't think along those lines. The motivating factor for me was just to kill them. I wanted to kill them. I really wasn't thinking about anything beyond that. I had a map. I knew I was gonna escape. I didn't think about money."

Charlie wandered the streets of Chester for hours. "I drove around the projects till morning, and then I saw this black girl walking the street, and she waved at me and kind of smiled. I figured why not, you know, and she got me a place. She put me up at her mother's house for the night, and I had to buy her some heroin or something. She needed some money. But she took care of me. She didn't try to rob me or anything. I just paid for staying up there in a room overnight, and then the next day I took off."

Ruth asked Charlie if he would be willing to discuss the murders of his mother and father. He answered, "Yeah, we can do—we can stick with the facts." He told them what happened that night.*

"November 12, 1988. My father was downstairs watching television, my mother was in the kitchen, and I was in my room listening to D.O.A. It was after suppertime, between eight-thirty and nine-thirty.

"I called my father upstairs to my room. I said, 'I want to show you my latest piece of artwork.' That's how I lured him up to my room with the intent of killing him. I had a dumbbell in my hand, a ten-pound dumbbell,

---

*Downs and Ruth had Cohen go through his story twice. The following quotations were compiled from both statements, and some of the material was rearranged so it appears in chronological order.

solid. I don't know what it's made out of. It's hard. And so when I had him looking, I had his back to me, I struck him repeatedly, and it didn't knock him out, but he went down, and I kept hitting him and bludgeoning him with it until he was unconscious. The first time I hit him he went down to his knees, and then I repeatedly hit him as he tried to stop me. And then I stabbed him repeatedly. [The knife] was ready on my dresser for what I intended to do. I stabbed him in the neck, the side, the back, or the stomach or the chest. I stabbed him repeatedly until he stopped breathing. I stabbed him until I was sure he was dead.

"Then I called my mother. I went downstairs and I said, 'Mom! Mom! Dad fell down. Come upstairs. Dad's hurt.' She came up the stairs and she asked me if I had called an ambulance, and I don't remember what I said. She made it up the stairs surprisingly quickly because she thought my dad was in trouble, but as soon as she got to the top of the stairs and her back was turned, I picked the barbell off the top of the banister. There's a flat ledge there, and I had the barbell sitting on the banister there. So as soon as she got up the stairs and turned her back to me, but she saw, she saw it coming. She realized I was gonna strike her, and she started to turn around, and I kept hitting her. She tried to defend herself, but she was too weak to stop me and I just bludgeoned her. It didn't take as many strikes to kill her. Although she was a big woman, she was frail, you know. And she quickly became unconscious and then I stabbed her in the neck, not as much as I stabbed my father, and she died more quickly. She died at the top of the stairs. The knife was just left there, lying on the floor."

Charlie broke down while discussing the murder of his mother, and he needed a few minutes before he could continue. "I took a shower to get the blood off of me, and I smoked a cigarette, and I watched out the window to see

if the police were coming. And when they didn't come I
ransacked the house, tried to find money. I went through
all their personal possessions, went through their bedroom drawers, the dressers, went through the kitchen,
anything, any place I thought they might have some
money saved or hidden, and any jewelry, any valuables I
could find. I believe I got around five hundred dollars,
maybe six hundred dollars, maybe seven hundred dollars.
Then I went to get some cocaine."

"There was six hundred dollars left in the house,"
Downs mentioned.

"Left in the house?"

"Uh-hum."

"I missed that. I didn't find that money. There'd been
no fight that evening, and you could say it was, you
know, it was premeditated. I was not under the influence
of any drug when I committed the murders. And that's the
facts. I think that pretty much covers everything."

Charlie declined to explain why he murdered his parents. "That's too long and drawn out an answer to discuss
in one sitting," he told Downs and Ruth, "and it's not
something I really want to get into at this time."

The interview ended at 4:45.

At seven-thirty Cohen was arraigned and ordered held
without bail on two counts of first-degree murder. Bail
was set at $10,000 for each of the weapons charges. By
eight he was at the Multi-Purpose Criminal Justice Facility in Wilmington, commonly known as Gander Hill.

Charlie told the prison officials at Gander Hill that he
wasn't suicidal. Nevertheless, they put him on full suicide
watch in the "pink room," a cell in the infirmary that contained nothing but a foam mattress on a concrete frame,
a toilet, and a camera so the guards could watch him. The
cell was painted pink, supposedly the most soothing
color.

All of his clothing except his undershorts was taken from him. He spent much of his time lying on the bunk reading the Bible. Occasionally, he did some exercises. Guards and medical personnel from the prison infirmary checked on him every couple of hours. He was allowed out to shower and watch TV for short periods of time.

He didn't have any contact with a lawyer or anyone from the Public Defender's Office over Memorial Day weekend. *America's Most Wanted* requested an interview, but he wouldn't speak with them.

On Memorial Day, May 28, 1990, at 10 A.M., he called Downs collect at police headquarters. He told Downs that he had been reading his Bible, particularly sections from the Book of Acts about Paul's conversion.

"I want you and Allen to come in, and I'll run down everything," he said. "Give you my whole travelogue." Charlie also asked Downs if he could help him get baptized in prison. Downs promised to look into it.

Downs and Ruth went to Gander Hill and conducted a second interview with Cohen at noon. They read him his Miranda rights again. Downs asked Charlie several questions to make sure he understood his rights. Charlie said he did, and he also declined to speak with a lawyer before making a statement.

Cohen told them about his sixteen months on the run. He started from the moment he left Chester, Pennsylvania, the afternoon of November 13, 1988, until he was arrested in Metairie, Louisiana, on April 2, 1990. Cohen wore blue denim prison clothing and smoked cigarettes. Downs and Ruth recorded the conversation. The interview lasted 2½ hours. At the end of the interview, Cohen explained why he'd spoken to them.

"I'm trying to give as honest an account as I can. I'm just doing what I feel is—trying to let the Lord work through me is what I'm trying to do. As long as I'm sure that what I'm doing is the Lord's will, that's what I'm going to do.... I want to tell everything I know that can possibly help you to resolve everything concerning crimes. I just want to do that."

The next morning, Cohen met with attorneys from the Public Defender's Office, J. Dallas Winslow, Jr., and Nancy Jane Perillo. Winslow was one of the most experienced lawyers in the Public Defender's Office. He'd handled several other high-profile cases in Delaware, including Roger Re's defense. He'd run for attorney general in 1986 and lost to Charles Oberly, the current attorney general, by fewer than 1,000 votes. Perillo didn't have as much experience as Winslow, but she was known for being persistent, knowledgeable, and always well prepared.

Winslow and Perillo were distressed to discover that Cohen had given lengthy statements to the police, and they made him promise not to speak with them again. They also had Cohen write a letter to the Department of Corrections and the Department of Justice stating that he would not speak with any police officials about his case. Winslow and Perillo knew there wasn't much they could do for him once he had given the confessions. They could fight the validity of the confessions, but that was a tough battle.

The infirmary staff noticed that Cohen showed no signs of psychosis or depression. His speech was clear, coherent, and logical, although he seemed to harbor some religious delusions. On Tuesday, his status was upgraded from full suicide to close psychological observation.

Cohen's confession to the Conrad Lutz murder came as a complete surprise to the San Francisco Police Department homicide investigators, especially Inspector Whitey Guinther, who had headed the Lutz murder investigation. Until the confessions, Cohen hadn't even been a suspect. In fact, even though Guinther had spoken to Downs on the phone just a few weeks after Cohen had murdered his parents, he couldn't remember ever hearing about the case. A person wanted for killing his parents in another part of the country was not usually a suspect in a robbery murder case involving a homosexual pickup.

On Wednesday, May 30, 1990, Guinther received a copy of Cohen's videotaped confession. The confession coincided with the facts from the Conrad Lutz murder scene. A copy of Cohen's fingerprints was also sent to the San Francisco police, and his prints matched the unidentified prints found in Lutz's apartment.

The next day the SFPD issued a warrant for the arrest of Charles Cohen. He was charged with robbery and first-degree murder. They also placed a retainer on Cohen. When his murder trial in Delaware was completed, he would be brought to San Francisco to face prosecution.

On Sunday night, June 3, 1990, *America's Most Wanted* aired a report on Cohen's courtroom confession. A recording of the actual confession he made in Gretna, Louisiana, was played on the show. On Tuesday, June 5, Dallas Winslow entered a plea of not guilty for Charles Cohen. Cohen attended "in absentia" via a closed-circuit video relay from a holding cell at Gander Hill.

In early June, Charlie wrote several letters. One was to Nina, the library security guard from the Bronx he had taken up with the previous fall. He wrote that he was sorry for the things he had done. He explained that Jesus had come into his life, and he asked her to tell Jason, her son, that he loved him. He also urged her to move to a safer neighborhood. He ended the letter with, "I know you're very angry, but I hope you can find it in your heart to forgive me. If you ever want to write back, you can, but if you don't, I'll understand."

He also wrote letters to his two aunts, Marcie Dolgin and Mae Lagana. Both letters were identical. "Writing this letter has been one of the most difficult things I have ever done," he wrote. He explained that he had found Jesus Christ as his Lord and Savior. He claimed that he was sorry for what he had done and that Jesus had forgiven him. He asked them to forgive him and to pray for him.

"All of what I now am is changed," he wrote. "If I could give my life and change things I would." He also pointed out that King David had been a liar, a thief, and a murderer. "Still, God loved David," Charlie added.

Both aunts sent copies of the letters to Downs, who passed them onto Walther. They would come in handy if the case ever went to trial.

chapter 4

- - - - - - - -

A Most Precious and Fragile Flower

In early June, Charlie requested that he be placed on protected status. He was concerned for his welfare, especially after all the attention his case had gotten in the Wilmington media the previous two weeks. He was moved from the infirmary to the protective custody pod of the prison, a housing unit containing 20 cells. The inmates in protective custody were separated from the general prison population for their own safety. They were locked down 21½ hours a day.

He soon received a letter from Diane, a young woman with whom he had become friends at St. Francis Medical Center in Peoria. "I just wanted you to know that I'm here if you need anything," she wrote. "I've been very worried about you for the past 1½ years. You don't have to tell me anything about what happened in Delaware. You helped me out when I was feeling bad, and I'm very concerned for you."

She wrote again a few days later asking about phone calls and visits. She also asked if there was anything he needed, like clothing or spending money, and she included a photo of herself in the envelope. Charlie was

very surprised to hear from her. They had worked together in the hospital's diet office in 1987, but they
hadn't dated. He remembered that she had been recovering from a bout with anorexia.

He read her letters several times and wrote back. First,
he told her that he was in deep trouble. Most of what she
had heard about him was true, and the case against him
looked cut-and-dried. "I've made my bed," he wrote,
"and now I have to sleep in it."

He told her that he spent much of his time feeling sorry
for himself, but her letters had cheered him up. He would
be delighted if she visited, but he suggested she "pray on
it first." He also asked her to send a money order for
shampoo, soap, cigarettes, and junk food.

By then John Downs had called the prison minister, Joe
Kadtke, and told him that Charlie wanted to be baptized.
Kadtke submitted Charlie's name to the warden for approval, but the warden denied the request. Cohen was a
high-risk, high-profile inmate, and there were questions
about his stability, so the warden suggested he wait.

Charlie met Reverend William Keichline in the protective custody pod. Keichline was the founder and pastor of
Mission of Care, Inc., a religious organization that do-
nated food and clothing to the poor in Delaware. Through
the '80s Keichline had added a TV show, a delivery service, and a campground to Mission of Care, and he received many awards for public service.

Mission of Care came tumbling down in March 1988,
when Keichline was charged with molesting a young
girl some fifty times over a three-year period. The girl's
family lived in a property rented to them by Keichline,
and according to the girl he had threatened to throw
her family out if she told anyone of the molesta-
tions.

Keichline denied any wrongdoing, but the police found
incriminating videotapes in Keichline's home. Allegedly

he had shown her pornography, had her pose for nude photos, and had sexual intercourse with her many times. In October 1989, he was found guilty of eleven sexual crimes against the girl and later sentenced to eight consecutive life sentences. Mission of Care went bankrupt soon afterward.

Reverend Bill frequently organized Bible study sessions in the protective custody pod, which Charlie attended. They also went to a chapel service every Thursday. Keichline quickly became Charlie's religious mentor and friend.

Charlie continued to receive letters from Diane, and she sent him money orders as well. He felt blessed to be getting so much attention from her. She was the only old friend who had written to him so far.

Diane, who was 25, was a nursing student at St. Francis School of Nursing in Peoria. She didn't know why, but Charlie was occupying all of her thoughts. It was crazy being obsessed with a murderer, and it wasn't right for a good, midwestern, Mormon girl. She didn't tell anyone except her closest friends about her association with Cohen.

Diane was living in a dorm and didn't have a phone in her room. She made arrangements to go to a friend's house certain evenings to take collect calls from Charlie there. She was writing to him two or three times a week, and soon she was receiving as many phone calls from him.

By late June she decided that she had to see him. She scheduled a flight to Philadelphia for the third weekend in July and made an appointment to see him at Gander Hill. Charlie was delighted. He believed that the Lord had brought her into his life, although he didn't know what type of relationship she wanted.

In 1987, six months before she met Charlie, Diane had been hospitalized for anorexia nervosa. Her weight had dropped to 75 pounds. When she got out of the hospital, she found a job at St. Francis Medical Center in the diet office.

Diane was still very insecure about herself and her eating habits. She couldn't bring herself to eat in front of other people. During lunch breaks, she'd get a salad and sit behind a large column in the hospital cafeteria. One day not long after Charlie had started working at the diet office, he walked up to her table with a bag lunch and sat down.

"You can't," she muttered.

"Why not?" he asked. He then proceeded to eat a lunch consisting of a dried apricot and peanut butter sandwich, yogurt, beans, and nuts. Diane was shocked. His eating habits were stranger than hers, and he didn't make fun of what she ate.

She liked him almost immediately. At night when there wasn't much to do in the hospital, they sat down and talked. She told him about her anorexia, and he told her about his cocaine problem and that he was attending Narcotics Anonymous meetings regularly. Diane couldn't believe it. He was so polite and innocent-looking. He didn't seem like a drug user.

He was funny, too. He was able to cheer her up at a time when she wasn't feeling very good about herself. There was nothing romantic between them. She was dating a medical student, and he had just broken up with Katie.

Diane thought everything about him was cute, even his baby picture, which was posted on the bulletin board at work. Everyone in the diet office had brought in a baby picture, and everyone else tried to guess who they were. They were only two guys in the diet office at the time, so it was easy to guess which picture was Charlie's.

Around Christmas, Charlie told her he was quitting to

join a band. Diane was upset and made him promise to keep in touch. His picture stayed up on the diet office bulletin board.

The following September, Diane enrolled in nursing school and continued working part-time at the diet office. She hadn't heard from Charlie since he'd quit.

When she came into work on the morning of November 15, 1988, someone asked her if she had seen the paper. She hadn't. She picked up the Peoria newspaper and saw a front-page article about the murders of Martin and Ethel Cohen in Delaware. Charlie was missing. She hadn't even known they had moved to Delaware, and she didn't believe he'd killed his parents: Something terrible might've happened to him. She looked up at the bulletin board. There was the picture of the smiling Charles Cohen as an infant. She was so upset she got sick.

Within two weeks Charlie was indicted for murder. He was also sighted with the car in Los Angeles, so it was obvious he had committed the murders. She decided that drugs had to have been involved. The Charlie she had known couldn't have done that.

The months rolled by, and there was no sign of Charlie. She wished that he would just stop by and see her. She thought of him out there somewhere all by himself, scared, confused, and lonely. She wanted to help and protect him. She got in touch with the Delaware police a few times and asked about Charlie. Each time they said that they hadn't found him yet. After a few months she took his baby picture down.

Diane flew to Philadelphia on Friday afternoon, July 20, 1990. She was nervous. She had never flown anywhere by herself before. She got a room at a Holiday Inn near Wilmington. She took a cab to the prison the next morning. Visits for protective custody inmates were limited to 45 minutes on Saturdays. Since she was visiting from out of state, the prison officials extended her visit to two hours.

When she was led to the visiting room, Charlie was sitting at a desk in a cubicle behind a thick piece of glass. It broke her heart to see him locked up and wearing prison clothes. She felt terrible that he couldn't just leave and go home with her. They spoke through two telephones.

"I know what you've done," she said. "We don't have to talk about it."

He thanked her profusely for being so supportive. He could barely express how much her visit and her letters meant to him. He told her about his last few years, how his family had moved to Delaware, and about the type of person he had become before the murders. He claimed that he had changed and had been saved, and he asked about her religious background. He also talked about growing up in Galesburg, his life on the run, and what it was like in prison.

Charlie was exactly as she remembered him, smiling and laughing. He wasn't the bizarre, drug-addled, punk rock killer as he had been portrayed in the press. Bill Keichline was visiting with his wife Marie that morning in the visiting room, and Charlie introduced Diane to Reverend Bill.

The two hours went by quickly. "You're not going through this alone," she said before leaving. "I'm sorry, but that's not going to happen. I'll be there. I want to help you."

By the time she got back to Peoria, she knew she was in love with Charlie Cohen. She also knew that she had to be with him. She spoke to him on the phone about the possibility of moving to Delaware. "I'd love to have you here," Charlie said, "but make sure that's what you really want to do."

Diane soon received a letter from Keichline. She

didn't know what he had done, nor did she want to know. "I talked with my wife Marie after our visit on Saturday, and she said that in the future when you come she would like to help...," Keichline wrote. "Diane when you next visit if you would write ahead to Marie she will help you. Like pick you up at the airport and maybe stay at her home."

Charlie spent much of his time in his cell writing letters to Diane and drawing sketches for her. He decorated many of his letters with ornate doodles and border designs. He meticulously scripted long poems he had written for her. He sent her artwork consisting of cutout pieces of color construction paper held together by toothpaste.

Charlie sent small religious pamphlets to her as well, and he outlined Bible studies that he expected her to do. Diane tried to keep their conversations and letters away from religious topics. She knew he had been through many different phases in his life, and she didn't want to be drawn into another phase just to see him drop it later. If he was serious about Christianity, fine, but she wasn't going to base their relationship on his religious fervor.

Despite Diane's unexpected and supportive presence in his life, Charlie suffered from severe mood swings and bouts of depression. He found comfort in the scriptures, but he was often fearful, confused, and lonely. He felt confident and happy for short periods, but inevitably a minor incident or comment sparked a flood of memories and guilt. When he looked back, he could see all the mistakes. At times he cried and couldn't stop. He thanked the Lord for caring enough to punish him. Sometimes Charlie claimed that his depression originated with a different source—"the father of lies, the author of confusion—that old serpent, the devil."

Diane constantly thought about moving to Delaware. She had a 4.0 grade point average her first two years in nursing school, but she decided not to reenroll in school for the fall semester. She was also sending him $20 almost every week. Charlie was costing her most of her spare cash, but she didn't care about the money.

Diane visited Charlie at Gander Hill again in August. Before her visit, she called Keichline's wife, Marie. Marie invited Diane to spend the weekend at her home in Wilmington. Marie lived with her younger sister, whose husband was also in prison for running a large investment scam. Many of Keichline's followers had been taken in by the scam.

Diane wasn't sure what she was getting herself into, but she agreed to spend the weekend with Marie, who picked her up at the Philadelphia airport. The Keichline home wasn't at all what she expected. Marie, her sister, and her sister's two daughters lived in a big, beautiful house. They were very religious, and Diane immediately felt comfortable there.

During her visit to Gander Hill, Charlie told her what a comfort she had been. He was overjoyed to have a friend like her. "I can't wait till we are in heaven together with Jesus," he told her.

In late August a young man a few cells away from Charlie's hanged himself. The pod was locked down all day. Without God to teach us and guide us, he decided, we are lost.

During the early morning hours of Saturday, March 17, 1990, Freeman Ballard, a 32-year-old white male, was murdered in his Metairie, Louisiana, apartment. Ballard, an engineer for a New Orleans television station, was a closet homosexual known to cruise the French Quarter for male prostitutes. He was said to prefer young white males, ages 17 to 25, with blond hair.

Ballard didn't show up for work that day. That evening a co-worker got a key, entered Ballard's apartment, and discovered his body. Ballard had been stabbed repeatedly about the head, face, arms, and chest. He had several defense wounds on his hands and arms. A bloody kitchen knife was found under the bed. Ballard was in a semisitting position, his head propped against the side of the bed. The greatest amount of blood was located at the head of the bed, so the police surmised that the attack had begun in the bed. He was wearing a black T-shirt and gray sweatpants.

Prior to the murder, Ballard had mentioned to several people that he had recently cashed an overtime check worth $2,000. No cash was found at the crime scene, and his wallet was missing. Ballard's car was found abandoned several miles away on a highway leading to New Orleans. It had run out of gas.

The police found samples of two different blood types in the apartment, indicating that the murderer may have been injured in the attack. Diluted blood was found in the tub, and the police assumed that the suspect had taken a shower after the attack. Several different types of hair were collected from the bathroom.

The Ballard murder went unsolved for months. After hearing the details of Charles Cohen's murder of Conrad Lutz, Detective Les Jones, who had escorted the Delaware authorities around New Orleans, realized that there were numerous similarities between the Ballard and Lutz murders. Cohen was also known to be living in New Orleans during March 1990, and he had been arrested in Metairie.

Jones contacted John Downs and asked for blood and hair samples from Cohen. Downs obtained a search warrant and went to Gander Hill on September 13, 1990. A nurse took the requested samples from Cohen in the infirmary.

When Nancy Perillo, one of Cohen's lawyers, found out about the warrant and Downs's visit to Gander Hill,

she was furious. Cohen had specifically invoked his right
not to be contacted by police, and Downs had violated
Cohen's rights. Perillo immediately sent a letter to the
warden complaining about Downs's conduct and sent
copies to Walther, Downs's superiors at the New Castle
County Police, the attorney general, and the judge handling the case, Jerome O. Herlihy.

On September 21, 1990, Cohen's lawyers filed a motion to suppress the confessions Cohen had given to
Downs and Ruth in late May. They claimed that the confessions had been coerced and that he had not understood
his right to have an attorney present during questioning.
The defense wanted the prosecution to be barred from using the confessions against him. A hearing on the matter
was scheduled for November 19.

Downs never heard from Les Jones of the Jefferson
Parish Sheriff's Office about the Ballard case. Cohen's
hair and blood samples didn't match those found in Freeman Ballard's apartment, and the Ballard murder remains
unsolved.

Diane visited Charlie again in September. By then she
had made up her mind to move to Delaware. Marie
Keichline suggested she move in with her and her sister.
Charlie and Reverend Bill both thought it was a good
idea, at least until Diane got on her feet.

By late September, Charlie was proclaiming his love
for Diane in each of his letters. No one had ever shown
as much concern for him in so pure a way. He felt unde-
serving of someone like her, but evidently it was God's
will for them to be together.

Charlie was so in love he felt like a little kid. He sat
and stared at her picture and sang love songs to her over
the phone. He danced around his cell and made funny
faces in the mirror. Diane sprayed her letters with per-
fume. They never mentioned the murders.

He often lay on his bunk imagining them all—Reverend Bill, Diane, Marie, and himself—in separate mansions, waving to each other and laughing joyfully. Another time he pictured them eating supper on his farm. He knew, of course, that no one could imagine the blissful peace that awaited them in heaven.

Diane made her longest visit to Delaware in October. She arrived Tuesday, October 16, and stayed through the weekend. She stayed at Marie's house and spent much of her time applying for nursing assistant jobs at health care facilities around Wilmington. The suppression hearing was starting in late November, and she wanted to be settled in Delaware by then.

That same week Charlie's friend and religious mentor, Bill Keichline, was moved to another prison in southern Delaware. "It's so sad to dwell on it," he wrote to Diane, "but the next time I see Bill could be at Jesus' feet."

On Wednesday night, October 17, Charlie called Diane collect at Marie's house and mentioned something about meeting in heaven. Then he talked about having children. "Well, I guess I should ask you to marry me," he suddenly added.

Diane was confused. She didn't know if the marriage proposal applied to when they were in heaven or on earth. He explained that he wanted to get married and have children in this world. He was serious about it. She immediately accepted. Neither of them knew if the authorities would allow the marriage, but Charlie said he would go to the Gander Hill law library to look up statutes pertaining to marriage in prison. "I know Jesus will surely give us the desires of our hearts," he wrote.

Besides her mother and sister, Diane didn't tell anyone about her plans to move or about her engagement. She didn't feel that anyone else needed to know. Her mother didn't try to convince her not to move to Delaware. She had learned a long time ago that once Diane set her mind to something, she did it.

A few friends from her church urged her to think about what she was getting herself into. Marie Keichline cautioned her as well and told her about the problems she could expect. Marie was living the life Diane was stepping into, and she knew it wasn't easy.

Diane didn't know what to think. Sometimes she felt confident, but sometimes she was very unsure of herself. She couldn't help wondering how things would have been if Charlie had never moved to Delaware. She had no idea when or if Charlie would ever get out of prison. She accepted the fact that people shouldn't get away with murder, but it was hard for her to be rational about his case. All she knew was that she would go to Delaware, visit him every Saturday, and give him as much support as possible. She knew it wasn't a normal situation, but she would have to cope with whatever happened, and things would somehow work out.

She tried to explain to everyone how she felt, but her feelings were almost impossible to put into words. Other people could be objective about it, but she was in love. She had agreed to be Charlie's wife, and she didn't take that kind of commitment lightly. Nothing else mattered to her except him. Couldn't anyone else understand that?

The week before she left, she got a call from a clinic in Wilmington. They offered her a position as a nursing assistant, and she took it. She sold her car, TV, and anything else she could find a buyer for. She flew to Delaware the second week of November and moved in with Marie Keichline and her sister.

While waiting in a checkout line in a grocery store during one of her first days in Delaware, she saw a picture of Charlie on the cover of the November issue of *Delaware Today* magazine, which was prominently displayed in the store. She tried not to look at the magazine, and she could barely wait to get out of the store. She didn't want to know what anyone else had written or said about him. They didn't know the side of him she knew. He was a sweetheart. He drew her pictures. He sang to her over the phone. He repeatedly promised his undying love. No one had ever done that for her.

Charlie was upset about the article, too. The guards in the prison read it, as did many of the inmates, some of whom asked for his autograph. He was worried that the other inmates would resent him because of his relatively comfortable upbringing. His parents had taken him on many expensive vacations, yet he had killed them, and now every inmate knew it. There was a harsh sense of justice in prison, and an even harsher way of carrying it out. He told Diane he never wanted to see another article written about himself.

Charlie believed that he would be free one day, and he repeatedly promised Diane that they would someday be together. He didn't know how or when, but he believed. The road that lay ahead of them would be difficult, but Jesus was his best friend now, so he couldn't lose.

"I dream, far too much," he wrote, "of wonderful times we will share when I am released." He pictured them embracing in the courtroom when the jury pronounced him innocent. He saw them walking hand in hand in the mountains with nothing but the sky, trees, and nature around them. Before she knew it, they would have a little house, a beautiful baby, and everything else she could dream of.

Charlie asked his "most precious and fragile flower" to be patient. Good things don't happen overnight, he told her, but good things come to those who wait. He knew that the suffering they were going through now was making their hearts and minds pure. As St. Paul had written, "For I reckon that the sufferings of this present time are not worthy to be compared with the glory which shall be revealed in us."

chapter 5

- - - - - - - -

The Happiest Man
in the World

Once a suspect has been read his or her Miranda rights and indicates either personally or through an attorney that he doesn't want to answer questions, all questioning by the police must cease. Richard Tompson, Cohen's court-appointed lawyer in Jefferson Parish, Louisiana, had asserted Cohen's right to not speak with the police twice, once to Walter Amstutz and once to Steve Walther.

If either John Downs or Allen Ruth had asked Cohen anything about the murders during their return to Wilmington from New Orleans on May 26, 1990, his Miranda rights would have been violated and the confessions would have been invalid.

However, once a defendant initiates further discussion about a case or indicates a willingness to speak, the police can follow up, assuming the defendant understands and waives his or her Miranda rights. Simply put, if a defendant wants to give a confession, he can, and the police are allowed to listen. Although Downs and Ruth may not have asked him directly about the murders, Cohen's lawyers hoped to show that they had preyed on his recent religious conversion and his guilt to subtly manipulate a confession from him.

Steve Walther and Bobby O'Neill were assigned to prosecute the case. Walther, the lead prosecutor, had been involved with the case from the night Martin and Ethel Cohen's bodies were discovered. He was a tough, experienced prosecutor. When he had a defendant on the stand, he went after him or her aggressively. O'Neill, the second chair, had been at the state prosecutor's office for three years.

Steve Walther knew the trickiness of the Miranda rights, and when he first heard about Cohen's statements to Downs and Ruth, he assumed there would be a suppression hearing. But he was confident that Downs and Ruth hadn't violated Cohen's rights. They were experienced police detectives, and they understood the law.

When Walther watched the videotape of Cohen's first statement, he couldn't believe what he was watching. Downs and Ruth had gone well beyond what the law required. It sounded like they were trying to talk him out of giving the confession. Cohen clearly wanted to talk. It was remarkable that he had even given the confessions after Downs and Ruth reminded him of his rights so many times.

How could Winslow and Perillo challenge the confessions? Downs and Ruth had read him his rights several times, he said he understood them, and he signed the rights waiver form. It was clean. They had proof on tape. Their only argument could be about what was said before the various tape decks were turned on, and the burden of proof would be on Cohen and his lawyers. It would come down to the detectives' word versus Cohen's. That would mean they'd have to put Cohen on the stand. And who was the judge going to believe, an ex-minister and an experienced detective or a parent killer?

Walther didn't care about Cohen's May 28 statement.

That simply detailed his travels. The May 26 statement, which contained the murder confessions, was worth fighting over, not only for the Delaware murder prosecution but for the Lutz murder case as well. With or without the confessions, Walther knew they had enough evidence to convict him on the Delaware murders. It was the San Francisco murder case that would be left high and dry if the confessions were ruled inadmissible.

The hearing to suppress Charles Cohen's confessions began on November 19, 1990, in the Daniel L. Herman Courthouse in downtown Wilmington, the Honorable Jerome O. Herlihy presiding. Testimony was scheduled to last three days.

Charlie was led into the courtroom in handcuffs by armed guards. He appeared alert and coherent. He had a thick mustache and wavy brown hair and wore a denim jacket and blue prison garb. Downs sat at the prosecutor's table. He had helped the prosecutors prepare for the hearing, and they wanted him on hand because he knew so much about the case.

Diane was the only person in attendance who supported him. None of his relatives or friends showed up. She sat in the first row directly behind the defense table. She was very nervous. Her fiancé's life was in the hands of lawyers and judges. Cohen turned and smiled at her whenever he had the chance. He was relieved that she would be there to help him through the suppression hearing and trial.

The prosecutors played the videotape of Cohen's May 26 statement during the first day of the hearing. Everyone in the courtroom listened as Cohen explained how he killed his parents and Conrad Lutz. They also heard him describe his activities immediately after his parents' murders. The videotape upset Diane. It was the most graphic description of the murders she had heard so far.

Downs took the stand on Tuesday, November 20, and continued with his testimony on Wednesday. Ruth was called to the stand on Wednesday. They were questioned at length about the events of May 26 and May 28. The content of their testimony was virtually identical. Both detectives claimed that they hadn't questioned Cohen in New Orleans or during either of the flights to Delaware. They said that once they were back in Delaware, Cohen expressed a willingness to confess to the third murder. Even then they reminded him of his rights, but he went ahead with his statements anyway.

"He was wanting to tell somebody, and we happened to be there," said Ruth. He later added, "I believe he is an intelligent person who understood his rights, and he made the comments on his own."

Downs testified that Cohen hadn't confessed because of any coercion. "He created a great deal of pain for other people," said Downs, "and he wanted to rectify the pain he had caused."

The defense questioned the detectives at great length, often covering the same material several times looking for inconsistencies. The prosecutors questioned the detectives as well, seeking to minimize any confusion the defense questioning had caused. For the most part the prosecutors kept their questions short and to the point.

"At any time did Mr. Cohen say, 'I want an attorney?' " Walther asked Downs.

"No, sir," said Downs.

"Who was the first one to initiate discussion regarding any of the murders?"

"Charles Cohen."

The suppression hearing recessed on Wednesday afternoon, November 21. Because of scheduling conflicts, it could not resume until Thursday, December 20.

* * *

Despite the stress of the suppression hearing, the relationship between Diane and Charlie intensified. They wrote longer and more frequent letters to one another and spoke on the phone almost daily. The inmates were officially restricted to one short phone call per night, but the guard on Cohen's prison pod often let him speak on the phone with Diane for as long as two hours. Cohen was so in love he sometimes kissed Diane's picture before going to sleep. His declarations of undying love and fantasies of their future together continued unabated. He never mentioned the suppression hearing in his letters.

One of their major concerns was getting married. He went to the law library but couldn't find any statute in Delaware law applying to marriage in prison, so he decided to write to the warden about it. Diane asked the bishop from the Mormon church she attended in Wilmington to marry them. After speaking with Cohen, the bishop agreed to marry them if they got permission.

They both knew that Charlie probably would be extradited to San Francisco once his Delaware murder trial was over, which was scheduled for May. They decided it would be best to get married after the trial but before he was sent to California, although they knew it was unrealistic to plan a wedding before his legal proceedings were complete. "I suppose it does take a leap of faith," he wrote to her. "Of course I believe in dreams coming true."

By December 6, his 26th birthday, he had changed his mind and wanted to be married before the trial. "If my wish comes true this is my best birthday ever," he wrote to Diane. He wrote to the warden that same day requesting a "quiet and anonymous" prison wedding. He asked to be married after his suppression hearing but before his trial in May. This "calm before the storm," he wrote, "could be our only opportunity to marry for who knows how long."

Diane promised to follow him wherever he went, even to California if necessary. It astonished him that she loved him so completely. He had always hoped for a woman like her to love him, but he had given up looking for her. She had made him the happiest man in the world. Even though they were separated by bars, walls, glass, and court officers, nothing could stand between them and the love they shared.

His euphoria over Diane was matched by equally intense periods of depression. On December 13 he broke down in tears in the chapel. He tried to stop weeping but couldn't. He couldn't help dwelling on what his life would be like if he were sentenced to death. No matter what happened, he decided, his feelings for Diane would not change. He would love her until the final moment.

The suppression hearing resumed on Thursday, December 20. Ruth and Downs spent most of the day and the next morning on the stand. Charles Cohen finally took the stand at 12:15 on Friday.

In response to questions from Dallas Winslow, Cohen described his background, his state of mind during the eighteen months he lived as a fugitive, which he called "a nightmarish journey," his conversion to Christianity in the Jefferson Parish jail, and the events leading up to his confessions to Downs and Ruth. He answered each question in a calm, thoughtful voice, sometimes pausing to gather his thoughts before answering.

He testified that the two detectives discussed his case and asked probing questions during the flights from New Orleans to Wilmington. He said that Detective Ruth asked him, "Why did you do it?" in the waiting room at the New Orleans airport. He testified that by the time he arrived in Delaware he felt very trustful of John Downs. He confirmed that he had asked about the FBI interrogating him and that he was the one who brought up the third murder. Nevertheless, he claimed that he had been manipulated by the detectives.

"To me it was obvious I was just manipulated and physically exhausted," he said. "I was emotionally under duress. I was mentally fatigued and I broke down. I was scared, upset, distraught, and confused. . . . I was so tired at this point that I wanted to get it over with. It was almost like a physical need to get it over with so you can go to sleep."

After a day of questioning by his public defenders, Steve Walther rose to cross-examine Charles Cohen. It was 10:50 on Christmas Eve. After a few questions about his background, Walther addressed Cohen's New Orleans courtroom confession.

> WALTHER: Isn't it true, Mr. Cohen, that you were bound and determined on May 24, 1990, in that Louisiana court to make a confession in spite of all the legal advice given to you from the public defender, from the judge himself?
>
> COHEN: Literally, yes.
>
> WALTHER: . . . You knew that could be used against you in a criminal prosecution. You understood that, didn't you, Mr. Cohen?"
>
> COHEN: I didn't really have time to understand much of anything at that moment.
>
> WALTHER: The judge asked you if you understood, correct?
>
> COHEN: I had made up my mind when I went in there.
>
> WALTHER: That wasn't my question. . . .
>
> COHEN: I knew what I was doing.
>
> WALTHER: You knew absolutely what you were doing because you said, 'I realize that, sir,' after the judge

told you that anything you said could be used against
you in a criminal prosecution, correct?

COHEN: Correct.

Walther got Cohen to admit that the Miranda warning
had been read and explained to him numerous times between May 24 and May 28 and that he'd understood the
warning. Walther also asked Cohen to recite the Miranda
warning, which Cohen was able to do. Walther then began questioning Cohen about his eighteen months as a fugitive.

WALTHER: Now, Mr. Cohen, isn't it a fact that in the
eighteen months after the murders of your parents one
of the things you resorted to, in order to survive, was
stealing?

COHEN: I only stole from—really one time I stole
property.

WALTHER: You stole your mother and father's LTD,
didn't you?

COHEN: Well, yes. Actually, I'm—

WALTHER: That was after the murders, wasn't it?

COHEN: Actually, on four occasions.

WALTHER: It jumped from one to four!

Nancy Perillo objected that Walther was badgering the
witness. Herlihy agreed.

WALTHER: I'm sorry if I badgered you, Mr. Cohen.
How many times did you resort to stealing in order to
survive?

COHEN: Four occasions.

WALTHER: On four occasions. The first occasion was
the theft of your mom and dad's LTD, correct?

COHEN: Yes.

WALTHER: You also stole cash from your mom and dad, didn't you?

COHEN: Yes.

WALTHER: . . . How about Conrad Lutz? Did you steal from him?

COHEN: Yes.

WALTHER: In fact, it was your intent to kill him and take his money, wasn't it?

COHEN: Yes.

WALTHER: . . . You stole from someone who took you in when you were homeless?

COHEN: Yes.

Walther paced the courtroom and asked questions quickly. If Cohen didn't answer quickly enough, Walther rephrased the question. He could barely conceal his contempt for the defendant.

WALTHER: In addition to stealing to survive, isn't it also true that you lied?

COHEN: Yes.

WALTHER: In fact, you lied every time you used an alias, didn't you?

WOHEN: Yes.

WALTHER: You were using aliases to survive and to keep from getting busted, weren't you?

COHEN: Yes.

WALTHER: In fact, you lied to the police when they stopped you during that eighteen months?

COHEN: Yes.

WALTHER: You lied to the police in Louisiana when you were arrested on April 2, 1990, correct?

COHEN: Yes.

WALTHER: You told them you were James McDowell, correct?

COHEN: Yes.

WALTHER: That was a lie, wasn't it?

COHEN: Yes, it was.

WALTHER: . . . Not only was that a lie, that was criminal, wasn't it?

COHEN: Yes.

WALTHER: . . . In order to survive, correct?

COHEN: Yes.

Walther's voice had been getting louder. Perillo objected that Walther was yelling at the defendant. Walther answered, "It keeps me awake, your honor." The judge let him continue.

WALTHER: . . . Mr. Cohen, can you give us some idea during that eighteen-month nightmare journey across the country after the murder of your parents, how many times you had to lie to survive?

COHEN: *No response.*

WALTHER: Just a ball park figure. Over 100?

COHEN: Certainly. Yeah.

WALTHER: Over 200?

COHEN: It's hard to say. I don't know.

WALTHER: Between 100 and 200?

COHEN: A lot.

WALTHER: A lot?

COHEN: Yeah.

Walther asked several questions about his manipulation of Conrad Lutz and his prostitution, both of which Cohen admitted to, before getting to his main point.

WALTHER: . . . Did you indicate Detective Downs and Detective Ruth, under oath, put their hand on the Bible and, according to you, committed perjury?

COHEN: Yes.

WALTHER: And what you have told this court is all the truth, correct?

COHEN: *No response.*

WALTHER: You wouldn't lie to us, would you, Mr. Cohen?

COHEN: ... No, I wouldn't.

WALTHER: You wouldn't lie to survive, would you?

COHEN: No.

WALTHER: Mr. Cohen, you realize the consequence of this hearing?

COHEN: Yes.

WALTHER: ... And you realize that if convicted of those crimes, you could face the death penalty?

COHEN: Yes.

WALTHER: And you're going to sit there and tell us that you wouldn't lie to save your life?

COHEN: Yes.

WALTHER: You lied for money. You murdered for money. ... Isn't that true?

COHEN: Yes.

Walther grilled Cohen about other deceptions he had committed as a fugitive before continuing.

WALTHER: ... Isn't it true that during this eighteen-month period of time, which you were trying to survive, you became a pretty good con artist?

COHEN: I don't know how good I was. ... If I was a con artist I probably would've made more money. I was more just like a street-hustler, panhandler. I didn't make much money. I kept it small because I wanted to keep it low-key. I guess I was good at fooling people.

WALTHER: ... Mr. Cohen, are you trying to con us today?

COHEN: No.

WALTHER: Mr. Cohen, how are we supposed to know

when you're lying and when you're trying to con us and when you're telling the truth? How are we supposed to know this, just because you say so?

COHEN: *No response.*

WALTHER: You choose not to answer that question.

COHEN: You have to take everything in the context of where we are today. I mean ... if you just don't take the time to know—know my whole life story, then you don't know me. You don't know me. You don't have enough to go on to really understand what took me to that point. ...

Walther then attacked the believability of Cohen's religious conversion.

WALTHER: Isn't it true that while you were in prison you said, 'Hey, look, enough is enough. Prison's not so bad, a roof over my head, three meals a day.' Did you come to the conclusion that it was better in prison than it was out on the street?

COHEN: No.

WALTHER: ... Weren't you tired of lying, stealing, and cheating?

COHEN: You can't equate that with prison either. There's lying, stealing, and cheating everywhere, in prison, out of prison, on the streets. ...

WALTHER: Did the fact that you were in prison with a roof over your head and three square meals a day, did that have any effect on your decision to confess or did it change your attitude at all?

COHEN: No.

WALTHER: ... Mr. Cohen, did Jesus answer you?

COHEN: Yes ... I could feel the burden of my sins lifted off me.

WALTHER: ... So you weren't hallucinating or anything like that? You weren't hearing voices?

COHEN: No.

WALTHER: . . . Did you include all those lies that you committed in this confession?

COHEN: I don't think it was necessary to pick out every specific sin you ever committed in your life. No one can ever remember that, except God.

WALTHER: Now this conversion you had, this salvation, I believe you indicated that you actually felt cool air hitting you in the face, correct?

COHEN: Yes.

WALTHER: . . . You weren't tripping out on some LSD or anything, were you?

COHEN: No.

One of the final questions Walther asked that afternoon was, "I believe you indicated that you also felt forgiven. Now you certainly didn't feel at that time that the State of Delaware was going to forgive you for these murders, did you?"

Cohen answered, "No."

Walther was surprised at how freely Cohen admitted to the murders, but he couldn't use these new confessions against him in a trial. However, if the taped confessions were thrown out and Cohen took the stand at his trial and denied the murders, Walther could bring up his suppression hearing confessions.

That evening Charlie and Diane spoke on the phone. He told her that this would go down as one of his worst Christmases yet.

On Friday, December 28, the prosecutor questioned Cohen at length about the details of May 26, the day he was brought back to Delaware. Cohen admitted that Downs and Ruth hadn't threatened him or promised him anything to get him to confess. He also admitted that he understood where he was and what was going on.

Walther asked him bluntly, "You understood your rights, correct?"

"Yes," Cohen answered.

It became clear that Cohen couldn't remember exactly what was said during the flights from New Orleans to Philadelphia on May 26, 1990. He also admitted that the detectives hadn't asked direct questions about the murders, and he kept trying to clarify how the detectives had manipulated him.

"They asked a lot of leading questions about the Delaware murders. . . . It was just continual badgering in the guise of friendship. They pretended to befriend me when actually they were trying to get a confession. . . . Actually Detective Downs wasn't badgering me. . . . [He] had me believing he was a friend. I really felt I could trust him. I see now that it was—a tool. . . . I think that's what really tripped me up. . . . He played it so subtly that he didn't appear obvious at all. . . . I was very scared, confused, and naive about the law. I needed a shoulder to lean on."

Walther asked Cohen to explain why he had said in the beginning of the videotaped statement, "You guys are being cool," if Ruth was bothering him so much.

"At the time I was—I had just been saved," Cohen answered. "I was very vulnerable to anyone, anyone at all. I was just so content and happy with my life at that time that that carried over into these very strained and very painful procedures. . . . Through it all I had this joy inside me, and you could see that I was trying so hard, just trying so hard to forgive these guys over and over again. . . . Suddenly I just completely yielded to what had been— what was being driven at all along. I just completely submitted myself to them. . . . That's when they actually won their little witch raid, their game to get me to confess."

Several times during the testimony Walther asked Cohen if Downs and Ruth perjured themselves. "Maybe nobody will believe me," Cohen said. "God knows."

"I'm sure he does," Walther answered.

Later in the day Walther asked him several questions about the purpose of suppressing the confessions.

> WALTHER: Now, Mr. Cohen, certainly you don't think the police don't have a case against you without this confession . . .
>
> COHEN: That's what I believe today.
>
> WALTHER: You believe that today. So . . . if you're successful in your motion to suppress these confessions, you're going to walk on these charges, the murder of your mother and father, aren't you?
>
> COHEN: I don't know. I don't know if I'm going to walk. I don't think they have a very strong case. I think they have a very, very weak case without it.
>
> WALTHER: And there's a good chance you could be set free on the charges of the murder of your mother and father?
>
> COHEN: I doubt it. I don't think I'll be free by any means.
>
> WALTHER: You think you'll be found not guilty if the state presented a weak case regarding the murder of your mother and your father?
>
> COHEN: I don't know. I just know that what they did was wrong, and that's the main point that should come out of this hearing.
>
> WALTHER: . . . If the statement is suppressed, Mr. Cohen, would you deny killing your parents?
>
> COHEN: No.
>
> WALTHER: You're saying you would take the stand whether or not the state presents a weak case and admit to everyone that you murdered your parents?

Perillo objected to the question, and Herlihy sustained the objection. The court was recessed until January 25.

* * *

By the end of the year Charlie was the head tierman in his pod. He was responsible for cleaning the common areas of the pod, and he helped distribute meals. He preached to the other inmates about the good news of salvation and tried to keep peace in the pod.

He was frustrated that so many of the inmates were rebellious and angry. He hated seeing young guys make the same mistakes he did, and he tried to live in a Christlike manner to set a good example. Many of them took to calling him "preacher" and teased him about his obsession with religion.

Charlie's fears and anxieties would not go away, but whenever he despaired, he thought of Diane and his worries vanished. Her love was a song in the night, and in the day the sunshine reminded him of her. Making love to her would be like leaving this world for a while. Going from prison to the warmth of her arms would be like going from night to day.

He imagined her dressed in the softest linen. Fresh flowers would be in her room and crushed flowers in her bath. She would have the finest perfumes and every precious jewel. Gold would adorn all the fixtures in her home, and woven tapestries would grace her walls. The softest music would play each morning as she rose. The treasures of her heart were the treasures he desired. There was no light or darkness, just his one true love for her. He gave everything of himself to her, and he could feel his love flow into her and hers into him.

Cohen answered more questions from Walther when the hearing resumed on January 25. It was his fourth day on the stand.

WALTHER: I think you also indicated on your direct examination that you were treated 'inhumanely.' I believe you even said 'like a monster.' You honestly be-

lieve that Detective Downs and Detective Ruth treated
you inhumanely and like a monster?

COHEN: Yes.

WALTHER: Did anyone threaten you with physical violence?

COHEN: No.

WALTHER: No one yelled at you or screamed at you,
did they?

COHEN: No.

WALTHER: Did anyone slit your throat or hit you
over the head with a barbell?

Perillo raised an objection, which Herlihy sustained.

COHEN: ... That's an irrelevant question. It's just a
matter of being considered innocent until proven
guilty. ...

WALTHER: Now I believe you indicated on your direct examination that they, meaning the police, had
control over you, correct? They kind of manipulated
you?

COHEN: Yes.

WALTHER: ... Isn't it a fact, Mr. Cohen, that you
were the one in control, you decided what murder to
talk about, and you decided that you were not going to
answer any questions about that eighteen-month period
after the murder of your parents? ... Isn't that a fact?
You decided, correct?

COHEN: I agreed to give the confession.

WALTHER: You did more than that, didn't you?

Walther pointed out several instances in the May 26
statement where Cohen refused to discuss a particular
topic and the police said, "Okay, it's whatever you choose
to do."

WALTHER: Yet it's your position today they were leading you, they were manipulating you, correct?

COHEN: Yes.

Walther then attacked Cohen's contention that he was mentally exhausted when he gave his confession to Downs and Ruth.

WALTHER: Isn't it true, Mr. Cohen, that in this confused, scared, emotional state that you say you were in on May 26, 1990, you nonetheless had the presence of mind to recall in exact detail how you murdered your mom and dad? . . .

COHEN: *No response.*

WALTHER: Mr. Cohen, do you understand my question? Do you want me to repeat the question, Mr. Cohen?

COHEN: No.

WALTHER: . . . You remembered how you murdered your parents, didn't you? You remembered where they were, what you did, exactly what you did, didn't you?

COHEN: I don't see a jury over there. I don't think I'm on trial.

WALTHER: Mr. Cohen, answer my question.

COHEN: . . . It's not something that is easy to forget.

The most dramatic moment of the day's testimony came when Walther and Cohen were verbally battling over whether Cohen had become a con man. Walther suddenly held up a picture of Conrad Lutz's battered and stabbed corpse and said, "You did a pretty good job of conning him, didn't you?"

Cohen didn't have a chance to answer because Perillo immediately objected. Herlihy sustained the objection.

Walther made one final point.

WALTHER: Mr. Cohen, I believe you indicated that
. . . you had done some ignorant things and some fool-
ish things in that eighteen months. You recall saying
that?

COHEN: Yes.

WALTHER: Wouldn't you agree with me, Mr. Cohen,
of all the things that have been said in this suppression
hearing, that is without a doubt the largest understate-
ment of any testimony in this case?

Perillo objected. Herlihy sustained the objection.

WALTHER: Nothing further.

The formal testimony in the hearing ended that afternoon. It had come down to a question of who the judge
believed, Cohen or the detectives. The lawyers' briefs
were to be delivered to Herlihy in March, and Herlihy
was expected to rule on the confessions in April.

chapter 6

- - - - - - - -

A Love As Strong As Death

The relationship between Cohen and Diane peaked during the winter of 1991. They were utterly devoted to one another. "Doesn't it seem like we can almost read each other's mind?!" he wrote in February. "I know this is true love happening! ... There's really nothing left for us to do but have children and die!"

In March he wrote, "Since you consented to be my wife I rarely feel all alone, I often wish I was in your arms, I listen to love songs I once thought were stupid, and I feel like I've got so much to live for."

With a ceaseless optimism he continued to reassure her that they would be together someday. He thought he'd be sentenced to life in prison, but he was sure his sentence would be commuted after nine years. "I believe it will be a difficult, and almost impossible at times, nine years," he wrote. "I guess the Lord blessed me with this promise because he knows what a doubtful and pessimistic person I am."

He wanted her to have lots of babies, and he promised to get her pregnant as soon as he could. "I'm going to keep you lazy and pregnant for a couple years," he wrote.

Somehow he got the idea that they would have twins, and he wrote to her many times about the names he would give them.

Diane was equally dedicated to Charlie. By the end of January 1991, she had sent him over 140 cards and letters during a seven-month period. Even though she didn't have a car, she somehow got to Gander Hill every Saturday morning to visit him.

Despite his fantasies, Diane knew the reality of the situation, and she assumed that he did, too. They didn't discuss the death penalty or the overall bleakness of his situation, and she never referred to his plans as "fantasies." If they comforted him, she felt she had no right to cast doubt on them. Perhaps, she thought, in his situation it was natural to dream.

In fact, she couldn't help but be drawn into the fantasies. She wanted his dreams to come true almost as badly as he did. She, too, fantasized about what their life together could have been like. Occasionally she let herself think about the possibility of having children with him. She wanted to believe that someday he could get out.

In late February Diane visited her family in Peoria, which made him think about his family. His aunts, uncles, and cousins wouldn't even speak with him, and he missed his parents. They had always forgiven and helped him, no matter what he had done. Now they weren't around to forgive or help him. "You are blessed to have your mother and sister and [nephew]," he wrote to her. "Always cherish their love because they have always been there for you."

At times he thought of giving up. Everything, absolutely everything, had gone wrong. He wondered if he would be better off dead. Sometimes the depression turned to anger and resentment, and he felt a profound lack of remorse. He was afraid he would have to face his past again as he had in the Louisiana prison, and he wasn't sure he could bear it.

During the first week of March, Charlie received word that the warden had turned down his request to get married. Marriage requests from unsentenced inmates were routinely denied within the Delaware prison system. He took the news well and promised Diane that he would wait patiently for the day she was legally his. The promise of a new life outside of prison with her was enough for him. In his heart, he already considered them married.

The trial had been scheduled for May, but because of numerous delays Herlihy postponed it to later in the year. All things considered, Charlie was relieved. "Now we can give more attention to mending our own lives day by day," he wrote to Diane.

Her visits with him at the prison were painful. They desperately wanted to be together, and being so close without being able to touch was excruciating. It seemed as though the world were conspiring to keep them apart. Sometimes they sat on the tables of the visiting booths and leaned against the glass to be closer.

Much of the time during their visits Diane simply listened as he described the pain, guilt, and frustration of his life. He regretted so much. There was so much he wished he could do over. Often his eyes filled with tears. She couldn't stand to see him suffering so much, yet there was nothing she could do to help. Every day he was reminded of what he'd done, and she saw what it was doing to him. She usually tried to change the subject because it was almost too painful to watch.

By the spring of 1991, Diane's feelings were beginning to change. She had a number of problems that were making her life difficult. First of all, she didn't have a car. Sometimes she got a ride to work, but most of the time she had to take public transportation. The trip involved two bus rides and a one-mile walk. She had to leave two hours early just to get to work on time. The trek began to wear on her. Getting to the prison on Saturdays and going to court weren't much easier. The stress of constantly worrying about Charlie wore on her as well.

Her anorexia started acting up again. Marie and her sister were both very thin. She knew it was irrational, but she felt fat and became jealous of them. Food no longer appealed to her. She started losing weight. Charlie implored her to eat regularly, but she couldn't. She saw a doctor, who prescribed Sinequan, an anti-depressant, but the stress kept mounting.

Diane was also having problems with her house mates. Marie was despondent over her husband's imprisonment. She could barely comprehend everything that had happened to them during the past two years. She argued that Bill had been framed and became virtually incapacitated with worry for him. She couldn't sleep at night, and she couldn't work.

There was yet another problem in the house. Marie's sister, whose husband was in prison, started seeing another man. Marie didn't approve, and they fought constantly. Diane was caught in the middle. The house was in turmoil. Eventually, Marie asked her sister to move out, and she did. Marie was a problem as well. She began making references to suicide. On one occasion Diane was so worried that she called several of Marie's relatives and asked them to come over and watch her. Diane just couldn't take it. The stress of Charlie's situation and Marie's depression was too much for her.

Charlie sensed Diane's unhappiness and began to fear losing her. She was all he had, and without her he was certain he would go mad, commit suicide, or try to escape. "We've got to fight to keep it together girl," he wrote. "I believe now more than ever that love is the strongest force in the universe."

Charlie was having problems of his own that spring at Gander Hill. He had several cell mates, none of whom he got along with and most of whom pestered him for sex. Gander Hill was overcrowded and beset with racial tensions. Fights broke out every day. An inmate named Doc walked around in the nude, practiced martial arts, and attacked guards and inmates without provocation. Another inmate in the pod set fire to his bed, and many of Charlie's belongings were stolen.

In June, Charlie shared a cell with a middle-aged black Muslim who hated white people. They were cooped up together in a six- by nine-foot cell 21½ hours a day. It was a psychological power struggle. Sometimes he felt so worn down he forgot everything but his name, Diane's name, and his shoe size.

Diane had become very good friends with Tim and Sandy, a couple from the Wilmington church she attended, and they wanted to help her. When the situation with Marie became intolerable, Diane moved in with them.

Tim and Sandy were very much against Charlie. They told her that she should forget him. He was dragging her down. They urged her to go back to school. You can't live like this forever, they said. It's not good for you. What kind of future will you have with him? Diane also spoke with another woman from her church whose husband had spent most of his life in prison.

"Diane, you don't really understand what this kind of life is like," the woman said. "It's a very lonely life, miserable most of the time. You end up working five-dollar-an-hour jobs, never have a good car, live in a dump apartment. Is that what you want?"

Diane told her that she had to help Charlie because no one else cared about him. If she left, she'd be deserting him.

"I understand how you feel. In prison relationships, everything's very intense. If you're in need of someone to care about you, it's powerful. The person in prison is so centered on you. It feels so good to get all that attention and love. It's addictive, but it's not a normal relationship. You're too young. You don't know what you're getting into. Get out while you can. Give yourself a chance to live."

At first Diane tried to block out their advice, but she did start thinking about her career. She wouldn't get anywhere unless she completed school, but getting her nursing degree was almost impossible in Delaware. She hadn't lived in Delaware long enough to qualify for in-state tuition, and even if she had, she couldn't afford to stop working. And how would she complete school if Charlie was extradited to California? She wasn't going to stay in Delaware by herself.

She thought about the year of nursing school she had missed. She would've been a year closer to graduating if she had stayed at home and waited this out. What could she do for Charlie in Delaware that she couldn't do from Illinois? Visit him once a week for 45 minutes? She could still speak with him on the phone, write letters, and visit occasionally. She could move back to Delaware or wherever he was after she finished nursing school.

Nothing about the whole mess was making sense to her anymore. Things weren't working out well at all. She'd never had to deal with such serious problems before. Charlie tried to be supportive, but he couldn't help himself, how could he help her? She was emotionally and physically worn out. She needed to get away from the situation just to think things out.

That spring, Dr. Robert L. Sadoff, an internationally known forensic psychiatrist on the faculty at the University of Pennsylvania, and Dr. Gerald Cooke, a well-known and well-respected psychologist from Plymouth Meeting, Pennsylvania, evaluated Cohen at the request of his lawyers. Both Cooke and Sadoff came to the conclusion that Cohen was mentally ill, and they both diagnosed him with a severe "borderline personality disorder."

The State of Delaware has two statutes regarding the use of mental illness as a defense of criminal liability. The first, not guilty by reason of insanity, is covered under statute 401a, which states, "at the time of the conduct charged, as a result of mental illness or mental defect, the accused lacked substantial capacity to appreciate the wrongfulness of his conduct."

Statute 401b describes the guilty but mentally ill defense, which has two parts. The first part states, "at the time of the conduct charged, a defendant suffered from a psychiatric disorder which substantially disturbed such person's thinking, feeling, or behavior." The second part states, "that such psychiatric disorder left such person with insufficient willpower to choose whether he would do the act or refrain from doing it, although physically capable." The plea is accepted if the defendant meets either of the criteria.

Since Cohen had fled and purposefully eluded capture for eighteenth months, Cooke and Sadoff agreed that Cohen understood "the wrongfulness of his conduct." Therefore, not guilty by reason of insanity was not a viable defense. They did, however, agree that Cohen met both criteria of 401b, guilty but mentally ill.

On May 2, 1991, Perillo and Winslow wrote a letter to the prosecutors, Walther and O'Neill, to "formally notify the state that the defense will be presenting evidence in support of a verdict of guilty but mentally ill."

Walther and O'Neill hired their own mental health expert, Dr. David Raskin, a psychiatrist from Wilmington, to examine Cohen. They wanted an objective opinion. If Cohen's psychologists were exaggerating his mental illness, they needed some ammunition to fight it. Raskin, who occasionally worked in the infirmary at Gander Hill, was familiar with Cohen and had met Dr. Martin Cohen just a few weeks before his murder.

In June, Diane went home to Illinois for a visit. She took all of her belongings with her because she knew she might not return. Within a week she registered for classes for the fall semester. She would stay in Peoria until she finished nursing school. She wrote to Charlie and told him that she would move back to Delaware when she graduated.

Charlie did not take the news well. "Is it me?" he asked her on the phone. "Are you having second thoughts about us?"

"That's not it at all," she said. "None of it's your fault. It's all the other things getting in the way and making it hard."

Charlie stopped communicating with her. She wrote to him repeatedly pleading with him to contact her. She knew he was hurt, and she felt guilty. After several weeks, she received a letter from him. "I'm having trouble writing this letter," he wrote. "All I want is you. . . . You belong to me and I am yours forever. . . . I'm really beginning to believe that our love is as strong as death. . . . Come home to me soon, darling. I'm waiting for you."

After numerous delays, Winslow and Perillo filed their opening brief for the suppression of Cohen's confessions in June 1991. It was 110 pages. The prosecutors, Walther and O'Neill, responded with their brief in July, and the defense filed a reply brief in August. The matter was finally in Herlihy's hands.

chapter 7

- - - - - - -

Life Is Beautiful

Since there were only a handful of protective-custody inmates at Gander Hill, the prison administration did away with the classification and moved Charlie to a pod in the general prison population in July.

He had not given up on Diane. He referred to her move to Illinois as "our first marital crisis." He wrote, "I will miss you tons while you're in nursing school but I trust it will be the best decision for our future together." In another letter he wrote, "Remember, I support you in whatever you do. All I ask in return is your loyalty and honesty."

He did not adapt well to being housed in the general population. He was afraid to leave his cell, and many of the inmates sensed his fear and harassed him. It seemed that almost all of the inmates were either homosexual or bisexual. He was terrified of being sexually attacked and tired of the constant come-ons.

In early August he was placed in a cell with a 200-pound inmate named Keith, who had, according to Charlie, "sometimes good intentions." Keith was well known and greatly feared in the prison population. Keith

reminded Charlie of himself a few years earlier, only
Keith was more physical and less psychological. He was
scared and confused, and it seemed that he had given up
on life.

Keith hated Charlie, and one day Keith threatened to
throw Charlie out of the cell if he didn't leave voluntarily.
The next night he screamed at Charlie and punched him.
Charlie didn't defend himself. He simply took it. A guard
in the tier heard the disturbance. By the time he got there,
Charlie was cowering in a corner of the cell holding the
side of his head. The guard moved him to a different cell.

Several inmates accused Charlie of snitching on Keith,
but Charlie knew better than to snitch on anyone. The inmates did terrible things to snitches. "You can just imagine the fun and happiness I've been feeling," he wrote to
Diane. Charlie was so afraid he decided to fast.

Charlie was interviewed by a mental health counselor
at the prison because of his fast. Cohen told the counselor
he was depressed over a personal situation and that he
would begin eating. He also explained that he was having
problems in the general population.

Dr. David Raskin, the psychiatrist hired by the prosecution, examined him on August 26. Charlie smiled oddly
and told Raskin, "The walls have ears." Raskin alerted
the staff at the infirmary that Cohen was showing signs of
a psychotic break—paranoia, bizarre behavior, inappropriate affect—and the next day he was admitted to the infirmary.

He was put on full suicide watch in the pink room. His
clothing was taken away, and he was put in a cell with a
bunk and a blanket. Guards and nurses checked on him
every couple of hours. He denied any intention of harm-
ing himself, but he admitted that he was depressed.

Charlie was polite with the infirmary staff, but the odd
smiling continued. He stated that he was reflecting on his
situation and knew who his friends were. Although the

complete isolation of suicide watch was stressful, he preferred the infirmary. He managed to get some sleep, and no one bothered him.

He spent much of his time in the infirmary writing to Diane and dreaming of a life with her outside of prison. He didn't care if the police read his letters anymore. "Maybe they'll read them in court and then the whole world will know how strong a love can be," he wrote.

Charlie fantasized of a happy, quiet, pastoral life with Diane once he was released from prison. His plans included a house on a lake in Maine or Canada, children, pets, and many outdoor activities. He would have his own ministry and a landscaping business and be a good husband and father. Most importantly, he would stop playing the fool.

He wanted to do good, normal things, like go shopping with her, fall asleep on her shoulder while she watched soaps, and go to church with her. He didn't want to hear a grown man eat with his mouth open, have to watch his door to make sure nobody stole his belongings, or have 200-pound bullies accusing him of imagined wrong-doings. He didn't want to hear about courts, judges, lawyers, or Delaware law ever again.

He remained withdrawn. He went out of his cell during short recreation periods, but he kept to himself. He claimed he wasn't suicidal, and on September 5 he was discharged from the infirmary and returned to the general prison population.

Once Diane started classes that fall, she and Charlie didn't communicate much, which worried Charlie greatly. His trial was postponed again, this time until November, and Judge Herlihy still hadn't ruled on his confessions.

On September 10, Charlie again met with a mental health counselor and claimed that he was being threatened by other inmates. He insisted on being moved to the prison in Georgetown, which offered protective-custody status. He refused to name those who were threatening him, but he told the counselor that he was having thoughts of suicide and of having to "defend" himself. He was admitted to the infirmary and put on full suicide status again. He had lost almost twelve pounds during the previous two weeks.

He seemed depressed and withdrawn and wouldn't answer questions posed to him by the medical staff. He said that the prison was too loud and requested earplugs. On September 19 he told a counselor that he would not return to the general population. "I like being alone here," he said. "I learn a lot about myself." He was still smiling inappropriately.

Charlie was discharged from the infirmary that same day and placed in administrative segregation, a prison pod where problem cases were kept. He was placed in a cell with a young man named Joe, who had also been on suicide watch recently. Joe seemed very strange, and Charlie was afraid of him. One night while Charlie was sleeping, Joe suddenly began pounding on the door and screaming for a guard. Joe was bleeding from his face, and he claimed that Charlie had cut him. Charlie was taken to a conference room and questioned while several guards searched the cell for a knife or sharp object. Charlie claimed that he hadn't cut Joe, and he didn't get back to sleep until 3 A.M.

In late September he wrote to Diane that the inmates running the tier would not let him use the phone to call her. They wanted him to 'marry' one of them, not a woman on the outside. "They can rearrange me but they can't change me!" he wrote.

Prison life was a very twisted game, he claimed. Even though he wasn't homosexual, he was expected to participate in sadomasochistic sex with the other inmates. He was constantly being pressured by them, and they told him that he would eventually break down. He felt like fighting all the time, but he prayed that he could make it through the next two months without any marks on his record.

A counselor met with Charlie on October 1. He answered a few of the counselor's questions but then abruptly and without explanation stated that he felt uncomfortable and wanted to end the interview.

By early October, Charlie was frantic about his lack of contact with Diane. He hadn't spoken with her or received a letter from her in weeks. He longed to have her near and constantly worried about losing her. He regretted not begging her to return to Delaware when he'd had the chance. "All I can say is I would surely die of a broken heart if you ever left me," he wrote.

Diane was very worried about him. His attitude was changing. He made strange accusations in his letters, which she didn't know whether to believe. He wrote that "someone was trying to set him up" and that someone "out there wishes I were dead." He also claimed that the inmates on his pod were withholding food from his meal trays and used food as bait for sex. He wrote that some of the ministers at the prison were working for the police and wanted "sexual favors" from him. "I guess I could understand a person working with the police," he wrote, "but I can't stomach someone using the Bible to get sex."

He saw a mental health counselor on October 7. Charlie spoke slowly and softly as though someone were listening. He said he hadn't been sleeping well because the other inmates were bothering him. Their objective, he claimed, was to make him tired, physically, emotionally, and spiritually, so he would break down. He also said he had been hearing voices, but he wasn't sure who the voices belonged to. Charlie was immediately admitted into the infirmary. It was his third stint on suicide watch in six weeks. He had lost another ten pounds.

After spending two days sleeping in the infirmary, he stated that he felt better and hadn't heard any more voices. He was discharged from the infirmary and transferred to the Transition Unit, a pod with a treatment program for inmates who were having problems adjusting to prison life. He was locked down 23 hours a day, but he was happy to have some protection and a private cell.

He often thought about his upcoming trial, which was scheduled to begin on November 5 and would last about a month. In a way, he was excited. It would be the culmination of everything that had happened in his life since the night of November 12, 1988. He was anxious to see if any of his relatives or friends showed up. He wrote to Diane's mother and sister and invited them to his trial. He was afraid his relatives wouldn't be on his side. He had found out that his aunts had turned over to the prosecution the letters he had written to them begging for their forgiveness.

He knew the jury would have to come to a unanimous decision to put him to death, so he figured his chances for a life sentence were better than 50–50. His lawyers told him he was lucky he wasn't in Florida, where just one person, the judge, determined the sentences in murder cases. They also told him that if he were sentenced to death, they would appeal the decision. The state hadn't executed anyone in a long, long time, and it wasn't likely that he would be put to death.

He discovered that the other inmates would leave him alone if he were dirty, so he stopped showering, brushing his teeth, and shaving. He also stopped sending his dirty clothes to the laundry because he didn't trust the inmate who picked up and delivered the laundry. By October 20 he smelled so bad that a guard ordered him to shower. He refused. Several guards escorted him to the showers where he was sprayed for lice and washed.

On October 23, Charlie met with a counselor. He agreed to shower regularly, but he stared at the counselor, and the session ended when he wouldn't speak with her anymore.

On October 31, 1991, Judge Herlihy denied Charles Cohen's motion to suppress his confessions. In a 64-page ruling Herlihy wrote that Cohen "initiated the conversation about his parents' murder," "did so voluntarily and not due to police pressure," and "fully understood and waived his right to counsel and his right to remain silent."

In every instance where the testimony of Cohen and the police differed, Herlihy "found more credible the testimony of the police." Herlihy said that any discussion of the Delaware murder case between the detectives and Cohen during the flights was "tangential."

"The Court is impressed with Detective Downs's thoroughness and his adherence to the constitutional ground rules then in effect," Herlihy wrote. ". . . Cohen's testimony indicated confusion about when the police discussed certain matters with him, if they were even discussed. . . .

"The Court finds that the police did not manipulate Cohen. . . . There is no evidence whatsoever of police pressure, questioning or badgering. . . . The Court finds that Cohen's decision to confess was the product of his own mind and volition and was not the result of any police manipulation or functional equivalent of interrogation."

Jury selection for Cohen's trial was scheduled to start the following Tuesday.

Winslow and Perillo talked to Charlie about changing his plea from not guilty to guilty but mentally ill. There was no use entering a not guilty plea since the prosecution could use the confessions, and they had no grounds to argue for an insanity plea. Guilty but mentally ill was their only option. He might still get the death penalty, but two life sentences were more likely. Even Raskin, the psychiatrist enlisted by the state to evaluate Cohen, had agreed that Cohen was mentally ill. Only one guilty but mentally ill defendant had ever been sentenced to death in Delaware, and that sentence was later overturned on appeal. Charlie was becoming distrustful of his lawyers, though, and was reluctant to change his plea.

During a phone call to Diane, he whispered that he couldn't talk because undercover people were listening. He also claimed that Nancy Perillo wasn't on his case anymore, and he told Diane that people had been following her when she had lived in Delaware. Diane expressed some skepticism, and he was insulted. Evidently, she couldn't be trusted either. He hung up and decided not to call her again. The next day he wrote to Diane that he wanted to terminate their relationship. The engagement was off.

Almost a year earlier, on December 12, 1990, four men from Philadelphia had driven a bright yellow rental van to a Delaware Trust Bank branch on Route 13, half a mile south of the Delaware State Hospital. They surprised two armored-car guards delivering money to the bank, shot them in the back several times, and fled with $613,000.

Police spotted the van on I–495 just north of Wilmington and gave chase. Numerous police cruisers and a police helicopter followed the van into Pennsylvania, through Chester, and over the Commodore Barry Bridge into New Jersey. As they were crossing the bridge, the suspects' van collided with a Chester police van, but the suspects managed to drive on. They drove several miles into New Jersey before crashing into a water tower and being apprehended. One of the armored car guards died that day. The other guard died a month later, just twelve hours after the birth of his third son.

In October 1991, all four suspects were convicted of first-degree murder. The prosecution requested the death penalty, but the jury could not reach a unanimous decision, so the defendants were automatically given sentences of life without parole. New Castle County juries had not imposed the death penalty for ten years. The prosecutors on the case, Eugene Hall and Steve Walther, were incensed.

"We live in a terribly jaded society if we've come to accept that type of conduct without returning the death penalty," said Hall. "It's just outrageous behavior. I don't know when the community is going to wake up. It's just unbelievable."

"I think it's time for all the politicians to stop talking about how tough they are on crime and enact a death penalty statute in this state that will work," Walther said.

The Delaware legislature took note of Hall's and Walther's harsh words. Just two days later the state legislature voted overwhelmingly for new death penalty sentencing procedures that made the judge, not the jury, responsible for sentencing in capital murder cases. The jury would merely vote on a sentencing recommendation, and a unanimous decision would not be necessary. Governor Mike Castle signed the bill into law on Monday, November 4, 1991. The new law took effect immediately and was to be applied retroactively to all pending cases.

As soon as Winslow and Perillo heard that the governor had signed the new bill, they filed a motion with Herlihy to preclude application of the new law to Cohen's case. They argued that it was unconstitutional to sentence Cohen under the new law since he had been charged under the previous law. They pointed to the "ex post facto" clause of the U.S. Constitution, which stated that the penalty for a crime could not be made worse after the

crime had been committed. Herlihy immediately postponed Cohen's trial, which was scheduled to begin the
following day.

On November 13 the Delaware Supreme Court agreed
to consider the constitutionality of the new law. Herlihy
requested that the courts be permitted to continue with the
guilty or innocence phase of the fifteen pending capital
murder cases, since the new law applied only to the penalty phase. The Supreme Court granted that permission.

Charlie took the news of the recent developments
badly. His precarious mental condition deteriorated even
further. Diane was also very upset. Charlie wanted to
break off their relationship, and he wouldn't call or write.
He didn't seem like the same person she had come to
love. He was changing for the worse, and she had no way
of helping him. She begged him to write to her. "Whatever I've done," she wrote, "I'm sorry."

She called Nancy Perillo and asked her about Charlie.
"You and I are the two people who care about him the
most," said Perillo, "and he's pushing both of us away."

Herlihy scheduled the guilt or innocence phase of Cohen's case for November 18. By then Perillo and Winslow had been able to convince Charlie to change his plea.

On the morning of Monday, November 18, Cohen was
transported to superior court. He filled out a guilty plea
form admitting to two counts of first-degree murder and
two weapons charges. He also indicated on the form that
he understood the charges.

In a legal procedure known as a colloquy, Judge
Herlihy questioned Cohen to make sure he was entering
the plea knowingly and voluntarily. At first Cohen stated
that he understood the plea and the nature of the proceeding, although he answered slowly and seemed oddly pas-
sive. He was thin and frail, and his eyes were bloodshot.

After a few more questions from Herlihy, he stopped responding.

> HERLIHY: Mr. Cohen, what I'm trying to do is make sure that since we're appearing here today in a proceeding without a jury, that you understand what rights you had that you would give up by going through the proceeding we have today. That's what I have to do, that you knowingly and intelligently and voluntarily give up those rights. Okay. Do you follow me?

Cohen looked down. He did not respond.

> HERLIHY: What I'm saying is we're having a nonjury hearing right now on the issue of whether there is a factual basis for accepting your plea of guilty but mentally ill, a nonjury hearing. But you also have a right to have a jury trial on that issue as well. I'm not talking about penalty, I'm talking strictly about guilty but mentally ill. You follow me? If you'd like to say something, you may do so.

Cohen again did not respond. Winslow leaned over and said to Charlie, "Do you have any questions you want to ask him?" After a long pause Charlie said he understood.

> HERLIHY: Okay. At that trial you would have been presumed innocent of any of the charges in the indictment until a jury decided that you were either guilty or guilty but mentally ill. Do you understand that?

Cohen didn't answer. He stared into the microphone on the podium in front of him and seemed to smile.

> HERLIHY: ... You understand what I mean? So you would have been presumed innocent at that trial until

and unless a jury decided that you were guilty or guilty but mentally ill. You understand that?

Cohen again did not answer. He didn't seem to be aware of what was happening.

HERLIHY: Is there something about that question which is confusing?

Winslow spoke to Cohen quietly for a moment but didn't get a response from him. Winslow requested a short recess, which Herlihy granted.

During the recess, Winslow again attempted to speak with Cohen but he wouldn't respond. Dr. Gerald Cooke, the psychologist who had shown up to testify for the defense, also spoke with Charlie, but he wouldn't respond to Cooke either.

After the recess, Cooke took the stand. He said that Cohen was "probably hallucinating. I say 'probably' because when I question him he won't respond." Cooke also said that Cohen had gone into a 'psychotic episode . . . approaching perhaps even a catatonic state." He was "responding to internal stimuli, that is, voices."

Cohen smiled oddly during Cooke's testimony. Cooke suggested that Cohen be hospitalized, medicated, and put on suicide watch. Walther vigorously opposed Cohen's hospitalization at Delaware State Hospital on grounds that he was a security risk.

"Do you think he's playing games with us today?" Walther asked Cooke.

"No, I don't believe he's playing games," said Cooke.

Walther got permission from the court to have Dr. Raskin examine Cohen before Herlihy ruled on Cohen's competency to continue with the legal proceedings. Cohen was returned to Gander Hill. He was immediately readmitted to the infirmary and once again placed on full suicide watch.

The next day Raskin examined Cohen. Charlie would not respond to any questions from Raskin or even acknowledge his presence. On November 19, Raskin wrote a letter to Walther about Charlie's mental state.

1) At the present time, Mr. Cohen is mute. He refuses to talk with me and, in general, refuses to talk with the nursing staff.

2) His chart does document behavior which is symptomatic of persons with psychotic illness, that is, irrelevant communication, muteness, and paranoid behavior.

3) I cannot rule out the presence of malingering behavior especially since his muteness did not start in any major degree until he was in court.

Recommendations:

I recommend that Mr. Charles Cohen be medicated with antipsychotic medications. If, in fact, he is experiencing a psychotic episode, these medications should within a brief period of time (days to weeks), bring him back to a level of competency to stand trial.

If on the other hand his behavior is more conscious and malingering, the medications may have no effect.

For the next several days, Charlie lay motionless on his bunk and stared as if he were in a coma. He wouldn't eat, drink, speak, or make eye contact with anyone, and he refused the medication prescribed by the prison psychiatrist.

On Thursday, November 21, he stared out the window of his cell with a blanket around his shoulders most of the day. He ate a little food on Friday, but his condition remained the same. Nancy Perillo visited Charlie on Sunday evening in his infirmary cell. He lay on the bunk with his hands at his side and his head under the blanket and wouldn't speak with her.

His condition had not changed by Tuesday, so Herlihy held a hearing to discuss Cohen's competency. Charlie was brought to court for the hearing, during which he stared straight ahead and seemed oblivious to the proceedings.

Herlihy called Dr. Antonio C. Sacre, the Gander Hill psychiatrist, to the stand. Sacre testified that Cohen "was lying in bed, refusing eye contact. We really had to shake him to see if he was okay." Sacre had prescribed medication for Cohen to "break his mute state and try to find out what is going on." Herlihy ordered that Cohen be medicated with psychotropic drugs, against his will if necessary.

Charlie was returned to Gander Hill. He silently walked into his infirmary cell with his head down, lay on the bunk, and covered his head. He stayed that way for several hours.

He ate some dinner, drank three glasses of water, and took the medication without objection. Sacre had prescribed 10 mg. of Navane, four times per day. Charlie remained uncommunicative but showed signs of improvement.

On November 29, the infirmary staff convinced him to take a shower, and he continued taking the Navane as prescribed. He also told a counselor, "I'm seeing things. I'm hallucinating, and I'm scared. I never had these before."

The next day he complained of shortness of breath and said his skin felt warm and moist. "I'm fasting, only drinking water to cleanse my body because I'm hallucinating," he said. "I see horrific faces that I know aren't real because of how they look, but I see them just as if they were here like you are."

On the following day he showered, ate, and made eye contact. When asked how he was doing, he said he was fine. He also said he was not suicidal. However, he still spent the majority of the day wrapped in a blanket staring out of his cell window.

On December 2 he made eye contact with a counselor and muttered a few words. "Life," he said, "is beautiful."

chapter 8

- - - - - - - -

A Strange Situation

Diane received a belated Christmas card from Charlie in January saying that he wanted to be friends. She was relieved to hear from him. The letter was lucid. It didn't seem paranoid or distorted. After the reports she had gotten from Nancy Perillo, she wasn't sure he would ever recover from the strangeness that had infected his brain. She wrote back, saying she wanted more from their relationship but that she would be his friend if nothing else.

The past few months hadn't been easy for her. She was doing well in school, but she felt as if her life were coming apart at the end of the semester, with tests to prepare for and papers to write, the demands of her part-time job, and the constant worry about Charlie. She needed someone to talk to, but Charlie wasn't there. She found herself breaking into tears at odd times. She hadn't realized how much she had come to rely on him.

In mid-December, Charlie was moved from the infirmary back to the Transition Unit in Gander Hill. He was still severely depressed and withdrawn. At first he was locked in his cell 23 hours a day. He was gradually given more freedom, and he participated in numerous counseling programs and self-help groups.

On Wednesday, February 12, 1992, Cohen was again brought before Judge Herlihy to enter a plea to charges that he had murdered his parents. First, the court took up the matter of Cohen's competency.

Dallas Winslow called Dr. Gerald Cooke to the stand. Cooke had been in court previously when Cohen had acted strangely. Winslow asked Cooke about Cohen's problems the past November.

"I was present in the courtroom when the judge was doing the colloquy, and basically it appeared that gradually Mr. Cohen became more and more absorbed within himself due to the depression he was experiencing," Cooke said. "When I interviewed him today, he tells me also that he was feeling very paranoid and distrustful at that time as well. And that is also part of the reason that he withdrew and he became relatively nonresponsive to the judge's questions. [He] appeared to be responding possibly also to internal stimuli, that is, perhaps hallucinating. Because of his mental state at that time, I felt he had become incompetent to proceed."

Winslow asked him about the treatment Cohen had received since November. "It really is comprised of two parts," said Cooke. "One was that he was placed on medication. I believe it was originally Navane, ten milligrams four times a day. Then he was gradually reduced in that amount, and it was discontinued sometime around the end of January.

"In addition, he was transferred to the Transition Unit, and I attribute that for much of his improvement. He had first been in the prison population and then in isolation, both of which he found very traumatic. And that being in the transition program, being in the counseling that was offered there, feeling safer in that environment, I feel has helped him come out of the serious depression and paranoid thinking that made him incompetent previously."

Winslow asked him about Cohen's current condition. "When I saw him this morning, it was my opinion that he was competent to proceed. He is still somewhat depressed, though not as depressed as before. He is still somewhat anxious, but he does not seem to be having the paranoid ideation. He is fragile by the nature of his personality structure, and he can regress under stress, but he seems to be in pretty good shape this morning.

"He was responsive to my questions. He was able to explain the purpose of this hearing. He no longer feels paranoid. That paranoia had included myself, yourself, the other attorneys, and the judge. And he no longer had that feeling. He felt he could trust and work with his attorneys. His thought processes were goal-directed. He wasn't hallucinating or delusional."

Walther cross-examined Cooke and asked him about Cohen's mental condition in future legal proceedings, such as a sentencing hearing. "If he remains in the mental state that I saw him in this morning, he should have no trouble," said Dr. Cooke. "My concern would be that as he hears some of these things, if he becomes upset and the depression worsens, we may see a repeat of what happened last time."

After cross-examining Cooke, Walther requested that Cohen be kept on medication to assure that he could face sentencing. He also commented for the record, "The state doesn't agree with the plea but won't offer evidence to the contrary. There is no agreement between the state and the defendant."

Cohen was then brought to the podium for the colloquy. As he had on November 18, Judge Herlihy posed numerous questions to Cohen to make sure he understood the ramifications of his guilty but mentally ill plea.

Cohen seemed alert and aware but frail. He had a short

beard and a scruffy haircut. He answered the questions from the judge in a quiet, halting voice. He said he understood his plea, and he was able to explain the purpose of the proceeding.

Herlihy asked if he understood the rights he was giving up by entering a guilty plea, such as the right to go to trial, the right to produce witnesses, and the right to be presumed innocent. Charlie answered, "I think I understand. In essence, this is it. There is no possibility of a defense."

Herlihy also made sure Cohen understood that there were only two sentences that could be imposed for any kind of guilty plea to first-degree murder—life without the possibility of release or death. Herlihy pointed out that if he received the former sentence, life, he would actually get two life sentences, one for each murder, which would run consecutively, not concurrently. Mandatory sentences of thirty years for each of the two weapons charges would also be tacked on. In other words, the best he could hope for would be life in prison without the possibility of ever getting out—a "natural" life sentence. Cohen said he understood.

Herlihy then asked him, "On or about November 12, 1988, in New Castle County, did you intentionally cause the death of Martin Cohen by stabbing him in the neck with a knife and striking him about the head with a blunt object?"

Cohen hung his head and quietly answered, "Yes."

The judge asked him the same question about his mother, and he again answered in the affirmative.

Charlie asked the judge about the date of his sentencing. Herlihy explained that the penalty phase of his case would be delayed until the Delaware Supreme Court ruled on the state's new death penalty sentencing procedures.

"We just don't know," Herlihy said. "We're in a strange situation."

Winslow then called Cooke back to the stand. Cooke had performed a psychological evaluation of Cohen in November 1990. He had performed a battery of psychological tests, interviewed Cohen several times, and reviewed much of the case material. Winslow asked him to describe the results of his evaluation.*

"At the time I saw him initially he had a very bland and superficial affect or emotional tone. In fact, it was rather inappropriate to the seriousness of the situation. That has obviously over time changed. At that time he had converted to Christianity, and he was using that, I believe, as a defense mechanism to deny and distance a lot of feelings about the situation. Since then he has obviously become depressed to various degrees at different times. So we've seen a lot of change in his moods.

"Also, at the time I saw him there was no clinical evidence of anxiety or depression for the same reasons. There was no evidence of thinking disorder or of psychosis or of hallucinations or delusions. And again, those are things that have subsequently been documented. I saw him before these things occurred. I indicated that because of the type of illness, he had the potential for such things, but at least to that time they had not been documented.

"As far as the history, he was an only child. And I think that's important because he tells me even from an early age he was very envious that his friends had siblings and he was envious of his friends' closeness to their siblings. And this theme of feeling that he didn't have sufficient closeness is something that runs throughout the evaluation. And this desire for closeness, I think, influences a lot of his future relationships.

"He described his mother as a person with a good

*Cooke's testimony has been abridged.

sense of humor, but also someone, I think, who overprotected him to the point of sometimes suffocating him. So his feelings about his mother are really rather conflicting. He described his father as a person who worked a lot, but also as someone who put a lot of effort and attention into him. So that he really was talking about his early childhood as a period that he perceived as very close family, lots of affection, lots of attention from his parents. However, that changed.

"At a certain point, probably around age seventeen or so, he went through a delayed adolescent rebellion. He perceived that his parents' pride turned to disappointment, and I think that began a vicious circle where his normal adolescent rebellion was met with a reaction from his parents that he was disappointing them, that he wasn't going to get the kind of support and nurturance that he got before if he didn't share their attitudes and values, which, in turn, made him more rebellious and which tested their love and caring, which, in turn, led them to be more rejective of him.

"I think part of what went into that vicious circling was this feeling from an early age that there was a condition, a contingency upon his parents' love and approval; otherwise, I don't think he would have had those concerns about not being close with others and being envious of his friends.

"He felt that he was very unsure about what he wanted to do at that point. He feels that his father pushed him and tried to squash his feelings of independence. He didn't really want to go to college but went and really felt sort of lost in the crowd. He also felt that all of a sudden after being overprotected, he had a lot of freedom and didn't know what to do with that freedom. And I think that was stressful for him, and this was part of the reason he got in with a crowd that was using a lot of marijuana.

"He said he stayed high a good deal of the time. And

he also got involved with other drugs. Obviously, as soon as he got involved with drugs and with people his parents disapproved of, that, in turn, heightened the conflict between him and his parents. That heightened his feelings of upset, rejection, and led to even more rebellion and drug use.

"From what he says, there were also other factors that led to a deterioration not only in his functioning but in the family dynamics as a whole. His mother had some physical problems and, I think, probably was going through a period of at least difficulty, if not depression. Around the same time his father lost the job he had had for many years. So the family was in a lot of stress.

"He went through a period of leaving home, living with friends, then moving back. He also went through a period in which he experienced very radical changes in his lifestyle and his attitudes. On the one hand he was involved in a sort of punk-rock lifestyle. Then he turned around shortly thereafter and enlisted in the Marines, which is a rather different lifestyle, but only lasted six days.

"I explored social relationships with him. Probably the two most important relationships were with a girl named Becky in 1984 and then Katie in 1987. My understanding of the dynamics of both relationships are pretty similar. I think in both cases, because of his exaggerated need to get close, he fantasized about these relationships. In his mind the relationships were far more advanced, far more serious, far more intense than they were in the minds of the women involved.

"When those relationships ended, the first one in 1984, he became very depressed. He did something that is an unusual sort of self-mutilation—he shaved his entire body. He increased his drug use. He began to suffer from bulimia and gained about 55 to 60 pounds. He went up to about 200 pounds. Prior to that he had been obsessed with being a vegetarian, eating the proper food, and had been down to about 135 pounds. Again, we see the extremes.

"He says he changed a great deal after the 1984 relationship, became more introverted, more of a loner, more morbid. And this is when the fantasies began. He had fantasies in which he dominated and controlled people, both aggressively and sexually. It seems pretty clear that on the one hand he was very inadequate, very vulnerable, and very powerless, and on the other hand, this resulted in compensatory fantasies of being dominating and powerful, sometimes in a very morbid and sadistic way.

"And again he tried at this point, after having tried the lifestyle of the Marines, to go to the other direction of trying to shock people. He got a Mohawk haircut, wearing a jacket with a skull and crossbones on it, other sorts of things like that.

"He was also very irreligious, almost antireligion for a number of years, and then indicates that he converted to Christ in May of 1990. Since that time his religion has waxed and waned, I think, in association with his illness. But that's another example of how he can go to one extreme or another in his attitudes, his values, and his beliefs.

"I also explored the second relationship, the one with Katie in 1987. The same sort of thing happened. When it ended, he became depressed again. I think, frankly, from 1984 on he was never totally free of depression, but it worsened after each of these rejections. His intense hunger for unconditional love or acceptance led him to fantasy or idealization, then the shattering sort of feeling when the rejection occurs. And again, I believe the fantasy exceeded the reality.

"He became very, very angry after that. I think for a period of time he had intense anger toward both Katie and his parents. Seems like he needed to blame someone for the things that were going on in his life. He began to feel he was a failure, his life was shattered, and that Katie and his parents were the ones primarily responsible for that. I think after the move to Delaware, though, in April of '88, perhaps the fact that Katie was no longer geographically present, the focus of his anger more and more became his parents.

"Gradually he began to withdraw emotionally from interpersonal relationships. He'd even stand back in relationships with others, be cold, aloof, view others with amusement, even contempt. He had been hurt so often by his rejections because of his overinvolvement that he would withdraw from them.

"I also explored various aspects of his sexual relations, and I think there's a sexual identity problem, too. He was never involved in homosexual relationships before the offense. According to what he told me, when he was living on the streets, he would allow men to perform oral sex on him for money, and he rationalizes that as needing to survive on the streets. But there are some other things in his past, such as being a nude model for art class while in college, things of that nature, which would say to me that his own sexual identity was also a conflict for him.

"Testing shows he feels trapped by his sexual concerns and sexuality, mixed up with his identity with aggressiveness. And he can get really preoccupied and obsessed with sexual issues, to the point of misperception of reality.

"I also went into his drug and alcohol use with him. I don't think there was such an alcohol problem, but there was a significant drug problem involving marijuana. It involved hashish oil and various pills, particularly stimulants. There was a period of time between 1983 and 1986 he estimates that he used LSD about one hundred times. He says the last ten to fifteen times he used it were what are classified as bad trips, became very paranoid, felt very angry. This is unusual. I think what was happening is he was really hanging on by a thread psychologically, that when he took LSD he may very well have gone over the line into psychosis for a brief period of time.

"As far as the events leading up to the killing, he says that about October 31st of 1988 he had such frequent and angry fantasies about killing someone that he felt that he had to get the anger out of his system. And he decided that he would go to New York City, wait in Central Park, and try to kill a stranger. And he did this, feeling that if he were to do that, maybe he could get himself back to normal and return home and get rid of that feeling of having to kill someone.

"When I asked him about wanting to kill someone, he used the term 'raw power' a number of times. And again, I think what we've got here is someone who feels so powerless and so inadequate that he's had to compensate for that through both fantasy and eventually through the killings.

"He said that after he failed to find someone to kill in New York City, he decided to kill his parents. And he said this was not only for the power feeling, but also a political statement. And he went on to explain to me that he feels that our system is screwed up. He saw his parents as a representation of that, and he wanted to shatter that. There's a certain paranoid grandiosity in there, too, the feeling that by killing his parents he almost creates in society a certain anarchy. On another level, I think, [the killing] would reduce others to the level where he felt himself.

"He says that the killing and subsequently eluding the police gave him a sense of power, pride, and confidence in his abilities, but that every time he felt secure and powerful something would happen, and he'd have to be on the run again. So he became more and more depressed. And then eventually he says that when he was arrested, he wanted to confess what had happened to him because he had gotten to the point where he just couldn't deal with it anymore. . . .

"Based on the testing, I would say that the killing, from a psychological perspective, really was directed more to his father than his mother. He perceived his father as the person who had given him love and approval when he met his father's standards and then as the person who withdrew it. It's my opinion that Mr. Cohen never really developed an independent sense of identity or self-esteem, that really his own sense of identity or self-esteem depended very heavily on his father giving or withholding of the approval.

"And the testing shows that the anger, the feeling associated with his perception of his father is significant enough to lead to misperceptions of reality. That when these distortions occur, there's a significant reduction in his ability to control his feelings, his thoughts, his fantasies, and his behavior. So that what happened is he came to see his father as a very evil and unapproachable figure. Same dynamics with his mother, but I think less intense than with his father."

Cooke then presented his psychological diagnoses of Cohen.

"The primary diagnosis, in my opinion, is borderline personality disorder, severe. I would have to say that I think his is among the more severe borderline personality disorders I've seen. The second is what we now call dysthymia, which is really the old depressive neurosis. I think that he did have a depressive problem from 1984 to at least May of 1990. It was in remission, I think, in part because of his conversion to Christianity and the kind of intensity that helped him deny the depressive feelings, but it returned subsequently.

"The most important aspect of the borderline personality disorder is an instability in the person's sense of identity, in their affect or emotion, and in their interpersonal relationships with others. And the *Diagnostic and Statistical Manual* lists eight criteria. I think he clearly meets six of those criteria. It says in order to make the diagnosis you have to have five. He has at least six and possibly more of the others."

Cooke then described the following eight criteria of borderline personality disorder: unstable and intense interpersonal relationships, self-damaging impulsiveness, marked shifts from normal mood to depression, lack of control of anger, recurrent suicidal threats or self-mutilating behavior, a persistent identity disturbance, chronic feelings of emptiness or boredom, and frantic efforts to avoid real or imagined abandonment. Cooke also explained that a person with a borderline personality disorder can go "over the border" and become psychotic in periods of extreme stress.

Winslow posed a question. "Doctor, do you have an opinion within a reasonable psychological certainty with respect to whether there's a connection between the disorders you mentioned and the killing of his mother and father?"

"I think the killings are directly a product and outgrowth of his disorder," said Cooke. "There was no argument or things of that nature. This was an outgrowth of morbid, aggressive fantasies that developed over time that helped him, in a pathological way, find some identity for himself. I think he had reached such a point of distortion in misperception of his relationship with his parents, his relationships with the world, that he felt that he had no alternative but to kill them."

"And do you have an opinion within reasonable psychological certainty as to whether or not, at the time of the killing of his parents, Mr. Cohen suffered from a psychiatric disorder that substantially disturbed his thinking, feeling, or behavior?"

"I do. That opinion is that he did, from both the borderline personality disorder and the dysthymic disorder. His thinking, feeling, and behavior were very much disturbed by them."

The court adjourned for the day, and Cooke met outside the courthouse with members of the local media to discuss his diagnosis of Cohen.

"Could he have faked it?" a reporter asked.

"No. The psychological tests have built-in indicators of whether a person is trying to fake it. In addition, there is so much consistency between the way he appears on interview, the historical information, the test findings, it would be very, very difficult for someone to pull all that together and fake it. If he's faking it, he deserves an Oscar."

"Has he expressed regret?"

"He has expressed regret for the killing in some ways, but it's not a full out-and-out regret. He still has many of the beliefs that I've described today. They're not gone. So he still believes that in many ways his parents were responsible for—to use the word he used—'shattering' his life and stood for a power structure he didn't believe in and things of that nature. So there is still a certain amount of feeling of justification in his mind. There is also regret. There is partial remorse. It's a complicated thing because he is a person who can often have two contradictory ideas in his head at the same time, and this is one of those areas where he does."

Herlihy made two rulings the following day. First, he ruled that Cohen was competent to proceed with the case and to assist his lawyers with his defense. Second, he accepted Cohen's plea of guilty but mentally ill to two counts of first-degree murder and two weapons charges. Herlihy did not attach a condition that Cohen be kept on medication, as Walther had suggested. He did note, however, that he would monitor Cohen's condition during the penalty phase.

Prosecutor Bobby O'Neill met with the media on the courthouse steps after the hearing and made an announcement. "The state is seeking the death penalty in this case because, contrary to the defense's opinion, the state feels that the defendant knew what he was doing when he murdered his parents. The state feels there are a number of aggravating factors that will justify the death penalty."

The next day, February 14, 1992, the Delaware Supreme Court ruled without dissent that the state's new death penalty law did not violate the United States or Delaware constitutions. In a 23-page opinion, the court found "the new law valid in all respects and fully applicable to all defendants."

"Designation of the trial judge as the sentencing authority does not violate the right to a jury trial," the court wrote in its finding. "The new law merely expresses the legislature's view . . . that a judge is the more appropriate person to make the ultimate sentencing decision in a capital case."

The court also ruled that the new sentencing procedures could be applied retroactively to all pending cases, including Cohen's. "Mere procedural changes do not prohibit retroactive application," the court noted.

Herlihy scheduled the penalty phase of Cohen's case, a sentencing hearing, to begin in early April. The state would not have to convince twelve people that Cohen should be put to death. It would have to convince just one, Judge Jerome O. Herlihy. The jury would merely vote on a sentencing recommendation. Herlihy would make the final decision.

chapter 9

- - - - - - - -

Die, All You Scum

In 1976 the U.S. Supreme Court allowed states to resume capital punishment. Between 1976 and 1991, eight death sentences were handed out in Delaware, although none were carried out.

On October 31, 1991, Steve Pennell, whom Charlie had met at Gander Hill, was sentenced to death. Pennell had been convicted of torturing and killing four women. He maintained his innocence but asked to be put to death to spare his family and the victims' families any further pain.

Pennell acted as his own attorney and refused to appeal the death sentence. He was scheduled to be executed on March 14, 1992, three weeks before Cohen's penalty hearing was to start. No one had been executed in Delaware in 46 years. As the execution date approached, numerous third-party organizations petitioned for a stay of execution, but they were all denied. On the morning of March 14, 1992, Steven Pennell was executed by lethal injection in a trailer on the grounds of the Delaware Correctional Center in Smyrna.

Steve Walther firmly believed that Charles Cohen deserved to be put to death. As far as he was concerned, Cohen was not insane. He may have been mentally ill when he committed the murders, but he knew what he was doing. He was a cold-blooded, calculating murderer, and he should be held fully accountable.

Walther didn't believe in capital punishment as a deterrent. Most murders were committed during emotional conflicts or during the commission of a felony. The death penalty wasn't going to deter those murders. The death penalty was retribution. If you intentionally murdered someone, Walther believed you should sacrifice your life. The only deterrent he could see was that the execution of Charles Cohen would deter him from murdering anyone else.

Walther realized that his chances of getting the death penalty were less than 50–50. Cohen's motive for murdering his parents was clouded over with a weird psychological drama that only the shrinks could explain. No matter how vile or reprehensible his acts, if the judge and the jury thought he was severely disturbed, they wouldn't put him to death. It would be difficult to convince anyone that a person who had murdered his mother was not completely nuts. People might be able to understand a son murdering his father during a heated argument, but to cut your own mother's throat—that just wasn't normal.

The defense had expert witnesses to testify that he was mentally ill. The state had plenty of witnesses to testify about the gruesomeness and despicable nature of his crimes, but they didn't have a credible witness to testify that he wasn't disturbed. They didn't even have a witness to testify that he was only slightly mentally ill, but Walther knew that psychologists and psychiatrists didn't play well in a courtroom. They offered explanations that didn't make sense. He and O'Neill would have to point out those weaknesses during cross-examination.

Their only chance for a death sentence would be to

convince the judge and the jury that Cohen was more evil
than mentally ill, more premeditated than crazy, but even
calling witnesses was tricky. If the judge and jury decided
that an evil act stemmed from Cohen's mental illness, a
prosecution witness could actually help the defense. In
fact, almost every witness and every piece of evidence
was like that. It was all a matter of the judge's and jury's
perception. Like all mental illness cases, the defendant
wouldn't be on trial, the skills of the lawyers would be.

Before the hearing began, Winslow and Perillo introduced several motions to bar the prosecution from presenting evidence of unadjudicated crimes. Cohen had not
yet been charged and found guilty of crimes in connection with the Lutz murder, the Los Angeles tow yard incident, and his assault and attempted theft in Metairie,
Louisiana. However, Herlihy denied the motions. The
state would be allowed to present witnesses and evidence
concerning those events.

The defense also asked Herlihy to bar information concerning Cohen's homosexual encounters while he was a
fugitive. The defense argued that his homosexual encounters could be used to exploit the jurors' possible prejudice
of homosexuals. The motion was granted. All evidence of
homosexual behavior on Cohen's part was removed from
the recordings of his confessions.

A representative of the attorney general's office called
several of Cohen's relatives and asked them if they
would be willing to provide victim-impact evidence—
information about how the crimes affected them. It is
used to counter character witnesses called by the defense.

However, all of Cohen's relatives declined to testify.
Marci Dolgin's response was typical. "I don't feel good
about the death penalty," said Dolgin, Ethel's sister.
"Some members of the family say fine—it's what he de-

serves. I am very angry, but I'm opting for him to spend his life in jail. It would hurt my mind to think of the day Charlie would have to die. What would he do if we came face to face [in court]. I'm not that way to take the bull by the horns and confront this. I don't know why he did this, what was in his mind. Ethel adored him so much. So did Martin."

Jury selection for the penalty phase of Charles Cohen's murder trial started Friday, April 3, 1992. After four days, a jury of seven men and five women was selected. The hearing began on Thursday, April 9, at 2 P.M.

Herlihy began by explaining the state's new death penalty procedures to the jury. At the end of testimony, he said, the jury would vote on two questions. Herlihy read the first: "Whether the evidence shows beyond a reasonable doubt the existence of at least one statutory aggravating circumstance."

Delaware law identifies twenty statutory aggravating circumstances, at least one of which must be present for a convicted murderer to receive the death penalty. The Cohen murders involved two: the crime resulted in two or more deaths and one of the victims was over the age of 62. Ethel Cohen had been 64 at the time of her death. Therefore, the question of a statutory aggravating circumstance would not be at issue.

Herlihy read the second question: "Whether, by a preponderance of evidence . . . the aggravating circumstances found to exist outweigh the mitigating circumstances found to exist. An aggravating circumstance is any factor relating to the crime or the offender that tends to make the defendant's conduct more serious or the imposition of the penalty of death appropriate. A mitigating circumstance is any factor relating to the crime or the offender that tends to make the defendant's conduct less serious or the imposition of the penalty of death inappro-

priate." Herlihy explained that Cohen had pled guilty but
mentally ill to the murders and that mental illness was a
mitigating circumstance.

"The jury shall then report to the Court its final vote,"
said Herlihy. "The court will then consider your answers
and will thereafter impose the appropriate sentence.
While the Court is not bound by your recommendation,
you should bear in mind that the jury's recommended answers will be given great weight."

Irrespective of the jury's vote, if Herlihy found that the
aggravating circumstances outweighed the mitigating, he
was required by the new law to sentence Cohen to death.
Cohen, who was wearing a coat and tie and had a new
haircut and a neatly trimmed beard, paid little attention to
the proceedings. Lawyers from each side then gave opening statements.

"The evidence will show the amoral nature of his character and his instinctive propensity to violence," said
Steve Walther. "Charles Cohen smashed ten- and twenty-
pound barbells against the faces of his parents, shattering
their skulls and causing massive brain damage. He then
took a knife and slit the throat of his mother with such
tremendous force that he almost decapitated his own
mother. As his father lay there defenseless, he plunged
[the knife] fourteen times into the body of his own father."

Walther concluded by calling Cohen, who sat at the defense table with his head down, "a liar, a thief, a robber,
a mugger, a manipulator, a drug abuser, a con artist, an
extremely dangerous man, and, of course, a convicted
murderer."

In her opening statement, defense attorney Nancy
Perillo did not dispute the facts of the crime. "The overwhelming question is why Charles would kill his parents,"
she said. "The answer is that Charles was a disturbed

young man. The mental illness of the defendant at the time
of the crimes is undisputed."

She said that Cohen "was compelled to kill in order to
psychologically survive. He had no choice but to do so.
The brutal nature of the murders shows his rage and how
out of control he was."

Perillo concluded by arguing, "The guilty but mentally
ill plea automatically establishes a mitigating circumstance, a very strong one. The totality of the evidence is
not overwhelming and doesn't cry out for the death penalty. The mitigating factors are very substantial. The aggravating circumstances in no way can possibly outweigh
them."

The prosecution set about calling witnesses. The first
was Detective Gregory Coughlin of the Evidence Detection Unit. He described the crime scene, showed photos
of the victims to the jury, and provided a running narra-
tive of a 30-minute videotape made at the crime scene.
The jurors and the judge saw the barbells and the folding
knife, the bloodstains on the walls, and gruesome close-
ups of the victims' bodies. Coughlin pointed out that
Martin Cohen's blood sprayed a yard high on one of the
bedroom walls.

On Friday, April 10, the prosecution called Dr. Ali Z.
Hameli, the state's chief medical examiner. The lights
were dimmed, and on a large screen Hameli showed color
slides of the wounds suffered by Martin and Ethel Cohen
and described them in great detail. A few of the slides
showed the barbells next to the Cohens' head injuries.
The edge of the barbells closely matched the grisly
wounds.

Most of the jurors appeared glum during Hameli's
presentation. Cohen couldn't see much of the screen from
the defense table. He showed no response to the coroner's

testimony or to the slides and spent much of the time drawing intently on a pad of paper.

While viewing a slide of the lacerations on Martin Cohen's neck, one of the jurors, a thin, pale, bearded young man in jeans and a flannel shirt, abruptly left the courtroom. The court waited silently for him to return. The hearing could not continue without him. When he returned several minutes later, he reported that he had felt faint but was well enough to continue.

John Downs took the stand and went through the evidence against Cohen that he had collected during his investigation. He also played the videotaped and audiotaped confessions Cohen had given to him and Allen Ruth almost two years ago.

Pio Hernandez was flown in from Los Angeles to describe how Cohen had taken off in his parents' '83 Ford LTD from Hollywood Tow's impound garage, almost running him over in the process. The state also called Hilda Sonderberg, Ronald Rowbatham, and Robert Rotherham, Jr., to describe Cohen's attack of Sonderberg, his fistfight with Rowbatham, and his subsequent arrest on April 2, 1990, in Metairie.

Inspector Whitey Guinther of the San Francisco Police Department and Dr. Ray E. Stephens, the chief medical examiner for the city and county of San Francisco, provided details of the Lutz murder, from Lutz's wounds to the condition of Lutz's apartment. Guinther had brought along photos of Lutz's blood-splattered apartment, some of which were shown to the jury.

James Williams, one of Cohen's art instructors at the University of Delaware, described some of the artwork Cohen did during the fall of 1988 and his demeanor in class. He specifically mentioned the "heads on hangers drawing," as it had come to be known, that Cohen had done for Williams's class. The drawing was shown to the jury and entered into evidence.

Val Starcher described Dr. Cohen's personality and his attitude toward his son. She and Randy Reed also described their discovery of the bodies of Martin and Ethel Cohen.

The state subpoenaed Rick Muncey from Illinois to read the letter he had received from Cohen in March of 1989. On April 16, Katie Adams described her brief relationship with Cohen in Peoria in 1987 and read the threatening letter he had written to her.

After approximately a week, the defense began calling witnesses. Winslow and Perillo called Mike Owens, Cohen's high school principal, and Phil Trapani, his high school tennis coach. Both testified that Cohen was a good kid in high school. Dorothy Cash, a friend of Ethel's from Illinois, testified that Charlie was a nice boy as a child.

Francis Cockroft, a senoir correctional counselor at Gander Hill who supervised the Transition Unit, described Cohen's improvement in the Transition Unit. She discussed the counseling sessions he attended and the various responsibilities he had taken on since being moved to the unit, such as morning clean-up supervisor and log book person. In his cross-examination Walther speculated that Cohen might have enrolled in the counseling sessions and taken on the extra responsibilities so he could have someone like Cockroft testify on his behalf.

Virginia Smith, a counselor at Gander Hill, testified that Cohen was quiet when he first joined the group counseling sessions but that he eventually opened up. "He was asked if he missed his parents," said Smith. "He said yes. He said he missed them very much. He cried. He cried quite a bit. He said he was sorry. He said he wished he had never done it."

Two guards from Gander Hill testified that Cohen was not a discipline problem in prison. A religious counselor who visited inmates at Gander Hill said that Cohen was "a repentant individual. Down deep I think he's a good person. A very compassionate, sensitive, caring individual."

Diane had returned from Illinois for the sentencing hearing, and she also testified. No one in the media or on the prosecution team knew who she was. Diane answered questions from Perillo about her relationship with Charlie. She described how she had fallen in love with him after his capture, how she had moved to Delaware to be near him, and their engagement and request to be married. She said Charlie was "caring, warm, honest, loving." She also said he was very remorseful. During O'Neill's cross-examination, Diane admitted that Cohen didn't think he'd get the death penalty and that he had hopes of eventually getting out of jail.

Dr. Gerald Cooke again testified that Cohen suffered from severe borderline personality disorder and depression. Walther questioned the validity of the psychological tests Cooke had used. He also pointed out that much of the basis of Cooke's opinion had come from an interview with the defendant, who may have lied to him.

Dr. Robert Sadoff, a psychiatrist who had also examined Cohen, testified that the defendant suffered from schizoid and paranoid personality disorders as well. Bobby O'Neill asked Sadoff how Cohen could have functioned for eighteen months as a fugitive and manipulated so many people if he were mentally ill. He skeptically questioned whether Cohen met the criteria for the paranoid and schizoid personality disorders. O'Neill also pointed out that many people have borderline personality disorders, but they manage to function without killing anyone. The prosecutors also got both Cooke and Sadoff to admit that Cohen could become violent in prison.

Ronald Hays, the art therapist from Philadelphia who had reviewed Cohen's artwork just after the murders, also testified for the defense. The police had originally hired Hays, and Downs had used Hays's conclusions to help bring murder charges against Cohen. Nevertheless, Walther vigorously grilled Hays on whether he could draw any valid conclusions about Cohen's mental condition at the time of the murders from his artwork.

The prosecutors were generally satisfied with their cross-examinations of Cooke and Sadoff. Walther and O'Neill had blunted the effect of their testimony by raising doubts about their diagnoses.

Diane visited Charlie at Gander Hill on Saturday morning, April 25. Charlie was antagonistic toward her. He told her that he hated her and wanted her to go home. He said that her testimony had hurt his case. "I think you have psychotic tendencies," he added. "As a friend, I think there's something wrong there."

As if to shock her, he told her about the incident with the girl from Chicago in Central Park in 1989. With a strange smile, he described in graphic detail how he had virtually raped her. He also told her that he had seen guys being raped in prison but that he had never had sex with anyone in prison, "not even with Nancy."

"With Nancy? What are you talking about?"

"Just go home," he said.

"I'm not going to leave you again."

"If you care, you'll go home."

Diane left the prison in shock. She felt physically ill and spent the rest of the day in bed.

Cohen's defense attorneys had subpoenaed Dr. David Raskin to testify. Raskin was scheduled to appear on Monday, April 27, and he decided to interview Charlie one more time before testifying. He met with Cohen on Saturday morning in an interview room at Gander Hill shortly after Charlie's hostile visit with Diane.

Raskin had interviewed Charlie many times during the previous two years, several times at the request of the prosecution. He had also read Sadoff's and Cooke's reports, but a diagnosis of borderline personality disorder didn't make sense to him. It seemed to fall short. First of all, Cohen was paranoid, which wasn't one of the criteria for borderline. Plus, borderlines didn't murder people. Cohen had told him that he had gone to New York in the fall of 1988 to murder someone to reestablish some balance in the world. To Raskin that did not sound borderline. That sounded schizophrenic.

"They've given you a better diagnosis from the point of view of the prosecution than I could give you," Raskin had told Walther. "I think he's crazier than their experts do."

Raskin asked Cohen how the hearing was going. "The futility of man, of me, of the defense witnesses, is being exposed," Charlie answered. He had his usual weird, chilling smile. The hearing was clearly starting to get to him. Charlie had been in court for over three weeks and had heard horrible things said about him. As Raskin had seen in the past, Charlie became more irrational as his stress level rose.

Charlie then began ranting about Dr. Sadoff, who had testified on his behalf. "Sadoff is a classic example of a sociopath. The man is disturbed sexually and socially. I don't think he wants to live. He reminds me of myself. The man is insane. His message is 'Die, all you scum.' It takes one to know one.

"It was clear what Sadoff was doing," Cohen continued. "He was in control, so domineering in his testimony. He's a big man, imposing. One can be afraid of him. He has no concern for his life. He could rape me and then kill me. He was out of control. He needs to seek help. I've had experience with psychopaths. I was one. I think he knows it."

Raskin had never seen this part of Cohen's thought processes before. Neither had Cooke or Sadoff. Cohen evidently trusted him more than the others, and he was opening up some bizarre ideas.

"[Sadoff] was reaching out for something, a lifeline," said Cohen. "The only thing he could grasp was sexual domination, a lot directed toward me. The man was out of control. He was obsessed with sex and satisfying his sexual desires. He was consciously trying to get to me because he thought that would be fun." Raskin, who had been in the mental health field for 25 years, knew what madness sounded like, and he knew he was hearing it from Cohen.

Raskin realized that Cohen was projecting his feelings about himself onto Dr. Sadoff. He saw himself as a socially and sexually maladjusted psychopath who needed to kill or be killed. Instead of experiencing those feelings within himself, he was projecting them onto Dr. Sadoff. Instead of Charles Cohen being the dangerous person, Sadoff had become the dangerous person.

Charlie added that Sadoff reminded him of his father because, like his father, Sadoff used intimidation to try to control him. Raskin suddenly understood that Charlie had seen his parents as incredibly dangerous to him, just as he was seeing Sadoff as dangerous. He had projected his fears, bizarre thoughts, and hateful delusions onto his father and mother, which made him feel justified in killing them.

How else could he explain why a young man who had grown up as an ideal child had suddenly gone bad and murdered his parents? He hadn't done it for money, they hadn't had a fight that night, and he hadn't been high on drugs. Charlie always said that he'd murdered them because of some vague, domestic problems, which never made sense to Raskin. Now Raskin was finally uncovering Cohen's real motivational system, and it was far more out of control and far crazier than he'd imagined.

Raskin asked him what he thought of the other participants in the hearing. "There's a lot of sexual innuendo in the courtroom," Cohen answered. "The judge is playing games, controlling like my father. He's a father figure, a sexual father figure. The bailiffs are young women who walk around in sheeny garb. There's no fidelity. It's all sex and power, cleverly washed over. Well practiced at deception are these people. The public defenders have sold out. The only people I can trust are the prosecutors. They're more sympathetic than my own lawyers."

Raskin questioned the validity of some of Cohen's claims, and Charlie suddenly became defensive. Raskin understood that Cohen was starting to view him as someone who was using him and making fun of him. He realized how dangerous Cohen was and hastily ended the interview.

The next day Charlie called Diane and told her that he loved her and wanted her to stay in Delaware. Diane didn't know what to believe. Did he love her or didn't he? She was beginning to wonder if Charles Cohen was worth all the trouble.

On Monday morning, April 27, Nancy Perillo called Dr. David Raskin to the stand. Raskin calmly reported to the court what Cohen had told him 48 hours earlier. Everyone in the courtroom was shocked. Herlihy grinned nervously, and the courtroom guards became visibly restless.

"Now, I will tell you I'm a fairly cool person when it comes to interviewing very crazy people," Raskin testified. "When we left that interview room, there was no guard outside that door, and I was very uncomfortable because he was very, very unhappy at some of the comments I was asking him and he was making, and the only reason I got this material is because his stress level was high enough so that his controls had basically broken down. He conceals these delusions until the stress level doesn't allow him to conceal them any longer.

"He's always trying to stay a step ahead to keep people from getting him. He feels everyone is trying to sexually or emotionally control and manipulate him. So he wants to control them before they control him. It's some pretty primitive stuff. But that's what his mind is like. That's how he experiences certain kinds of people and relationships, as dangerous, as being capable of hurting him, sexually attacking him. He's deluded into feeling someone is trying to destroy him, and it's a fairly frightening thing to hear that and to feel that. It's hard to describe what goes on in this man's mind unless you see it in stark terms."

Raskin went on to diagnose Cohen as a paranoid schizophrenic. "He was almost a too good child. In adulthood, things began to unravel, which is common with schizophrenics. Characteristically, they do okay until adolescence. Schizophrenia can be set off by factors like drugs and family disorders, but it has a biological base. It's a genetic disorder. He used drugs to gain distance from what was going on inside, but they also fueled his problems. His bizarre artwork is consistent with the diagnosis. Creative work loosens the control and breaks down the defenses."

Raskin also pointed out another unusual aspect of Cohen's personality. "He wants everyone to think he is a normal person. He's the opposite of a malingerer. He's malingering sanity. People who malinger fake hallucinations, hear voices, see things. Charles is just the opposite. He doesn't pretend he's sick. He pretends he's sane. Why? The answer is staring us in the face—because his father was a psychologist. He had a battle with his dad. To admit mental illness would be to lose the battle with his father. He greatly feared his father. His psychological life or death hinges on his denial of his mental illness. His behavior is a facade, a fake, used to throw people off.

Charles Cohen is desperate not to let people know what goes on inside Charles Cohen."

Perhaps the most important point Raskin made was to relate Cohen's comments to the murders of his parents. "His delusions about Dr. Sadoff were analogous to his delusions concerning his parents. Those same fantasies were operative around his parents. He had such bizarre fantasies about his parents and about what they would do to him. He selects people who are imposing male authority figures, and they become the target of his paranoid ideas. There's no way to understand the murder of his parents without understanding his thought processes. The homicide was the only option he felt he had for parents he thought were killing him. I'm really talking about a very sick person. Common sense is not something that takes place in this man's mind. His thinking is very atypical. He's really a tragically sick person."

Perillo asked Raskin if Dr. Cohen could have seen Charlie's sickness. "Parents often miss the boat because they don't see the boat," said Raskin. "Nobody wants to see their son as a paranoid schizophrenic. They would rather believe that he was just having some problems. . . . Dr. Cohen would've been devastated if he had been forced to confront his son's mental illness."

Steve Walther had always respected Raskin, but when he heard Raskin's surprise testimony and the more serious diagnosis of paranoid schizophrenic, he was absolutely disgusted. Borderline personality disorder was one thing, but paranoid schizophrenia was something else altogether. Raskin wasn't saying that the kid was mentally disturbed but that he was out-and-out crazy. He'd even used the word "crazy," which wasn't a valid psychological term. Plus, he was the first mental health expert to clearly connect Cohen's mental illness to the murders.

They had been shanghaied. The whole case was shot.

He and O'Neill had neutralized the other mental health experts, but Raskin had blown them out of the water. The death sentence was down the toilet. The opposite of malingerer! Malingering sanity! That was a new one on him. He had paid Raskin good money to evaluate Cohen, and look what he had gotten in return—a ream job.

The lying, manipulating, murderous little jerk was going to beat the death penalty. Cohen had sat through the entire hearing. Was it just a coincidence that he had come up with this crazy scenario just a few days before the hearing ended? Cohen was more manipulative than Walther had given him credit for. Cohen had realized he might lose the case and decided that Raskin was his last hope. Then he'd convinced a smart guy like Raskin that he was crazy. Walther couldn't prove that Charles Cohen had read the *Diagnostic and Statistical Manual,* but his father had been a psychologist, for God's sake. Martin Cohen probably had several copies of the *DSM* lying around the house. The kid could probably quote from it.

When Walther saw Raskin in the hallway after his testimony, he joked, "I want some of the money back that we paid you." The state had paid Raskin $500 per hour to evaluate Cohen the previous summer.

Both the prosecution and the defense presented closing arguments on Wednesday, April 29, and they were similar in content to their opening statements, although they were given by different lawyers. Bobby O'Neill reminded the jury of Cohen's many despicable crimes, while J. Dallas Winslow, Jr., reminded the jury of Cohen's mental illness.

The climax of O'Neill's closing came when he stood in front of the jury and held one of the barbells Cohen had used to bludgeon his parents in one hand and a folder of psychiatric reports in the other. "When you place them on a scale like this dumbbell and these reports," he said, lowering the barbell and raising the reports, "the aggravating circumstances clearly outweigh the mitigating."

O'Neill also reminded the jury that while he was on the lam Cohen had written, "I have accepted the fact that I will probably die of a fatal drug injection or electric shock. This does not bother me."

"With his own words he has judged himself," O'Neill noted. "There's no question he knew what he did was wrong. The defense talked about treatment. He's had treatment. Now it's time for punishment."

Winslow was emphatic and emotional. "There's no good news here for Charles Cohen," he said. "It's all bad news—life without chance of parole or death. Even if he gets life, the next time he hits the street is going to be in a box, a pine box, and he's going to be dead.

"When you have someone who is substantially impaired, do you treat them the same as someone who is not?" Winslow asked. "We don't punish as much people who are mentally ill. We treat them as well as punish them. [His parents] were killed because he was mentally ill. If he hadn't been mentally ill, they wouldn't have been killed. He would've been the same Charles Cohen he was before his mental illness.

"Are you going to put to death someone who was mentally ill, someone who couldn't control his thoughts or feelings, when his punishment can be reasonably satisfied by a life in prison?" Winslow asked the jury. "The only reason we're here today is because he is mentally ill, and that's not his fault."

The jury began deliberations on Thursday morning, April 30, 1992, and continued to Friday. At noon they reported to the judge that they were ready to report the result of their vote. The lawyers, Cohen, Diane, the press, and dozens of onlookers gathered to hear the results. The spectators' section was packed. The jury of seven men and five women filed into the jury box.

The jury foreman stood and reported that by a count of eight to four, the jury had voted that the mitigating factors outweighed the aggravating. They were recommending that Charles Cohen receive a life sentence rather than death for the murders of his parents. Cohen smiled and thanked his attorneys. Winslow patted him on the back, and Perillo hugged him.

"Clearly, Charles Cohen was mentally ill," said Steve Walther stoically to a group of reporters on the steps of the courthouse afterward. "The bottom line is, can we execute someone who is mentally ill? That's an extremely difficult thing to ask lay people to do or even to recommend."

Diane visited Charlie at Gander Hill the next day, Saturday, May 2. She was returning to Illinois that afternoon.

"Nancy wants to break us up," he said. "She wants me all to herself."

Diane knew the comment was ridiculous, but she didn't question it because she didn't want to upset him. As the visit progressed, he became antagonistic toward her again.

"You're a mess," he said. "I can't take any more of this." He asked the guard to take him back to his cell, but the guard couldn't take him back right away, so Charlie stood in a corner of the visiting room and stared at the wall. Diane remained seated in the visiting booth. She didn't know what to do. Was he testing her commitment, or did he genuinely dislike her? He eventually came back to the booth and picked up the phone, but he wouldn't speak with her or look at her. Diane left for the airport directly from the prison.

* * *

The following Monday morning, May 4, 1992, lawyers for both sides recommended to Judge Herlihy that he follow the vote of the jury. A short time later, Herlihy announced that he had accepted the recommendation of the jury and was sentencing Charles Cohen to life in prison. Referring to the jury's recommendation, Herlihy said, "The conscience of the community has spoken."

In his twelve-page sentencing decision, which he read in court, Herlihy acknowledged that the murders were "intentional" but cited Cohen's mental illness as the reason for not sentencing him to death. Herlihy specifically mentioned Dr. David Raskin's testimony, which he called "chilling" and "pervasive."

Herlihy wrote that Cohen "shall be imprisoned for his natural life ... without benefit of probation or parole or any other reduction." He also sentenced Cohen to consecutive, mandatory terms of thirty years for each of the weapons offenses.

"As to all counts," Herlihy concluded, "as much as it is within this Court's power and prerogative to say or direct, based on the unanimous psychiatric and psychological testimony, the defendant should never be released from prison."

The only way Cohen could be set free would be by a pardon from the governor, and a Delaware governor hadn't pardoned a convicted murderer in over two decades.

chapter 10

- - - - - - - - -

The Ping-Pong Ball

At times Charlie felt good about himself because he knew his parents were in heaven. He also knew that they had forgiven him and wanted him to carry on. However, as the ramifications of his long prison sentences sank in, he lapsed further and further into depression. He was eating less and losing weight. He looked tired and haggard, spent almost all of his time alone in his cell, and rarely communicated with anyone. A minister advised him that the only way he could overcome his depression would be to stop thinking about his situation and to focus on others, but he couldn't follow the advice.

Charlie was scheduled to graduate from the Transition Unit on Thursday, May 28, 1992. As part of the graduation, the inmates were given a party. Friends and relatives were permitted to attend, so Diane planned a trip to Delaware for the graduation. However, just a few days before she was to leave, she received a strange letter from Charlie.

"You believed everyone else when they told you I was gay, but you never even thought to ask me," he wrote. "I told you everything, and you still chose to take a stranger's word before mine."

He also wrote that she made him sick, and he asked her a series of odd questions. Did she want to have sex right now? Did she want to marry a man with money? Was she so lonely she could die? "I could have a woman," he added. "I'm not that undesirable. I could have sex with a woman in prison. It's possible." She didn't know what he was talking about, but she was used to being confused by Charlie and his strange ideas.

Diane flew to Philadelphia and attended the Transition Unit graduation party at the end of May. Charlie seemed lucid and polite but quiet. She was supposed to visit with him again two days later, but the next day, Friday, May 29, Cohen was abruptly transferred to the Delaware Correctional Center in Smyrna.

Cohen was classified "maximum security," which meant he would be housed in the Maximum Security Unit of the penitentiary, commonly known as MSU. It was a prison within a prison, a separate building on the penitentiary grounds surrounded by two tall rows of razor-wire fencing.

MSU was the most secure facility in the state prison system, and it housed the worst and most dangerous inmates in the state. Most of them were discipline problems, inmates who ignored the rules, started fights, or repeatedly tried to escape. The inmates were locked down 23 hours a day, and their privileges were severely restricted. Mentally ill inmates were routinely classified for MSU.

When Nancy Perillo heard of Cohen's transfer and his MSU classification, she immediately called Robert Watson, Commissioner of the Department of Correction, to protest. Perillo knew that there was nowhere worse for Cohen than MSU. She also knew that once an inmate was in MSU, it was very hard to get him out.

Perillo informed Watson that if the Department of Corrections could not or would not place him within the correctional system where he could get treatment, she would formally request that he be transferred to the Delaware State Hospital, as stipulated by Delaware law. She also requested that he be kept in the infirmary until the medical staff at Smyrna had a chance to evaluate him. Commissioner Watson agreed to keep Cohen in the infirmary, at least temporarily.

Perillo also arranged for Dr. Raskin to evaluate Cohen. Raskin saw Cohen in the infirmary at Smyrna on Wednesday, June 3. He reported to Perillo that Cohen was not acutely psychotic, although he was once again fasting. Raskin also reported that Cohen was not on medication and had refused the medication offered to him.

Perillo wrote to Judge Herlihy and Commissioner Watson on June 11, 1992. She reported Raskin's findings and told them, "Mr. Cohen has been considerably withdrawn from others, his affect has been often inappropriate, there have been indications of some continued paranoid thinking, and he has lost a significant amount of weight."

Perillo also reminded Herlihy and Watson of Title 11, Sections 408b and 408c of the Delaware code and wrote, "We hereby request on behalf of Mr. Cohen that he be transferred promptly to the Comegys Building of the Delaware State Hospital, under whatever special security arrangements may be deemed necessary, for further evaluation and treatment."

Delaware Code, Crimes and Criminal Procedure, Section 408b:

Such defendant [found guilty but mentally ill] shall be committed into the custody of the Department of Correction, and shall undergo further evaluation and be

given such immediate and temporary treatment as is
psychiatrically indicated... The Commissioner shall
thereupon confine such person in the Delaware State
Hospital.... The Delaware State Hospital ... shall
have the authority to discharge the defendant from the
facility and return the defendant to the physical custody of the Commissioner whenever the facility believes that such a discharge is in the best interests of
the defendant.

After three weeks in the infirmary at the Delaware Correctional Center in Smyrna, Charlie was placed in the
Maximum Security Unit. He quickly became withdrawn.
Some inmates and counselors tried to speak with him, but
he wouldn't respond. Dallas Winslow drove to Smyrna to
visit him, but Charlie refused to meet him.

On Thursday, July 2, 1992, Judge Jerome O. Herlihy
convened a hearing to consider Perillo's request. Charlie
was ushered into the courtroom by two guards. He had
clearly lost a lot of weight. His hair and beard had gone
uncut, and matted tufts of hair and beard stuck out from
his head and chin at odd angles. He wore bright orange
prison overalls and seemed dirty, sickly, and disoriented.

When Herlihy entered the courtroom, everyone stood
except Charlie. Winslow told him to stand. Charlie slowly
stood, but he didn't make it to his feet until everyone else
had sat down. He stood, half crouched, alone for several
seconds. Everyone was watching him. He seemed confused and slowly sat back down. He sat with his head
down throughout the remainder of the 90-minute proceeding, drooling on a table in front of him.

Perillo and Winslow argued that Cohen wasn't getting
treatment at Smyrna and that the Department of Corrections had placed him in the worst possible prison environment, which had caused his mental condition to
deteriorate.

Raskin testified that he had spoken with Charlie that morning. Cohen had wept in Raskin's presence and said he was sure he would be attacked and sexually molested in MSU. Cohen then withdrew and wouldn't answer any more of Raskin's questions.

Raskin claimed that Cohen was "on the road to a breakdown" and needed treatment and a better environment. Raskin said that a therapeutic environment, such as Delaware State Hospital, would be best for Cohen and that MSU was the worst of all possible environments for him.

"If he remains in MSU without medication," said Raskin, "I have no doubt that he will deteriorate to a psychotic state."

Herlihy was not happy with the situation. He scolded the Department of Correction's lawyer, stating that Cohen shouldn't have been placed in MSU and that by doing so it made the hearing "totally predictable." Herlihy added that he didn't want Cohen moved around like "a Ping-Pong ball."

A mental health counselor from the Delaware Correctional Center testified that very little mental health treatment was available at Smyrna. Walther and a lawyer representing Delaware State Hospital argued that the Comegys Building at the hospital wasn't secure enough for a high-risk inmate like Cohen. Perillo and Winslow pointed out that several murderers were housed at the Comegys Building without problems.

The lawyers debated various placement options for Cohen, but they couldn't come to an agreement. Herlihy was being squeezed from all sides, and he was becoming frustrated. He offered to move Cohen back to the Transition Unit at Gander Hill, but no one at the hearing seemed to think the Transition Unit was anything more than a temporary solution.

Clearly out of options, Herlihy ordered that Cohen be

transferred to the state psychiatric hospital his father had been running when he murdered him. "Commissioner of corrections will have additional security at Delaware State Hospital; twenty-four hours a day, seven days a week," Herlihy wrote in his order.

On his way back to Smyrna, Cohen told one of the guards, "I've got them eating out of my hands." Perillo heard about the comment and later asked Charlie for an explanation. He didn't have much of an answer.

Herlihy also heard about the comment. He had also found out that Cohen would soon be extradited to San Francisco, so on July 7, just five days after ordering Cohen to the state hospital, he rescinded his order. Commissioner Watson agreed to move Cohen back to Gander Hill and assured Herlihy that Cohen would receive the necessary medical and psychological treatment.

Charlie was returned to Gander Hill on July 16. His mental condition had deteriorated so far that he was immediately admitted to the infirmary on suicide watch and placed on antipsychotic medication. It marked the sixth time in just over two years that Charlie had taken up residence in the pink room.

By early August, Charlie's condition had improved. He was discharged from the infirmary on Friday, August 7, although he continued to receive small doses of Navane and was placed back in the Transition Unit.

Diane did not receive any word from Charlie during June, July, or August. She had written to him many times, but he hadn't responded. She didn't know if he had lost interest in her or if his mental condition was interfering with his ability to communicate. She assumed the former and, by late August, had become very bitter. She had put so much effort, time, and money into the relationship that she felt like a fool. She took his pictures down from her bulletin board and began dating a resident at the hospital.

She finally received a letter from him in early September. He told her what he had been through the past few months and that he was fighting extradition to California. He felt that Conrad Lutz's family had been through enough without a murder trial. He also felt that his two Delaware life sentences would satisfy the California authorities, but he was mistaken. The San Francisco district attorney's office fully intended to try him for the murder of Conrad Lutz and to seek the death penalty.

"I'd prefer it if our relationship became platonic," he wrote. "I'm really not prepared to be married or to try to treat you as my wife." He looked at his life as one of service to God, and he didn't foresee them getting married after he was released. He asked her to respect his decision. "After all we've been through," he wrote, "it seems like the obvious choice for us."

In mid-October, William Fazio, a deputy prosecutor in the San Francisco district attorney's office, came to Delaware and initiated extradition proceedings against Charles Cohen. On October 21, 1992, Charlie was arraigned on a governor's warrant and ordered to San Francisco. A week later Inspector Whitey Guinther of the San Francisco Police Department escorted Charlie to San Francisco to face charges for the murder of Conrad Lutz.

On December 18, 1992, J. Dallas Winslow, Jr., appeared in Court of Chancery in Wilmington representing Charles Cohen and waived his client's claim to Martin and Ethel Cohen's estate. The court ruled that Charles Cohen was "deemed to have predeceased his parents for purposes of determining the identity of the heirs." The court also ruled that Martin and Ethel Cohen "died more or less simultaneously" and divided the estate among their remaining close relatives.

Charlie was indicted for robbery, burglary, and first-degree murder by a grand jury in San Francisco on Tuesday, January 26, 1993. The grand jury also found two special circumstances: that the murder was committed during the commission of a robbery and that the defendant had previously been convicted of murder. Only one special circumstance was necessary for the state to seek the death penalty.

Bob Berman, Cohen's public defender in San Francisco, offered the district attorney's office a deal. Cohen would plead guilty to first-degree murder if the district attorney would not pursue the death penalty. Cohen would receive a life sentence without parole and be transferred back to a Delaware prison, where he would spend the rest of his life. The entire process would be completed quickly and at little expense to the taxpayer.

Fazio recommended that the offer be accepted, but his superiors turned down the deal. Chief Assistant DA, Bob Podesta, argued that the motive for the Lutz murder was, as Cohen had admitted, strictly for financial gain and clearly premeditated. He also claimed that Berman had presented little, if any, mitigating evidence. However, he invited Berman to present such evidence in the future.

Berman felt that the decision was politically motivated. He claimed that Arlo Smith, the district attorney for San Francisco, planned to run for state attorney general in 1994 and didn't want to leave himself open to charges of being soft on crime. Smith had lost a close race for state attorney general two years earlier.

Berman began preparing the case for trial, although he hoped it would never get that far. He knew it could drag on for years and cost several million dollars. He hoped to eventually persuade the district attorney's office to accept the original deal.

Berman spoke with Dr. David Raskin about the Lutz murder. Raskin did not agree that Cohen's motive for murdering Lutz was money. He felt that Cohen was hiding or perhaps not even aware of the real motive.

"Charles describes the Lutz murder as a crime of convenience, to steal some money, but it's a helluva way to get a few bucks, so that makes no sense," Raskin said. "And Charles says, 'Gee, I just felt that murdering someone was the only way.' But what did he really mean by that? The whole issue of homosexuality and his own sexuality and his being inclined to violence and attack—in a sense he was acting out a fundamental psychological feeling, which is his fear, and I don't believe he's been gay at any point in his life.

"If you were using old-style psychology, circa 1950 and 1960, you would say he was both fascinated and frightened at this whole issue of male dominance and male sexuality and being attacked by men, which was his concern about Sadoff. He was also concerned about being sexually attacked in prison. His identity, his sexual identity, his aggression—in a sense the Lutz murder pulls it all together. This whole thing about relationships with older men, sexual fears about older men, crazy mixed-up stuff about sex and violence all gets combined in this one crime. He literally gets into an almost sexual encounter. He's massaging Lutz's back, and he stabs him violently, right before the sexual act is to take place. This is not just about money. It's a fascinating crime because it really explains Charles Cohen."

Berman knew that Raskin's analysis might save Cohen from the death penalty.

Charlie was being held in the maximum security unit of the San Francisco County Jail, and he was locked down 23 hours a day. The stress of his uncertain future began affecting his mental condition. He stopped eating, talking, and bathing. Two other prisoners in maximum security threatened to kill him. Charlie came to the conclusion that he probably wouldn't live much longer. If the state of California didn't execute him, an inmate would.

He was transferred to a locked psychiatric ward at the San Francisco General Hospital on March 12, 1993, and placed on medication. Five days later he was returned to the county jail. Before the end of March he spent another short stint in the psychiatric ward.

"I don't know what will happen," he wrote to Diane, "but I know I'm back on my feet and living for God now. So whatever happens will be for His glory."

But Charlie wasn't back on his feet. He wouldn't come out of his cell or speak with anyone. During a visit with Berman in May, he stared at the wall of his cell silently until Berman left. Nancy Perillo went to see Charlie while she was visiting friends in San Francisco, but he refused to meet with her as well.

As of the fall of 1993, the charges against Cohen for the murder of Conrad Lutz had not been resolved, and it didn't look like they would get resolved anytime soon.

He has still not been baptized.

Postscript:
- - - - - - - -

You Don't Just Freak Out

Elizabeth:

I still can't comprehend that this happened. It's like it's not true to me. I still carry a picture of Ethel in my billfold. It's so difficult for me to believe that this is the same young man that I saw grow up. Most people in Galesburg thought he was a wonderful little boy. Martin and Ethel would've given Charlie the world if they could have. They were older when they had Charlie, and they just idolized him. They just didn't know how to handle it, as brilliant a couple as they were. Ethel and I used to speak after we moved, and she used to say, "There's so much I can't tell you on the phone." Martin said to me once that they didn't know where they went wrong.

Kevin:

He always had delusions of grandeur, but he never followed through with anything. He couldn't focus on his school work. He went from one extreme to another. He was also very impressionable. He had new friends all the time. He was like a chameleon. He would become that other person. He talked about being in a band, but he just wanted the spotlight. He always told me that he dreamed about getting all his friends together and living in some mansion.

The only way I can make sense out of it and still cherish my friendship with Charlie is to think—I mean, you just can't possibly understand what it's like to do that much cocaine and how it affects your life. A lot of people say, "Don't be so naive. You know people who have done cocaine. You've done it yourself. You don't just freak out. The problems are deep-seated." But over an extended period of time, it can take its toll. When you have a dreamlike vision of what your life is going to be like, and it doesn't happen . . .

Mick:

He was easy-tempered and gentle. He hated any type of violence. That's the way he was. He couldn't hurt a fly. He was completely nonviolent. I mean, completely! He never got in any fights. We'd play basketball and if it got a little rough, Charlie would get upset about it or he'd get hurt. He'd get mad about things, but it wouldn't be aggressive or physical.

During high school, I'd go hunting. Charlie would get mad about it. He'd say, "You're stupid. I don't know how you can kill a defenseless little animal." That's why it was so weird that he would, you know . . .

Bobby O'Neill:

During the eighteen months he evaded the authorities, he survived by manipulating and deceiving others, and he quite obviously manipulated his parents the night he murdered them. How could he manipulate all these people if he was mentally ill? His father worked with mental illness every day, so it's curious that he never picked up on any mental illness. What about the videotape of Cohen's interview with Downs and Ruth in May 1990? He seemed alert, calm, and lucid. Nearly two years later, and he's totally out there, paranoid schizophrenic. And how much of that was induced by the prison environment? Was this a legitimate change or another attempt to manipulate? There's no doubt in my mind that he's a fiendishly clever person.

Jonathan:

It was always so rewarding just to talk to him because he had a profound sensitivity. One of the strongest, most palpable things that came off him was that he was a good person in a really visceral way. He listened and really gave people's concerns very serious, very sensitive regard. It's not bullshit, especially when you consider the number of people who took care of him. You can't have that many people from that many different parts of the country responding the same way to someone unless there was something to it.

Virginia:

Spoiled rotten, rotten, rotten. He took advantage of them. He had her wrapped around his little finger. From the time he was eight they had problems with him. Not behaving. Getting into trouble. He was always a problem. He could wheedle anything he wanted. The more he wheedled, the worse he got, until he got involved with drugs, then he was impossible. He was just a rotten kid. He was born bad. They should have put their foot down. They should've done something early.

He never did anything worthwhile in his life. He was constantly begging, wanting this, wanting that. And his slightest wish was her command. He spent money like water, money he got from his parents. Ethel's eating problems were Charles. She would get so upset. If I had to testify, I'd say electrocute him. That may sound hard-boiled, but that's the way I feel.

Pete:

I'm still in shock. I feel sad that he has to spend the rest of his life in prison. I'm mad as hell at him for what he did because I could've helped him. I could've gotten him away from there. But like I tell my mom, "Hey, it's a sad thing, but they did it to themselves." I'm sorry it came to that. I wouldn't wish ill on anybody, but I know exactly why he did it. That was the only way he could get away from them. He couldn't find any other way out. When he killed them, he was finally free of them.